WEAPONS OF MASS DESTRUCTION:
New Perspectives on Counterproliferation

WEAPONS OF MASS DESTRUCTION:
New Perspectives on Counterproliferation

Edited by
Stuart E. Johnson
William H. Lewis

National Defense University Press
Fort Lesley J. McNair
Washington, DC 20319

National Defense University Press Publications

To increase general knowledge and inform discussion, the Institute for National Strategic Studies, through its publication arm the NDU Press, publishes McNair Papers; proceedings of University- and Institute-sponsored symposia; books relating to U.S. national security, especially to issues of joint, combined, or coalition warfare, peacekeeping operations, and national strategy; and a variety of briefer works designed to circulate contemporary comment and offer alternatives to current policy. The Press occasionally publishes out-of-print defense classics, historical works, and other especially timely or distinguished writing on national security.

NDU Press publications are sold by the U.S. Government Printing Office. For ordering information, call (202) 512-1800, or write to the Superintendent of Documents, U.S. Government Printing Office, Washington, DC 20402.

First printing, April 1995

For sale by the U.S. Government Printing Office
Superintendent of Documents, Mail Stop: SSOP, Washington, DC 20402-9328
ISBN 0-16-047822-7

Contents

SECTION III
Preventive Approaches

Foreword

The National Defense University recently hosted a major symposium to address the challenges to U.S. national security and international stability posed by the spread of weapons of mass destruction: nuclear, chemical, and biological weapons, and missiles as a means of delivery. The need to examine such issues is clear. Perhaps no problem facing civilian and military decision makers today is as urgent and important as the effort to control the proliferation of such weapons. Put simply, WMD proliferation represents one of the most complex and fundamental threats to security today.

Attended by many of the premier experts in the field, the NDU Symposium explored a broad spectrum of issues ranging from the incentives and disincentives for proliferation to non- and counterproliferation policies and programs. The panelists discussed such critical issues as how effectively present controls to prevent proliferation are working and how to protect against proliferation when it occurs. Most impressively, the participants ventured to identify alternative perspectives and approaches that may contribute to meeting the common challenges.

All this unfolds in the pages that follow. It is a search for wisdom, for, as Cicero said twenty centuries ago, "Weapons are of little use on the field of battle if there is no wise counsel at home."

ERVIN J. ROKKE
Lieutenant General, USAF
President, National Defense University

Introduction

THE UNITED STATES HAS ACHIEVED A GREAT DEAL OF SUCCESS IN THE post-Cold War era. Our forces are more capable and better equipped than those of any conceivable adversary. The quality of our troops is good and morale in the armed forces is high. Analysts do point out that we might have problems in executing a strategy of fighting nearly simultaneously two major regional contingencies. But these problems lend themselves to straightforward analysis, and the solutions are straightforward if challenging in an era of tight defense budgets. In the immediate future, there does not seem to be a threat to our interests from a nation that we cannot handle militarily.

Yet, a handful of weapons of mass destruction, especially nuclear weapons in the hands of the wrong country, can change this situation overnight. The use of a few of these weapons, or even the threat of their use, changes the context in which our national command authority makes decisions about the terms under which we go to war or whether we go to war at all.

Unlike classical force planning against a hostile nation with conventional forces, coping with weapons of mass destruction is a complex issue, and the tools we have at our disposal are imperfect. Motivations for developing or attempting to develop an arsenal of weapons of mass destruction differ from region to region and from country to country. An approach that is appropriate for one region or class of nations may be useless in addressing proliferation in another.

This volume presents a broad look at the problem facing U.S. policy makers. In the first section, *Challenges to Policy,* Dr. Robert Joseph examines the trends at work that define the strategic context in which our policy must be reviewed and in some cases reformulated. This is followed by a detailed explanation of U.S. policy initiatives in the area of counterproliferation by Dr. Mitchel Wallerstein. As he points out, the U.S. government has not been sitting still. It is moving forward to strengthen the full range of traditional nonproliferation tools, such as by promoting the indefinite extension of the Nuclear Non-Proliferation Treaty and enhancing effective export controls designed to prevent the spread of weapons of mass destruction. Moreover, acknowledging that a determined proliferator is likely, over time, to succeed, the administration is undertaking those prudent defense responses required to protect against proliferation. In such cases the United States must be prepared to defend its interests. The next essay, by Dr. Lewis Dunn, focuses on nonproliferation with primary attention to technical constraints. He proposes the issue be given more prominence within the U.S. policy making community to reflect the complexity (and criticality) of dealing with this multi-faceted problem.

Ultimately, developing a program of counterproliferation must be tailored to the situation prevailing in different regions of the world. The next section, *Regional Challenges,* includes chapters by key opinion leaders from countries where proliferation is already a reality or near-reality. These chapters provide an insight into the motivations and intentions of key nations that possess (or seek to possess) weapons of mass destruction. Their perspective is important. Whether we agree with their conclusions or not, we must understand how they arrived at them if we are to tailor our own policy appropriately.

For example, Pakistan and India launched programs to develop the capability to build nuclear weapons in response to a more powerful neighbor already in possession of, or about to develop nuclear weapons—in the case of India, in response to China; in the case of Pakistan, in response to India. Neither enjoys the security guarantees from the United States (or another nuclear armed power) that have played such a critical role in discouraging nations such as Germany and Japan from developing their own arsenal of weapons of mass destruction.

The chapters by Messrs. Subrahmanyam and Sundarji lay out the perspectives of two influential opinion leaders in India on the importance to them of maintaining their nuclear weapons capability. They are frank in their view that the NPT is a flawed agreement that favors the five major nuclear weapons states. Munir Ahmed Khan gives a perspective from Pakistan in which he reviews the motivations for Pakistan's nuclear program and a series of proposals to alleviate tensions in the region. He recommends a strong role for the United States to ensure that the conventional military balance between Pakistan and India not get too lopsided.

George Perkovich then reviews a number of models for managing proliferation on the subcontinent. While unabashedly confessing to viewing the issue as an outsider, he makes a cogent case for nonweaponized deterrence—a regime in which both parties agree not to assemble and deploy nuclear weapons despite their competence to do so. Such a regime lends itself to a verification regime that could give India and Pakistan confidence that the other was not moving ahead secretively to assemble a ready arsenal of nuclear weapons. Dr. Perkovich further argues for stopping short of building a full-up force of nuclear weapons, pointing out that those states that have done so have found the economic, environmental, and societal costs to far exceed initial predictions.

Another category of nation is the rogue state. Unfortunately, these nations are located in precisely the regions where the United States has in the past and may well in the future want to intervene with conventional military forces: the Korean peninsula and the Middle East. The critical need to deal with North Korea's nuclear program on an ongoing and vigilant basis is underlined by Dr. Leonard Spector. Dr. Zalmay Khalilzad addresses the problem of proliferation in the Middle East with a focus on Iraq, Iran, and Israel. With respect to Iraq, he points out that if Iraq had nuclear weapons, our deployment to the region in Desert Shield/Desert Storm would have been complicated. We may have been reluctant to prosecute the war as aggressively, and Saudi Arabia would surely have been more reluctant to host our large deployment.

A Chinese perspective is presented by Wenguang Shao, who describes a China that broadly supports U.S. nonproliferation goals but sets limits on the degree of cooperation we can expect. Sergei Kortunov outlines Russia's perspective and delineates a broad range of areas where the United States and Russia can cooperate. A primary concern is the need to construct and maintain a strict regime to prevent the leakage of fissile material from Russia. Dr. George Mamedov lays out a broad set of proposals to strengthen and expand nonproliferation efforts. Again, conceptually, there is ample room for cooperation with the United States, including support for indefinite prolongation of the NPT, conclusion of a comprehensive test ban treaty, extension of security commitments to nations that agree to forego the development of weapons of mass destruction, and prevention of non-Russian states of the former Soviet Union from becoming nuclear weapons states.

The book concludes with a series of chapters that provide roadmaps for the future. David Kay reviews the role that inspections play in hindering states from acquiring weapons of mass destruction. He argues that imperfect though they be, they are an indispensible tool in building a program of nonproliferation or counterproliferation, and he offers suggestions on how to strengthen the utility of inspections. Janne Nolan provides a similar analysis of the Missile Technology Control Regime.

The concluding paper by William Martel and William Pendley states frankly and iconoclastically what many feel: The genie is out of the bottle and, in any event, all proliferation is not bad. Indeed there are cases where they argue that it has stabilized a region and probably has limited the extent of conflict between India and Pakistan. They argue for a nonproliferation and counterproliferation policy that evaluates a nation's attainment of weapons of mass destruction on a case-by-case basis and focuses on preventive or accommodating efforts only for those states that are truly threatening or destabilizing.

One theme is common throughout this volume: We need to encourage a serious and sober search for effective responses to the proliferation of weapons of mass destruction. The authors make a responsible contribution to that search and lay solid groundwork for continuing discussion.

Stuart E. Johnson
William Lewis
Washington, DC
April 1995

SECTION I

Challenges to Policy

WMD:
A Proliferation Overview

Robert G. Joseph

THROUGHOUT THE COLD WAR, THE PRIMARY CONCERN WITH weapons of mass destruction focused on the nuclear weapon stockpiles of the Soviet Union and the United States. Considerable debate and deliberation went into the development of an appropriate strategy and force structure to deter attack by the Soviet Union. From 1960 through 1990, close to 15 percent of total U.S. defense spending went toward building and maintaining a credible nuclear deterrent posture. While several other nations openly, and in some cases covertly, developed nuclear weapons and long-range delivery systems, their holdings were a small percentage of those of the two superpowers. Efforts to limit deployed nuclear weapons were almost exclusively conducted in bilateral negotiations between the United States and the Soviet Union.

With the end of the Cold War, the situation has changed. The United States and Russia are reducing their deployed strategic nuclear arsenals to about one third of their 1990 size. Russia, despite its economic problems, is continuing to develop new strategic missiles, although its

Dr. Robert G. Joseph is currently Director of the NDU Counterproliferation Research Center and Professor of National Security Policy at the National War College. He has held the positions of U.S. Commissioner to the Standing Consultive Commission (ABM Treaty) and U.S. Representative to the Bilateral Consultive Commission (U.S.-Russia nuclear testing). He is also a former Principal Deputy for International Security Policy and Deputy Assistant Secretary of Defense for Nuclear Forces and Arms Control Policy. He holds a Ph.D. from Columbia University and an M.A. from the University of Chicago.

progress in modernizing strategic nuclear forces will be subject to the military obtaining adequate resources. The United States is not developing any new nuclear weapons, and the last U.S. strategic missile program was cancelled in the early 1990s.

The number of countries capable of obtaining weapons of mass destruction (WMD)—nuclear, biological, and chemical—is growing. Despite several notable successes in impeding and actually reversing WMD proliferation, the post-Cold War environment is characterized by an increasing number of states seeking to acquire such weapons and their delivery systems. For this reason, preventing and protecting against WMD and missile proliferation has become one of the highest national priorities for the United States.

In responding to the above changes, especially WMD proliferation, U.S. policy makers are faced with a new set of challenges. A strategy to deter a nuclear strike against the United States is still critical, but no longer sufficient. As Moscow and Washington implement the first Strategic Arms Reduction Treaty (START I) and move toward START II levels of nuclear forces, it is necessary to consider the implications of no longer having a nuclear force that dwarfs those of medium-sized powers such as China. Moreover, possession of WMD by new regional powers will greatly complicate the U.S. ability to deter such countries from aggressive actions, as well as the ability to deploy forces to those regions. The Persian Gulf and Korea are examples of places where weapons of mass destruction in the hands of hostile regimes put U.S. forces at grave risk in crises or conflicts. Likewise, possession of WMD and the prospects for covert delivery by rogue states or terrorist groups present new security threats to the U.S. homeland.

Defining Trends

Deep Reductions in U.S. and Russian Nuclear Weapons are Underway

The implementation of the Intermediate Range Nuclear Forces (INF) Treaty and the first START agreement has resulted in the first real reductions in the nuclear forces of the United States and Russia.

President Reagan and General Secretary Gorbachev signed the INF Treaty in December 1987 at the Washington Summit. This agreement prohibited the United States and the Soviet Union from developing and deploying ground-launched missiles with ranges between 500 and 5500 km. As a result, the United States eliminated its Pershing and Ground Launched Cruise Missiles and the Soviet Union destroyed its SS-20, SS-12 and SS-23 missiles. While the total numbers of INF weapons were small compared to strategic forces, the treaty was important for two reasons. First, it represented the first time both sides had actually agreed to eliminate nuclear weapons, rather than just control their growth. Second, it created an intrusive verification regime that led to a high degree of confidence on both sides, thereby paving the way for the deep cuts in strategic forces contained in the START agreements.

At the July 1991 Moscow Summit, after a decade of negotiations, Presidents Bush and Gorbachev signed the START I agreement. In expectation that the treaty would be implemented fully by the parties, the United States and Russia began the elimination of substantial numbers of strategic nuclear weapons before formal entry into force. All parties have now ratified START I.

The START II Treaty, signed by Presidents Bush and Yeltsin in January 1993, limits each of the two sides to between 3,000 and 3,500 strategic weapons and, most significantly, eliminates all MIRVed ICBMs, including the heavy SS-18. Neither the U.S. Senate nor the Russian Duma has begun consideration of the agreement. Although the future of START II is open to question, Presidents Clinton and Yeltsin agreed in September 1994 to pursue the prospect for accelerated implementation of the agreed reductions. The United States, for its part, is structuring its future strategic force posture consistent with START II limitations.

Demand for Nuclear Weapons Is Growing

On the demand side, the trend toward further proliferation has accelerated, with a few notable exceptions. The relative discipline and general predictability of the bipolar Cold War relationships have been replaced in several key regions of the world by the expansion of regional arms races, including the aggressive pursuit of WMD and missile delivery capabilities. In several regions, for example the Persian Gulf and Northeast Asia, there appear to be few, if any, limits on the ambitions of unstable actors to acquire the most advanced and deadly weapons available, either through internal or external sources. Increasingly, the currency of power for these countries is a WMD capability. These weapons are perceived as both a status symbol and an instrument of political and military power for the pursuit of hegemonistic objectives.

In some regions, however, the trend is positive. Argentina and Brazil have apparently resolved their security concerns and abandoned their nuclear programs. South Africa has agreed to dismantle its nuclear weapons program and the six nuclear weapons it already possesses, and to join the Nonproliferation Treaty as a non-nuclear weapons state.

Despite these successes, an increasing number of countries have or are seeking the capability to produce and deliver nuclear weapons (see DNA Report, "Global Proliferation: Dynamics, Acquisition Strategies, and Responses," 1994). These states can be divided into several distinct groupings:

States with Undeclared Nuclear Capabilities. Several states are judged to possess either fully developed nuclear weapons or the capability to assemble and deliver such weapons in short order. Israel is in the first category, and is believed to possess a large and sophisticated stockpile of nuclear weapons. India and Pakistan are in the second category, with both believed to possess relatively crude weapons, but to be acquiring greater capabilities over time. All three countries have or are acquiring the ability to deliver WMD warheads with ballistic missiles; in the cases of Israel and India, their missiles are developed and produced domestically.

Instant proliferators. The dissolution of the Soviet Union resulted in the creation of three *de facto* nuclear weapons states in addition to Russia: Belarus, Kazahkstan, and Ukraine. In these three countries, proliferation was not the result of a determined effort to acquire weapons. Following independence, both Belarus and Kazahkstan expressed their intention to de-nuclearize and join the Treaty on the Nonproliferation of Nuclear Weapons (NPT) as non-nuclear weapons states. Ukraine, on the other hand, pursued a more ambiguous course. While allowing the return of "non-strategic" nuclear weapons to Russia, Kiev resisted the transfer of strategic forces (SS-19s, SS-24s, and air-launched cruise missiles), pending additional security and financial assurances. By the fall of 1994, Kiev had received the necessary assurances and joined the other two countries in ratifying the NPT.

States With Established Nuclear Weapons Programs. Several states, including Iraq, North Korea, and Iran, have established nuclear weapons programs that can or seek to produce weapons-grade fissile material. Although the Iraqi program has clearly been dealt a major setback by

Iraq's defeat in the Gulf War and the imposition of UN inspections, few believe the program has been permanently abolished. The leadership has not changed, and Iraqi nuclear expertise remains intact. The fact that the Iraqi nuclear weapons program was discovered to be much more advanced than had been believed prior to the Gulf War sounds a cautionary note for those seeking to evaluate the status of similar programs, such as North Korea's. Moreover, membership in the NPT, along with IAEA inspections, did not prevent the Iraqi and North Korean programs but may in fact have been used as a cover to gain access to weapons technology. This is a clear lesson for Iran and points out the importance of denying Iran the technologies necessary to produce fissile material, such as those to be attained in the pending purchase of Russian reactors.

States With Basic Expertise and Infrastructure. Potential proliferators such as Algeria and Syria appear to be acquiring the basic expertise and infrastructure needed to provide a nuclear weapons option, often through the acquisition of nuclear power reactors for ostensibly peaceful purposes. While some countries have explored the nuclear weapons option and backed off—for example, Taiwan and South Korea—others have decided to move forward on a weapons program. Even those that have not gone forward could quickly restart a weapons program if they believed their security interests demanded it.

States with the Necessary Expertise and Infrastructure. A growing number of non-nuclear weapons states possess the necessary scientific and industrial infrastructure to initiate a weapons program and rapidly field an effective weapons system. Countries such as Germany, Japan, and Sweden are in this group. The only factor which prevents such states from acquiring nuclear weapons is the political decision to eschew them. Many have felt more secure without national nuclear forces, relying for their security instead upon regional alliances and the U.S. strategic deterrent force. Others, especially the neutrals, have judged the financial and security costs of going nuclear to far outweigh the perceived advantages.

In addition, concerns about nuclear weapons coming into the possession of terrorists and organized crime groups have intensified in recent years. The end of the Cold War has heightened fears that terrorists could acquire such weapons, threaten to use them, and perhaps use them under certain circumstances. Moreover, concerns about a loss of control over the former Soviet Union's stocks of weapons-grade nuclear material have led to fears that organized crime elements could begin to traffic in nuclear materials as they have already done in other arms.

Chemical and Biological Weapons Offer Advantages to Potential Proliferators; Missiles Are the Delivery System of Choice

Some potential proliferators are pursuing chemical weapons (CW) and biological weapons (BW) programs, often at the same time they are pursuing nuclear weapons. CW and BW offer a number of advantages over nuclear weapons for such states (see Seth Carus, "The Proliferation of Biological Weapons," in Brad Roberts, ed., *Biological Weapons: Weapons of the Future?*, Center for Strategic and International Studies, 1993).

First, while nuclear weapons are very expensive, CW and BW provide a much cheaper route to WMD capability. Although the expense of producing and weaponizing large quantities of chemical weapons can be substantial, a small arsenal can be acquired relatively inexpensively. Biological weapons are also a relatively low-cost option in part because their suitability for unconventional delivery can reduce the delivery cost. BW is much more lethal than an equal quantity of CW. A small stockpile of biological warheads can have a devastating effect across a broad area, provided the problem of fratricide can be resolved.

Second, almost all of the technologies and materials required to produce CW and BW are dual-use in nature, and widely available for commercial purposes. For example, fertilizer production can be adjusted to produce chemical weapons, and pharmaceutical production techniques can be adapted to produce biological agents.

Third, CW and BW programs are much easier to conceal from international inspectors, and much more secure from air strikes. Production facilities for CW and BW do not have the unique signatures of nuclear facilities, and can be concealed in relatively small spaces—perhaps within legitimate chemical or pharmaceutical industrial plants. Similarly, defensive CW and BW programs, which are allowed under the various conventions that seek to ban such weapons, can be used as ready cover for offensive CW and BW programs.

Finally, the majority of potential WMD proliferators see missiles, and especially ballistic missiles, as the delivery system of choice. More than a dozen of these countries have operational ballistic missile programs.

Although the missiles possessed by today's proliferators are generally limited in range to about 600 km, much longer range missiles are being pursued. Iraq, for example, was able on its own to significantly increase the range of its Soviet-supplied SCUDs. North Korea is actively exporting longer range SCUDs, has flight-tested the 1,000 km NODONG, and has under development missiles with a range of 3,500 km or more, (the TAEPODONG II). Potential buyers for these Korean missiles are numerous. Similarly, as cruise missile technology becomes available with growing access to navigational aids such as the Global Positioning System, cruise missiles will become more attractive as a low-cost but highly effective WMD delivery system.

Responding to the Challenge

Maintaining Strategic Nuclear Deterrence

While U.S.-Russian relations have been fundamentally altered by the end of the Cold War and while common interests have grown and areas of rivalry have declined, Russia remains the only nation with the ability to destroy the United States. Thus, it is essential for the United States to maintain a strategic balance with Russia and to monitor closely Russian implementation of the START agreements, as well as to promote greater transparency regarding the entire nuclear stockpile—including reciprocal exchanges regarding numbers, locations, and other information, as well as greater security for nuclear material. Washington must be prepared to adjust force structure planning if relations sour, if Moscow decides that further reductions are not in Russia's interest and does not go forward with START II ratification and implementation, or if the United States is prevented from verifying Russian compliance.

In this context, it is proving difficult to establish a consensus on a new strategic framework which can be used to determine how nuclear forces fit into the overall U.S. security strategy now that the global competition with the Soviet Union has abated. The September 1994 Nuclear Posture Review (NPR) established a rationale for U.S. nuclear forces. The NPR outlines the U.S. post-START II force structure for 2003, maintaining the triad of submarine-launched ballistic missiles, heavy bombers, and silo-based ICBMs. The recommendations of the NPR resulted from a combination of factors, including START limits, budgetary constraints, and a desire to preserve manufacturing expertise in key areas.

However, the NPR raises but does not answer some key questions relating to the future U.S. nuclear posture. For example, it mentions the possibility of negotiating new agreements for deeper reductions than START II, and intimates that Washington will explore whether unilateral reductions to levels below those prescribed by START II could still yield a sufficient nuclear force. Yet another set of issues, also addressed in the NPR, relates to the ability of the United States to maintain a credible—reliable and safe—nuclear weapons capability without nuclear testing. For example, how might the United States maintain the capability to design, fabricate, and certify new warheads under a Comprehensive Test Ban Treaty? The future of the U.S. nuclear infrastructure and national weapons laboratories are central issues in this context.

Assisting the Destruction of WMD in the Former Soviet Union

One of the most potentially important nonproliferation initiatives currently underway is the assistance being provided to Ukraine and Russia to help achieve the de-nuclearization of the former and help the latter in ensuring safe and secure nuclear weapons dismantlement as well as to meet its legal obligations to destroy its CW stockpile. However, questions continue to be raised about Moscow's capability and, in some cases, commitment to comply with its arms control obligations, especially those in the areas of chemical and biological weapons. Unconfirmed but persistent public reports of continuing offensive CW and BW programs in Russia undermine support for Nunn-Lugar funding and could, if not convincingly countered, do serious harm to U.S.-Russian relations.

Overall, the future success of U.S. cooperative reduction initiatives is far from certain. Progress has been made with Ukraine, most notably in the January 1994 Trilateral Agreement on de-nuclearization. However, a variety of problems have arisen with Russia and Ukraine in the implementation of the Trilateral Agreement.

Controlling the Spread of WMD Technology

On the supply side, the diffusion of advanced technologies has become exceptionally difficult to control, despite the strengthening of export control regimes directed at preventing WMD and missile proliferation.

The emergence of alternative suppliers, the development of greater indigenous capabilities, and the consequences of the collapse of the Soviet Union make it unlikely that those countries determined to acquire such weapons can be stopped.

Many of the technologies and material used for WMD production are also used for legitimate non-weapons purposes. Such dual-use technologies are increasingly available on the open market and, where they cannot be openly bought or bartered, appear to be increasingly available through illicit channels. In this context, the exponential growth of organized crime in Russia and the possible leakage of tightly controlled nuclear weapons materials are indicative of a larger problem. While a decade or more might be needed to acquire nuclear weapons, a determined leadership with sufficient resources is likely to succeed. For chemical and biological weapons, the time and costs are significantly less.

The United States, along with a majority of industrial nations, have actively supported the establishment of multilateral export control regimes designed to deny potential proliferators access to sensitive technologies and materials needed for WMD and missiles. These include the Nuclear Suppliers Group, the Australia Group for chemical and biological weapons, and the Missile Technology Control Regime. Washington has also sought to re-orient the former COCOM, which was designed to prevent the transfer of strategic technologies to the Eastern bloc, to a nonproliferation mission. Domestically, the United States has enacted national legislation to control trade with, and provide sanctions against, proliferators and those who support their programs. Under such legislation, Washington has imposed sanctions against Russian and Indian firms, and more recently against China for its assistance to Pakistan's missile program.

The strengths and weaknesses of export controls were vividly illustrated in the case of the Iraqi nuclear weapons program. Clearly, export controls succeeded in delaying and increasing the cost of this program. Nevertheless, post-Gulf War discoveries about Iraq's nuclear program revealed it to be much more advanced than most analysts had suspected. Iraq acquired critical dual-use components both on the open market and through illicit trade with companies from states that are members of export control regimes. As with arms control treaties, export controls can be an important nonproliferation tool but, by themselves, will not stop determined proliferators.

Promoting International Norms and Incentives Against WMD Proliferation

On the demand side, the United States has taken the lead in strengthening multilateral arms control treaties to halt further nuclear weapons proliferation, such as through supporting the indefinite extension of the NPT, and to ban the development and use of chemical and biological weapons. Moreover, the United States has attempted to create incentives for potential proliferators not to pursue WMD and disincentives for those who do. One element has been diplomatic dissuasion, which has been a consistent element of U.S policy. It has in some cases made a major contribution to U.S. nonproliferation efforts, for example, in influencing Argentina's decision to end its CONDOR ballistic missile program.

Another approach involves encouraging regional stability through greater dialogue and transparency among regional states, including confidence-building and security measures in such areas as the Middle East and South Asia. Such diplomatic approaches represent a low-cost, non-threatening approach to containing the spread of WMD. In the case of nations that have chosen to remain outside the regimes for controlling the diffusion of WMD, diplomatic dialogue is sometimes the only option for Washington. A more direct approach to preventing proliferation is through security assurances, either in the form of positive security guarantees to individual states (for example, South Korea) or negative security assurance, such as those associated with NPT membership.

Preventing WMD Attacks on U.S.Territory and Forces

The substantial reduction in the threat of a strategic nuclear war has not made the United States secure from WMD attack. The bombing of the World Trade Center may portend future terrorist attacks on soft, unprotected targets such as cities. American cities are also becoming directly vulnerable to attacks by long-range delivery systems of new WMD-capable states. An even more immediate concern is that U.S. forces deployed abroad are increasingly at risk from WMD and missile proliferation.

To bolster deterrence, it is imperative for the United States to maintain a credible military capability to respond decisively to WMD attacks. The logic of deterrence still applies: if those who would contemplate the use of WMD against U.S. targets know that this is likely to result in swift, sure and devastating retaliation, they may well consider the price of such actions to be unacceptably high. For example, if the leaders of a rogue regime understand that the employment of WMD against U.S. forces engaged in a limited military action will result in the expansion of that action's objectives to include the destruction of the regime in question, this may be sufficient to deter the regime from using WMD, even in the absence of an in-kind counter-strike. As a party to the biological and, if ratified, the chemical weapons conventions, the United States has given up the option for retaliatory BW and CW strikes In many cases, an overwhelming conventional response may be the preferred, if not the only, credible option.

Strengthening Counterproliferation

Experience and prudence dictate that, ultimately, some proliferators will succeed in their quest. Thus, in addition to strengthening efforts to prevent WMD and missile proliferation, the United States is undertaking a number of measures to protect against such proliferation when it occurs. The 1994 Counterproliferation Initiative is designed to ensure that the necessary defense acquisition, doctrine, and training are in place to provide the United States with the ability to deter and defend against the WMD and missile threat.

To achieve these objectives, the Department of Defense is pursuing enhanced and, in some cases, new capabilities in a number of areas, including:

• Detection and assessment of nuclear, chemical, and biological weapons development programs, as well as tactical detection of CW and BW use;

• Active missile defenses such as an improved Patriot system and the more capable THAAD;

• Counterforce capabilities designed for use against WMD targets, such as deep penetration precision munitions for destroying underground WMD facilities.

A central issue is the U.S. ballistic missile defense program. When President Reagan launched the Strategic Defense Initiative in 1982, the focus of the program was defense of the U.S. and its allies against a massive attack by Soviet strategic nuclear forces, with potentially thousands of warheads. By the end of 1990, relations with Moscow were changing and clear progress was being made in the START negotiations.

The threat of a much smaller attack, for example from an accidental launch or by a regional power with limited numbers of missiles, was seen as more likely. Accordingly, the program shifted to an emphasis on global protection against limited strikes (GPALS), designed to handle up to a few hundred warheads threatening the U.S. homeland. In the past two years, the program has again shifted focus almost exclusively to theater missile defense, designed to provide protection to U.S. forces deployed in regions where they may face weapons of mass destruction mounted on ballistic missiles.

Whether the above counterproliferation programs will be successful and sufficient will be determined by several factors. For instance, the rate of technological progress in BW detection and in development of non-nuclear weapons to kill deep underground targets are controlling factors for success in these areas. Another factor is resource limitations, in particular whether—if the DoD budget continues to decline—the United States will be able to maintain the conventional superiority necessary to deter the use of WMD. Finally, concerning active missile defenses, arms control policy could foreclose U.S. options to respond to the emerging threat. For example, negotiating limits on theater defenses in the name of strengthening the ABM Treaty would undercut the U.S. ability to develop and deploy missile defenses able to counter longer range theater missiles, such as those being developed by North Korea.

Preparing for Regional Instability Resulting From WMD Proliferation

Some analysts argue that proliferation of WMD capabilities—particularly nuclear weapons—may in some cases actually serve U.S. interests by moderating the behavior of potentially antagonistic states. Two examples often cited are India and Pakistan and, more recently, Russia and Ukraine. Such ideas are largely derived from the Cold War strategic experience, in which the balance of terror imposed by nuclear weapons provided stability by deterring the superpowers from conflict.

However, stable deterrence requires more than the deployment of nuclear weapons. On the hardware side, it requires sophisticated command-and-control arrangements and technologically challenging measures to ensure weapons survivability. Absent such capabilities, adversarial relationships can be rendered more, not less, unstable as a result of nuclear weapons. This is a major concern regarding nuclear weapons on the Asian subcontinent, where "use it or lose it" considerations provide both sides with an incentive for first use.

Stable deterrence also requires rational leaders on both sides who, although hostile to each other, hold essentially limited and pragmatic objectives, and are unwilling to commit national suicide for religious, ideological, or personal purposes. This condition also may not hold for a number of aspiring proliferators and, as a result, has fundamental implications for U.S. security policy.

Concepts to Capabilities:
The First Year of Counterproliferation

Mitchel B. Wallerstein

ONE YEAR AGO, ON THE 7TH OF DECEMBER, A DATE THAT IS otherwise notable for more infamous reasons, then Secretary of Defense Les Aspin launched the Defense Counterproliferation Initiative. This initiative represented an opportunity to reassess the military threat posed by the proliferation of nuclear, chemical, and biological weapons and their means of delivery and to give this threat greater emphasis in our military planning. At least twenty countries, many of them hostile to the U.S. and our allies, of mass destruction. The greater the proliferation of these weapons the larger the constellation of consequences for us—from attacks on our citizens and our cities by terrorists, to use of these unconventional weapons against our forces of friendly populations in some regional war, to the possibility that we might be deterred from involvement in some future conflict where our interests do not seem sufficiently immediate or direct to justify the risk.

My charge in this administration is to develop and promulgate those defense policies necessary to prevent proliferation, roll it back where possible, and to assure our forces are prepared to defeat challengers armed with weapons of mass destruction. I see these as wholly complementary goals that must be pursued in parallel if we are to achieve success. Through the Defense Counterproliferation Initiative we are

Dr. Mitchel B. Wallerstein currently serves as Deputy Assistant Secretary of Defense for Counterproliferation Policy. Prior to joining the Department of Defense, he was the Deputy Executive Officer of the National Research Council of the National Academy of Sciences. Dr. Wallerstein also teaches at the Johns Hopkins University School for Advanced International Studies and at the Georgetown University School of Foreign Service. He holds a Ph.D. and M.S. from M.I.T., a Masters from the Maxwell School of Public Affairs at Syracuse University, and an A.B. from Dartmouth College.

giving greater attention the military implications of proliferation, and therefore to defense planning to ensure we are able to fulfill our responsibilities for national security and defense. I welcome this opportunity to discuss our initiative in terms of the needs we identified in 1993 and what we've done in the course of the last year to meet those needs. First, I'd like briefly to review how the counterproliferation concept came about.

How CP Got Started

DoD's motivation for its counterproliferation strategy derived largely from a convergence of two factors: 1) military necessity resulting from our Gulf War experiences with Iraq, and 2) a reorientation of our conventional force structure as a result of the Bottom Up Review.

I have always believed that experience is the best teacher. In the Gulf War with Iraq, we had the best kind of experience from which to learn about the military implications of WMD: our forces performed brilliantly, but we also caught a glimpse of how, when confronted by an adversary with weapons of mass destruction, our capabilities were limited in some important ways.

• Saddam Hussein repeatedly fired SCUD missiles at our troops and civilian populations of our allies. While not militarily decisive, we learned that our ability to defeat the missiles—either on the ground or in the air—was limited.

• During the conflict, we learned that Saddam Hussein had facilities to develop biological weapons. When we planned to attack suspected facilities, however, we discovered that our knowledge was equally limited regarding how to attack such a target while limiting collateral effects to the surrounding area.

• We knew Saddam had an extensive chemical weapon arsenal and had experience using it. Saddam's army had used chemicals against Iraq's Kurdish minority and against Iranian forces. But Saddam did not use chemical weapons against the UN forces during Desert Storm. We would very much like to know why, but again our understanding is limited.

• Finally, after the UN began dismantling Iraq's nuclear weapon infrastructure, we learned that our understanding of the size, scope, and progress of Saddam's nuclear program had been very limited.

Our Gulf War experience revealed too many limitations on our forces when they are required to confront an adversary armed with WMD. Through our counterproliferation initiative we are making sure to put the lessons of this experience are acted upon.

The second factor motivating our new initiative, was the Bottom Up Review. With the end of Cold War competition on a global scale, this administration undertook a Bottom Up Review and reoriented our force structure on the ability to fight and win two Major Regional Contingencies or MRCs. When you look at the planning factors associated with these MRCs, it becomes readily apparent that a high probability of WMD use—or threat of use—exists. So, we had the convergence of a real world demonstration of our limited capability to address the military strategy that directed us to prepare for those very types of real world contingencies.

Of course, we would prefer not to face threats from adversaries armed with nuclear, biological and chemical weapons. Preventing proliferation from occurring in the first place remains our paramount objective. The Defense Department has a strong record of support for international regimes against the proliferation of WMD and for export controls on sensitive technologies. For example, we have loaned equipment and personnel to the UN to enhance the effectiveness of the UNSCOM mission in Iraq. Here at home, DoD personnel with technical expertise of weapons development are extremely important to determining whether specific exports have military applications. Indeed, I want to emphasize that, in no way, have we given up on preventing proliferation, nor do we see counterproliferation as an alternative course of action to nonproliferation.

However, we realize that determined proliferators are likely to succeed. And that certain countries of concern to us are some of the most determined. For proliferators, the end of the Cold War and the break up of the Soviet Union has increased the potential for access to WMD technology, material, and expertise, although the successor governments to the Soviet Union are taking steps to maintain—and actually expand—their export controls. At the same time, the global economy is enjoying a rising tide of trade and technology that improves the ability of a proliferator to produce indigenously, or leap developmental hurdles and purchase key components "off the shelf." Thus, where proliferation succeeds, we must be prepared to protect our troops, our interests, and our allies. This military preparedness is at the very heart of what constitutes the Defense Counterproliferation Initiative.

The Defense Counterproliferation Initiative

The Defense Counterproliferation Initiative is not a single, acquisition-oriented program within the Department. Rather, we are working to integrate a greater emphasis on the threats from and military implications of WMD into all of the activities of DoD. This is a large task and we will only be able to accomplish it over time but I think we have made some significant progress in the short year since we launched the Initiative.

Let me spend a few minutes to review the five elements of this initiative and the progress we have made in each.

Policy Framework

As we began to formulate our thinking about counterproliferation, we realized that a well-articulated policy statement was essential to direct the myriad of relevant Defense Department activities. Secretary Perry issued this guidance to the Joint Staff, the Services and the Major Commands, directing them to take account in their defense planning and programming of the increased threat posed by the proliferation of WMD and the new DoD counterproliferation policy. Appropriate modifications have also been made to the Contingency Planning Guidance and Defense Planning Guidance documents. Additional policy development will be required as the military departments and warfighting CINCs continue to wrestle with the many dimensions of this tough problem.

Military Planning

Following from this policy guidance, the Joint Staff is leading a study of the missions of the CINCs and functions of the Services to determine how best to respond to proliferation and implement counterproliferation. This study has the full participation of the CINCs and Services themselves and is fundamental to bringing about a sea-change, if that is necessary, in the thinking of the Department on how to handle these new threats. The study will be completed in January 1995, when Chairman

Shalikashvili is expected to make his recommendations on Service functions and CINC missions to the Secretary.

An important tool for military planning is the ability to model or simulate future battlefields. In the past, nuclear, chemical, and biological weapons effects were analyzed by a small group of experts, but were often not included or marginalized in scenarios developed for our conventional wargaming. There are many reasons for this lack of integration, primarily that the modeling of unconventional effects is extremely difficult. But the result was that military planners had few tools for determining the full impact of WMD on their plans. However, now we are seeing a greater effort in many wargames to combine conventional and unconventional weapon effects as the importance of NBC/M on the conventional battlefield is becoming more widely understood. We have a long way to go, but the growing demand for modeling NBC/M effects is encouraging. As a natural progression from our wargaming experience, we have planned for further educational requirements at our senior and intermediate service schools as well as a need to facilitate CP doctrinal development. Here, the National Defense University has established a new Center for Counterproliferation Research to infuse the senior leadership of our military with a greater understanding of the political and military implications of WMD.

Intelligence Support

As I discussed earlier, most of the lessons we learned in the Gulf were related to the orientation of our intelligence collection requirements, and specifically to our increasing need for operational intelligence. We now place far broader and more detailed demands on our intelligence assets than simply to determine if proliferation is occurring so we can notify the relevant nonproliferation regimes. We know that proliferation *IS* occurring. To prepare our forces to meet the consequences of that proliferation on the battlefield, the quality of our intelligence gathering and analysis must be measured in terms of its operational utility: Exactly what agents is a state developing? Have the agents been integrated into weapons? Have the weapons been deployed? Where are they deployed? How does the state intend to use them—What is the doctrine? Where are the WMD facilities?

To answer these questions and others, the Intelligence Community's Non-Proliferation Center has created a new directorate for military planning and DoD has assigned personnel to help the NPC better understand and meet these operational requirements. The Defense Intelligence Agency also has instituted a Counterproliferation Issue Manager position to coordinate assets in support of the military intelligence requirements. In a moment when I discuss acquisition activities, I'll again highlight some of the areas where we are augmenting existing funds to operationalize intelligence.

Acquisition Strategy

To match our new policies, our new functions and missions, and better intelligence, we are also looking at ways to better equip our forces should they have to engage an adversary armed with WMD. In designing our acquisition strategy, we have been guided by our goal of integrating counterproliferation throughout the Department. Therefore, we are adapting, where possible, current systems and platforms rather than building specialized ones. We do not want anyone to think that there is a single solution to the problem of proliferation and risk ignoring other necessary preparations of our forces.

The first analysis of where we should focus our acquisition strategy came from the interagency Nonproliferation Program Review Committee, chaired by Deputy Secretary John Deutch. The Committee recommended several "areas for progress" where additional funding of programs already in development could significantly enhance counterproliferation and nonproliferation capabilities.

- Real-time detection and characterization of biological weapon and chemical weapon agents
- Detection, characterization, and defeat of WMD-related underground facilities
- Detection, location, and rendering harmless of WMD inside and outside the U.S.
- Personnel and equipment protection and decontamination versus BW/CW agents
- Rapid production of BW vaccines
- Intercept of low-flying, stealthy cruise-missiles
- Boost phase intercept of ballistic missiles
- Prompt mobile target kill

The Committee's report not only served as a catalyst for action within the Services and Defense Agencies, but also garnered funding support from Congress in several important areas. Congress provided $60.0M in FY 95 to accelerate DoD efforts to fix capability shortfalls in the following areas:

- BW/CW detection and characterization
- Hard target characterization and defeat
- Paramilitary/terrorist WMD threats
- Detect and track WMD shipments at sea
- Individual/collective protection and decontamination

Counterproliferation International Cooperation

The final major element of the Defense Counterproliferation Initiative recognizes that in future conflicts where NBC/M may be involved in all likelihood, we won't be fighting alone. We will be engaging along with allies or coalition partners, and most likely will be operating from the homelands of regional partners. I spend much of my time in very constructive dialogue with representatives of other governments, explaining our ideas about counterproliferation, gaging their reactions, clarifying misunderstandings, and in general creating an environment where we can come together on a multilateral basis to work on these very difficult issues of mutual concern.

We embarked on a premiere initiative for international cooperation at NATO in January of this year when NATO Heads of State and Government agreed that NBC/M proliferation represented a risk to the alliance and that NATO should act. The Alliance established a new structure to address this issue and established the Senior Defense Group on Proliferation, which Assistant Secretary Ashton Carter co-chairs with his counterpart from the French MoD Jean-Claude Mallet. Those of you familiar with NATO history will appreciate the significance of French participation, much less co-leadership, with the United States, of a NATO group working on defense planning. I see this as another indication of the consensus building around the military implications and the threat to our common security.

The Defense Group on Proliferation has a three phase plan: assessment of risks, analysis of the impact on Alliance capabilities, and analysis of necessary improvements. The first phase of NATO's DGP workplan, development of a risk assessment, is scheduled to be completed this December. The final meeting of the DGP, where the Risk

Assessment is to be approved will be held in mid-November, 1994. This assessment:

- Identifies countries of concern to NATO and provides technical detail on their NBC capabilities.
- Seeks to outline potential WMD threats out to 2010 as an input for defense planning.
- Begins discussion on the operational impact of use or threatened use of these weapons against NATO populations, territories, and forces.

Future work will evaluate necessary military capabilities and make programmatic recommendations. This risk assessment will lay an excellent foundation for all of the work at NATO on proliferation, not just that of the Defense Group on Proliferation.

We also are pursuing counterproliferation discussions with the Russian Federation, through the Strategic Stability Working Group. In October 1994, we presented our counterproliferation conceptual framework to members of the Russian general staff, and engaged the Russians in a constructive dialogue. The Russians offered to present their views about proliferation threats at a subsequent meeting, and we look forward to another constructive exchange.

We also continue to explore a possible relationship with Japan built around theater missile defense issues and technology sharing. Of course, the situation today in Northeast Asia represents a critically important venue for further counterproliferation and nonproliferation discussions, planning, and negotiations.

Conclusion

I will be the first to say that the progress we have made in the past year represents only the first step of many that will be necessary to improve the capabilities of our forces when confronting an adversary armed with nuclear, biological or chemical weapons and advanced delivery systems.

In the coming year, we look forward to further progress on the military side as a result of the review of service functions and CINC missions. And the first fruits of our acquisition strategy also will be ripening.

At the same time, our policy work will continue to move ahead. I am convinced that the key to combatting the spread of weapons of mass destruction lies in expanded international cooperation. We plan in the coming year to work for the unconditional and indefinite extension of the NPT and the entry-into-force of the CWC. Complementing these international regimes against proliferation, will be our continuing efforts at NATO, as we work to ensure that alliance forces also are prepared for the military problems posed by WMD conflict.

The Defense Department's fundamental responsibility for the national security of the country and the requirement that we be prepared against any and all risks posed by the proliferation of WMD would be reason enough for our counterproliferation efforts.

But there is another rationale as well. As potential adversaries come to understand that the possession and/or blandishment of WMD is not sufficient to deter or dissuade the United States from defending its interests—and those of its allies around the world, as we have for decades—they will be compelled to reconsider the value of the huge investment of time, money and international credibility they are making to develop such weapons. This would be the optimal outcome of our efforts, since our primary goal remains to stop proliferation from occurring in the first place.

Proliferation Prevention: Beyond Traditionalism

Lewis A. Dunn

THE CHALLENGE POSED BY NUCLEAR, CHEMICAL, AND biological weapons proliferation is now widely-acknowledged to be one of the major threats to U.S. security in the post-Cold War world. Reflected in the counter-proliferation initiative announced by then-Secretary of Defense Les Aspin in December, 1993, efforts have begun to identify needed defense-related responses—from acquisition to doctrinal development—to protect against future proliferation threats. This new emphasis on the defense planning implications of proliferation is both to be welcomed and long overdue. Nonetheless, it is equally clear that putting in place effective military responses to proliferation will be operationally difficult, technically complex, costly, and in some instances not fully feasible. For that reason, measures to preserve and strengthen U.S. efforts to prevent proliferation remain essential. Indeed, preventing proliferation in the first place ultimately may be the best means of proliferation protection.

Traditional non-proliferation measures—most often symbolized by non-proliferation export controls—remain critical. These measures need to be preserved and strengthened. But non-proliferation traditionalism alone is insufficient. Instead, such measures need to be complemented by new non-traditional initiatives. In that spirit, the following paper first briefly reviews more traditional proliferation prevention activities before

Dr. Lewis A. Dunn is Vice President and Manager of the Weapons Proliferation and Strategic Planning Department of Science Applications International Corporation. Formerly he was the Assistant Director of the U.S. Arms Control and Disarmament Agency and served as Ambassador to the 1985 Nuclear Non-Proliferation Treaty Review Conference and as Ambassador to the 1987 United Nations Conference on the Peaceful Uses of Nuclear Energy. Dr. Dunn earned a Ph.D. in Political Science from the University of Chicago.

proposing some possible new thrusts. Its purpose is not to make an unshakable case for these additional initiatives but to encourage more thinking "out of the box."

Non-Proliferation Traditionalism

Traditional U.S. non-proliferation policies, supported by likeminded countries, have emphasized three main thrusts. These have respectively sought to: buttress technical constraints; reduce proliferation incentives and enhance disincentives; and to build non-proliferation institutions. Consider each in turn.

Enhancing Technical Constraints

Over the past two decades, multilateral export controls and suppliers' restraints have been put in place to enhance technical constraints and make it more difficult for countries to acquire NBC weaponry. These controls have not been expected to block proliferation outright. Instead, their purpose has been to "buy time."

In some instances, buying time has allowed other diplomatic and political actions to be taken (e.g., use of U.S. influence in the mid-1970s to persuade both South Korea and Taiwan to shut-down questionable nuclear activities). Buying time, however, is also valuable in its own right. Regional security and domestic political changes can lead to unexpected decisions to renounce or rollback NBC programs. This is perhaps best typified by South Africa's decision in the early 1990s to dismantle its rudimentary nuclear arsenal and join the Nuclear Non-Proliferation Treaty (NPT), a decision made possible by the withdrawal of Soviet and Cuban forces from Angola in the late-1980s and made necessary in the eyes of the new government of President de Klerk by the inevitability of black majority rule.

Reducing Incentives and Increasing Disincentives

Equally important, traditional prevention policies have sought to reduce proliferation incentives. Diplomatic persuasion and non-nuclear jaw-boning, use of conventional arms sales to help buttress defense capabilities of U.S. allies and friends, political support in crises, and efforts to encourage regional stability and confidence-building all have played a role. The threat of economic and other sanctions, reflected in U.S. legislation, has also been used in attempts to enhance disincentives to pursuing NBC weaponry.

Perhaps the most important measure for reducing proliferation incentives over the past decades, however, has had little explicitly to do with non-proliferation. This is the *U.S. alliance structure in Europe and Asia.* By providing a framework for stability and security during the Cold War era, that structure was an essential underpinning of decisions by major countries in Europe and Asia not to seek a nuclear arsenal. (The two exceptions, France and the United Kingdom, both acquired nuclear weapons more because of concerns for their great power status and prestige than about their security.) But throughout this Cold War period this alliance structure was, in effect, a "free good" for non-proliferation. Henceforth, its maintenance will need to be partly justified—and paid for—on non-proliferation grounds.

Institution-Building

Beginning with the creation of the International Atomic Energy Agency in 1957, institution-building has been the third major non-proliferation thrust. In an incremental process, major institutional advances have been made over the ensuing decades. Their purpose has partly been to reinforce, legitimize, and help implement the preceding efforts to enhance technical constraints and reduce proliferation incentives. Equally important, this process of institution-building has helped to create and extend an overall norm of non-proliferation.

Specific advances include the:

• Treaty of Tlatlelcolo, creating a nuclear free zone in Latin America (1967);

• Nuclear Non-Proliferation Treaty, with its legally binding obligation not to acquire nuclear weapons as well as its provisions for international inspections and export controls (1968);

• Biological and Toxin Weapons Convention, at least creating a norm—even if virtually unverifiable—against acquisition of BW weaponry (1972);

• Zangger Committee "trigger list," identifying specific exports to be controlled under the NPT (1974);

- Nuclear Suppliers' Group and Guidelines, buttressing supply restraint and extending it to encompass technology as well as equipment, components, and materials (1978);
- Establishment of the Australia Group to enhance export controls on BW and CW-related items (1986);
- Missile Technology Control Regime (MTCR), restraining sales of missiles, missile components, and related technologies by key industrial countries (1987);
- Periodic upgrades of the Zangger Committee trigger list and the Nuclear Suppliers' Guidelines, culminating in controls on dual-use exports (1991);
- Creation and use of the United Nations Special Commission for Iraq, valuable for the future both as an institutional-model and as a precedent for Security Council involvement in proliferation crises (1991); and
- Conclusion of a Chemical Weapons Convention (CWC), which includes the most comprehensive challenge inspection system yet negotiated (1992).

Key challenges are ahead to preserve and strengthen this fabric of non-proliferation institutions. Indefinite or long-term extension of the NPT in 1995 is not assured. With its limited verifiability, the BWC remains at best a partial success. The CWC has yet to be ratified by the United States Senate or to enter into force globally. Countries of proliferation concern continue to seek new ways to circumvent export controls. Regional confidence- and security-building has to be accelerated in regions of proliferation concern, whether South Asia, the Middle East, or Northeast Asia. Key outsiders need to be brought fully into these regimes, not least China and the Newly Independent States. How well these challenges are met will greatly affect the prospects for containing proliferation.

Beyond Non-Proliferation
Traditionalism Alone

Over the first five decades of the nuclear age, the United States took the lead in each of the preceding areas. The resulting creation of an overall non-proliferation regime has been and remains a major policy success.

Nonetheless, for several reasons, continued non-proliferation traditionalism alone will not suffice.

Traditional approaches to proliferation prevention fail to take advantage of potential synergies among global, regional, and national non-proliferation efforts. Traditionalism also lacks a credible national or international response to non-compliance with non-proliferation obligations and norms. Perhaps most important, it offers too limited a solution for dealing with countries that may be seeking WMD not due to insecurity but as instruments of regional domination and hegemony or to pose a direct threat to the United States.

In light of these weaknesses, new thinking about proliferation prevention is needed in least four areas. These are: leveraging global arms control and non-proliferation actions to encourage regional restraint; institutionalizing a presumption of Security Council action in response to non-compliance and to deal with proliferation threats to the peace; deterring acquisition of WMD by potential regional hegemons; and contingency planning to provide an option of *in extremis* recourse to military options to block proliferation.[1]

Leveraging Global Nuclear Initiatives

During the Cold War era, nuclear arms control and non-proliferation were pursued in isolation from each other. The former focused on measures to stabilize U.S.-Soviet nuclear competition; the latter sought to convince individual countries not to seek nuclear weaponry for themselves. By contrast, future proliferation prevention activities should seek to integrate U.S. nuclear arms control and non-proliferation policies. In effect, the U.S. goal would be to leverage global arms control initiatives both to help define the context of national nuclear decision-making in several key proliferation problem countries and to offer an alternative means of regional restraint.

Efforts already are underway to begin negotiations on a global convention cutting-off the production of plutonium and highly-enriched uranium for nuclear explosives or not under safeguards, a *fissile material production ban*. Such a ban could offer a more palatable vehicle for decisions by India and Pakistan to cap their nuclear weapons programs short of open nuclear competition. Similarly, should the Middle East Peace Process remain on track, Israeli decision-makers could well find eventual adherence useful to demonstrate nuclear restraint and to help legitimize a tough international stand against Iraqi and Iranian nuclear pursuits.

Short of conclusion of a fissile material ban, preliminary steps might be taken with important non-proliferation payoffs. Discussions of verification issues involving China, Pakistan, India, the United States, and selected other countries could reinforce the confidence-building process within South Asia. It also would begin to engage China more fully as a player in that region, thereby meeting India's concerns. An early Israeli indication of its readiness to participate in cutoff negotiations, and to adhere should an agreement be reached, would reassure its Arab neighbors and help strengthen the NPT regime.

Similarly, *bringing China, France, and the United Kingdom fully into the global nuclear arms control process* is important not only for the success of future negotiations but also for its potential non-proliferation payoffs. In particular, a cap on the further expansion of China's nuclear arsenal would reassure countries in Asia, while shaping, as well, the debate in New Delhi about India's future nuclear choices. More broadly, the prospect of reducing the nuclear arsenals of all five acknowledged nuclear powers would strengthen the global non-proliferation norm and help ensure the longer-term legitimacy of the NPT. Success in on-going negotiations for a global nuclear test ban would have comparable impacts.

Greater *transparency*, that is voluntary openness, about nuclear activities—from doctrine to dismantlement of surplus nuclear warheads—increasingly characterizes the U.S.-Russian nuclear relationship. Over time, the other acknowledged nuclear powers may come to accept the principle of increased transparency. This will provide an opportunity for the United States to seek to encourage new transparency initiatives in the non-proliferation realm and more effective implementation of existing ones. Examples could include requiring all NPT parties to inform the IAEA of nuclear-related exports and imports; enhanced implementation of transparency measures under the BWC; and new regional non-proliferation-related visits to sites and facilities, e.g., between the two Koreas and perhaps in South Asia and later the Middle East.

Institutionalizing a Presumption of Security Council Action

The lack of credible and effective response to non-compliance with countries' obligations under the NPT, the BWC, and a future CWC stands out in any assessment of non-proliferation traditionalism.   Recent experience has been decidedly mixed.

Since 1991, the United Nations Special Commission on Iraq has played a vital role in rooting out Iraq's NBC programs. At key junctures, moreover, the members of the Security Council have also shown their readiness to stand behind UNSCOM's efforts. But it owed its existence to the special circumstances of Iraq's defeat in the Gulf War, a fact undoubtedly not lost on other potential violators. By contrast, throughout the summer of 1994, members of the Security Council, especially China, resisted U.S. efforts to forge a consensus to impose sanctions on North Korea unless it remedied its violation of the NPT. Ultimately, the United States struck its own bilateral deal with the North Korean regime, aimed at blocking North Korean access to growing stocks of plutonium but at the price of deferring special IAEA inspections and a full accounting of past North Korean actions for at least five years.

North Korea's success in resisting international pressures to honor its NPT obligations risks sending a signal that other aspiring proliferators may seek to emulate.   More generally, lack of effective international responses to non-compliance can only encourage countries contemplating treaty violations. Over time, if some countries are perceived to be able to violate with impunity their non-proliferation obligations, the credibility of the overall regime will erode. Still other countries are all but certain, as well, to rethink their own decisions not to seek NBC weaponry.

For the short-term, the task is to *limit the North Korean deal's damage* to global norms and institutions. For its part, the United States needs to use its remaining leverage, e.g., the carrot of improved political relations, to press for timely and full implementation of the agreement. Chinese diplomatic intervention in Pyongyang to make clear that it, too, expects timely implementation would back-up U.S. actions. Another step would be to use suitable multilateral forums, e.g., the IAEA and the United Nations Security Council, to serve notice to Pyongyang that backsliding will be met by an international response. To lessen the precedent set by North Korea's successful resistance of IAEA special inspections, both the IAEA General Conference and other forums could be used to reiterate support for such inspections. Efforts might be made, as well, to hold a few special inspections soon, perhaps in the process of developing initial inventories of to-be-safeguarded nuclear materials in one or more of the Newly Independent States.

For the longer-term, however, more far-reaching efforts need to be explored to create a presumption of Security Council action in support of non-proliferation. This could help not only to fill this "non-compliance gap" but also to build norms and lessen insecurities that could shape still other countries' proliferation decisions. A number of specific steps could be considered.

The January, 1992 Summit of the members of the Security Council declared the Council's readiness to respond to violations of IAEA safeguards and that it considered proliferation to be a "threat to the peace." Going a step further, the Council could pass a formal *Security Council resolution on proliferation* to give legal status to that declaration. The Council could also state its readiness to respond to violations of non-proliferation treaties.

To help institutionalize Security Council involvement, a second Security Council *non-proliferation summit* could be held and a commitment made to do so annually in the future. Similarly, the position of a *"Non-Proliferation Rapporteur"* to the Council might be established.[2] The rapporteur's responsibilities could include keeping the Council informed of matters of non-proliferation concern, providing an annual report on non-proliferation, and serving as a source of information for Council members lacking the intelligence capabilities of the great powers. Moreover, the process of increasing Council involvement—and that of the members of the Council as well as their national bureaucracies—would be as important as the specific substance of a rapporteur's reports.

Successful use of the Security Council to buttress and backstop traditional proliferation prevention presupposes continuing bilateral U.S. consultations with the other permanent members of the Council members, especially China. With regard to the latter, U.S. policymakers should think in terms of a long-term effort to *integrate China fully into the overall non-proliferation regime* and to influence Beijing's approach to proliferation. Multiple points of engagement with Chinese officials should be pursued—with political, economic, military, energy, and other constituencies in China. China's participation in international non-proliferation organizations, from the Nuclear Suppliers' Group to the Australia Group, should be solicited. Periodic difficulties are to be expected. But over time, China's policies may come to approximate more closely those of the other Perm-5 countries.

Deterring Acquisition by Denial of Gains

Deterrence of acquisition has been a modest and not very successful element of past non-proliferation efforts. Almost exclusively, deterrent efforts have emphasized the threat of punishment. They have frequently foundered, however, on the reluctance either of the United States or of other countries to carry out such threats. Faced with aspiring proliferators whose goal is regional hegemony and aggrandizement, actions are needed, as already suggested, to lay a better political foundation for great power punitive action under the Security Council. At the same time, the United States and its allies need to take other steps to buttress proliferation deterrence not by the threat of punishment but by the prospect of denial of gains.

In that regard, U.S. policies should consciously seek ways to convince aspiring regional hegemons that even if they acquire NBC weaponry, they still will be unable to achieve their regional and extra-regional goals. To the contrary, such countries need to fear that acquiring these weapons will make them less not more secure. In effect, proliferation deterrence by denial would seek to send a clear signal to countries like Iran, Iraq, and others that "they shall not gain."

More specifically, a mix of *political and military actions* need to be explored by the United States, unilaterally and with its closest allies. To the extent that alliance or less formal security ties exist with countries potentially threatened by aspiring regional hegemons, such ties need to be reaffirmed and preserved. Political and diplomatic signals of U.S. readiness to persist in the face of new NBC threats would figure as well. This could include joint exercises, joint planning, and joint acquisition programs with potentially vulnerable friends in key regions. It also might involve articulation of a new declaratory policy to make the point that countries seeking NBC weaponry as a means of coercing U.S. friends, allies, and the United States itself will find themselves less not more secure. Continued prudent military preparations—from enhanced active and passive defenses to changes of operations—to neutralize the advantages of NBC use against U.S. forces are especially essential.

Deterrence by the prospect of denial of gains also has a *NATO dimension*. Currently, NATO's Senior Defense Group on Proliferation is assessing the military implications of proliferation for the Alliance. This is the first step to ensure that NATO has the required military capabilities to neutralize future proliferation threats against NATO territory, NATO peacekeeping operations, and NATO forces operating out-of-area.

Active Measures for Proliferation Prevention

Traditional approaches to proliferation prevention need to be complemented, finally, by new attention to the option of more active measures to block or set back pursuit of NBC weaponry by aggressive, radical regimes. Forcible military interdiction, covert or special operations, or outright use of conventional military power—or at least the threat thereof—all fall into this category. Each of these military options has significant downsides and risks; but each also could prove the least bad alternative in certain situations.

Under some conditions, *forcible interdiction* may be the only means possible to block particularly dangerous proliferation transfers. This could be so, for instance, in response to attempted shipment of diverted nuclear weapons materials or nuclear weapons from Russia to an aggressive aspiring nuclear power. Sale of nuclear-weapons materials or longer-range ballistic missiles by a rogue supplier to an aggressive proliferator would be another example.

The military and technical risks of attempted forcible interdiction of proliferation transfers would vary from case-to-case. Tailored military forces will be required, backed by timely and accurate intelligence and with the right on-call technical experts. Depending on the specific situation, the political costs—both at home and overseas—also are likely to vary. They could range from intensely critical in the case of interception of questionable but legal dual-use transfers to widely-welcoming in the event of use of military forces to block transfer of or recover stolen NBC weaponry or critical materials.

The likely dangers of acquisition of nuclear or biological weaponry by potential regional aggressors equally warrants exploration of possible recourse to *covert or special operations* for proliferation prevention. Theoretical possibilities cover a spectrum from tampering with shipments of critical inputs before they reach a proliferator to sabotage of production facilities in such a country. While unlikely to block pursuit of NBC weaponry indefinitely, successful covert or special operations could slow that pursuit considerably. The political risks and operational difficulties, however, would be high. This is especially so if such operations entailed activities within a proliferator rather than "off-shore" actions. A sound understanding of technical vulnerabilities—whether of specific shipments or targeted facilities—also would be vital as would be intelligence about the overall proliferation profile of the country in question. Here, too, however, the likely dangers of acquisition of nuclear or biological weaponry by aggressive regional powers could in some cases tip the balance for covert or special operations as a last resort.

By contrast, *use of conventional military forces* to attack a proliferator's nascent NBC-weapons infrastructure in situations short-of-war appears far more questionable. Once a program has been underway for some time, the military requirements of successful conventional military preventive action—from accurate intelligence on *all* facilities and sites to target destruction with a politically acceptable risk of collateral or environmental damage—are likely to be very high. At an earlier stage when the military requirements may be more manageable, the political will to act is very likely to be lacking since more traditional measures will have yet to be fully tried.[3] Both early and late, "out-of-the blue" recourse to force will most likely be widely condemned internationally, including by neighboring countries.

Nonetheless, the *threat of preventive military action* could possibly prove a useful adjunct to other proliferation prevention initiatives. An implicit threat of recourse to military force could back-up political and diplomatic initiatives, as may have occurred in recent negotiations with North Korea. Similarly, the risk that acquisition of NBC capabilities would prove a lightning rod not a deterrent of U.S. military strikes in the event of conflict could reinforce other ongoing efforts to buttress deterrence of acquisition by a strategy of denial of gains.[4]

The Tasks Ahead

Fears during the Gulf War that Iraq would use chemical or biological weapons against coalition forces, reinforced by postwar revelations about the scope of its nuclear weapons activities, have served as a proliferation wake-up call for the U.S. defense community. The civilian defense policy and acquisition communities, the Joint Staff, and the individual military services all have been seized with the "proliferation problem." Prudent defense planning to ensure that the United States and its allies can deal effectively with the consequences of possession of NBC weaponry by hostile third world countries (and sub-national groups) clearly is essential. Equally important, proliferation prevention activities increasingly need to be complemented by new initiatives that build on but go beyond non-proliferation traditionalism. For in the final analysis, enhanced proliferation prevention remains the first line of defense against future proliferation threats to the security of the United States and that of our friends and allies.

Notes

1. As already suggested, non-proliferation traditionalism also needs to be supplemented by greater attention to the defense planning or counter-proliferation aspects of dealing with the proliferation threat. These issues, however, go beyond the scope of this short essay.

2. My colleague Burrus Carnahan first proposed this idea to me. More recently, establishment of a Security Council non-proliferation rapporteur has be proposed by French Prime Minister Balladur and by the United Nations Association of the United States.

3. This likely inverse relationship between the military feasibility of preventive proliferation action and the political willingness to act was first pointed out to me by Peter Engstrom.

4. Conversely, fear of preventive military action might only serve to encourage proliferation hard-cases more to disperse, harden, and move underground their NBC infrastructures. The balance of positive and negative impacts is likely be highly scenario and case specific.

SECTION II
Regional Challenges

The Emerging Environment: Regional Views on WMD Proliferation

Krishnaswami Subrahmanyam

Current Status of Weapons of Mass Destruction

Biological Weapons

WEAPONS OF MASS DESTRUCTION FALL INTO FOUR BASIC categories—biological, chemical, radiological and nuclear. Biological weapons are banned under the terms of the Biological Weapons Convention of 1925. However, there is strong international opinion that the treaty requires updating give, the recent advances in biotechnology. Some hold that a rigorous, universal, nondiscriminatory verification regime on the lines of the one developed within the recently concluded Chemical Weapons Convention should be established.

Chemical Weapons

The Chemical Weapons Convention was signed in January 1993 and is expected to come into force in 1995. The ratification of the convention is slow mainly because most of the signatories are waiting for the lead of the nations having the largest stockpiles of such weapons. If the major stockpile holders of chemical weapons begin ratification, the process will accelerate. The Chemical Weapons Convention has been hailed by some

Dr. Krishnaswami Subrahmanyam is Consulting Editor (Foreign Affairs), The Economic Times. Prior to his present position, he was a Contributing Editor, Business and Political Observer, New Delhi. Dr. Subrahmanyam retired from the Indian Administrative Service in 1987. Dr. Subrahmanyam received a M.Sc (Chemistry) from Madras University.

as the first such multilateral disarmament measure and as a model for outlawing and eliminating similar weapons of mass destruction in circumstances which are nondiscriminatory. India, Pakistan, Bangladesh, Nepal and Sri Lanka have all signed the convention. There is also a bilateral India-Pakistan agreement on "the complete prohibition of chemical weapons" signed in 1992.

Radiological Weapons

Though some discussion on the prohibition of radiological weapons has taken place in the Committee on Disarmament, the subject is not on the active international agenda at present. However, the Indian offer to Pakistan to conclude an agreement not to be the first to use nuclear weapons against the other also encompassed the use of radiological agents.

Nuclear Weapons

There are at present five declared nuclear weapon powers—the U.S., Russia, U.K., France and China—and it is believed that Israel, Pakistan and India either have nuclear arsenals or the ability to assemble such weapons at short notice. The U.S. State Department Report to Congress on progress toward Regional Nonproliferation in South Asia says: "We believe both India and Pakistan could assemble a number of nuclear weapons in a relatively short time frame." North Korea which, according to recent U.S. Government statements, is believed to have one or more nuclear weapons, has recently entered into an agreement with the U.S. to suspend operations of its present reactors, shut down the facilities it was setting up for energy generation, and to accept two light water reactors in their place. Though there is a provision in the agreement to relocate the irradiated fuel rods into a third country no details are available about the status and extent of any plutonium that might have been reprocessed. Nor has there been any clarification from U.S. Government sources about the earlier official statements that North Korea might possess one or more nuclear devices.

There has been speculation in the U.S. press about Iranian aspirations to acquire nuclear weapons, but it is believed Iran is some years away from achieving nuclear weapons status. Iraq's nuclear capability has been completely dismantled under UN supervision.

Ukraine has carried out partial dismantling and transhipment of missile warheads. While Ukraine is committed to accede to the non-proliferation treaty, recent reports indicate that the Chairman of the Foreign Affairs Committee of Ukraine has declared that his country might delay joining the NPT. The future of the Ukrainian arsenal is still unclear.

There are reports of clandestine trade in nuclear materials originating from Russia and other former Soviet republics. Germany's Federal Chancellor Helmut Kohl and Russia's President Boris Yeltsin have exchanged letters on the subject. German officials have also visited Russia and there were meetings between the officials of the two countries concerning foreign and domestic intelligence. The two sides have agreed to work together in preventing the smuggling of nuclear material, by tightening border controls and exchanging information. The Director of the U.S. Federal Bureau of Investigation has also met his counterpart in Russia to seek his cooperation in fighting organized crime, especially in the nuclear field. He has pointed to the threat posed by criminal associations obtaining nuclear material and selling it to terrorist groups or states with clandestine weapon programmes. The FBI director signed a memorandum of understanding with Russia's Interior Ministry providing for joint efforts to fight organized crime.

While there are reported attempts to smuggle nuclear materials across Russia's western borders there is no information available about such smuggling on Russia's southern borders. However, there are unconfirmed reports of intensive activity by organized criminals to transport narcotics from Afghanistan into Central and Western Europe. It is difficult to exclude the possibility that criminal networks are attempting to smuggle nuclear materials across the southern borders of Russia. According to *Programme for promoting Nuclear Nonproliferation, News brief, Number 27*, Israeli authorities are said to have discussed with their German counterparts reports that nuclear material smuggled from Russia is ending up in Iran.

A former diplomat from Saudi Arabia, Mr. Al Khilewi, who has been granted asylum in the U.S. has alleged that Saudi Arabia gave financial support to Iraq's nuclear weapons programme in the magnitude of five billion dollars, hoping to obtain nuclear weapons and nuclear technology from that country. He further alleged that Saudi Arabia, prior to 1971, gave financial assistance to the Pakistan nuclear programme and had tried to buy into a Pakistan covert programme. It is to be recalled that Saudi

Arabia has acquired some 30 Chinese CSS-2 long range missiles.

According to the testimony of the Director of the CIA to Congress in July 1993, China is the country that is probably most aggressively recruiting CIS Scientists to help with a wide number of weapons programmes.   Subsequent to this testimony, a spate of press reports indicated that the flow of CIS weapons designers to China continued on a large scale in late 1993, according to the SIPRI 1994 Yearbook. More recently, U.S. Defence Secretary, William Perry, during his visit to China, has offered China technology for computer testing of nuclear weapons.

It may be recalled during the Security Council summit of January 1992 the Indian Prime Minister raised the issue of possible leakages of materials and technology arising out of the dissolution of the Soviet Union.

Nuclear Doctrines

The possession of nuclear weapons and the building of vast stockpiles of such weapons were justified on the grounds of the ongoing Cold War. After the signing of the Nonproliferation Treaty, the nuclear weapon states quadrupled their arsenals.   The underlying doctrines were not persuasive at that stage and the size of the arsenals did not appear to be rationally justified.   Now that the Cold War is over, none of the five nuclear weapons powers acknowledge any adversaries.   The former adversaries have become partners for peace.   Russia and China have entered into a "no first use" agreement in regard to nuclear weapons and, once again, China is a large scale recipient of Russian defence technology. In these circumstances, the rest of the world, which are not as fortunate as the five nuclear weapons powers are not able to comprehend the rationale for the continued possession of very large nuclear arsenals by the five nuclear weapons powers. The justification advanced by the three Western powers—the U.S., UK and France—are as follows: 1) They have to keep their nuclear weapons because others have them; 2) They need them as insurance against strategic uncertainties; 3) They cannot be certain at this stage that Russian progress towards marketisation and democracy will not be reversed and, hence, would not pose threats; and 4) They need them against rogue states like Saddam Hussein's Iraq developing nuclear weapons clandestinely and posing a threat to international peace and security. Though Russia and China do not articulate their justifications in these terms, it would appear their reasoning is also broadly along similar lines. This reasoning applies perhaps with more force and justification to other countries which are situated closer to Russia and China and in the region where potential Saddam Hussains are likely to appear. So far there is no literature which explains the rationale of nations not facing any threats at all keeping large nuclear arsenals, while nations actually facing nuclear threats are being asked to surrender their nuclear capabilities.

The Nonproliferation Treaty

The Nonproliferation Treaty was a compromise agreement concluded at the height of the Cold War. The common purpose that brought the U.S. and the Soviet Union together to promote the Treaty was their concern about Germany and Japan acquiring nuclear weapons. At that stage, it was anticipated that within the next twenty five years some 25-30 countries could acquire nuclear weapons. India and Israel used to feature in that list but not Iraq, North Korea, Iran or Pakistan. The language of the Treaty makes it clear that it was an interim arrangement. The preamble to the Treaty specifically refers to the liquidation of all the existing stockpiles and the elimination from national arsenals of nuclear weapons and the means of their delivery pursuant to a treaty on general and complete disarmament under strict and effective international control. Article VI mentions cessation of the nuclear arms race at an early date and to nuclear disarmament and general complete disarmament under strict and effective international control. The Nonproliferation Treaty did not stop the proliferation of nuclear weapons by the nuclear weapon powers. The U.S. and the Soviet Union continued to proliferate until the middle of the eighties and then started bringing the stockpiles down. In the case of the other three nuclear weapon powers the proliferation continues.

The Treaty was no doubt successful in preventing other industrial nations from acquiring nuclear weapons and this was secured by extending the deterrence of the nuclear arsenal of the U.S. and USSR explicitly in most cases and implicitly in the case of others. Israel and India acquired their nuclear capabilities within the first few years of the NPT coming into force and the world has lived with these capabilities for over two decades. Neither of these two countries has behaved with less than the highest standards of responsibility and restraint.

India made attempts to obtain security guarantees from the nuclear weapon powers against the Chinese nuclear threat during 1966-67 but failed to secure them. Faced with a line-up of Pakistan, the U.S. and China in 1971, at the time of the Bangladesh crisis when ten million refugees were pushed into India, India concluded a Peace and Friendship Treaty with the Soviet Union to generate a sense of deterrence vis a vis China. The U.S. Administration's pro-Pakistan tilt in 1971 and the despatch of the aircraft carrier Enterprise against India presumably influenced India in its attitude towards acquisition of a nuclear capability. Through the sixties and most of the seventies, India faced an active threat from China then under the dominance of Mao Dze Dung. Even at that stage, India exercised utmost restraint. It carried out its first and only nuclear test as a peaceful nuclear explosion and not an above-ground test with all weapon parameters being monitored. This was a period when the U.S. and USSR were conducting dozens of peaceful nuclear explosions. When the U.S. and USSR came to the conclusion that PNES were not viable, India conducted no further tests. India did not embark upon building an arsenal following its test in 1974. This restraint is unparalleled.

The Nonproliferation Treaty did not prevent nations signing the treaty from embarking upon a clandestine programme as happened in the case of Iraq. Nor were the obligations undertaken by the industrial powers (both nuclear and non-nuclear) not to transfer nuclear technology to non-nuclear weapon nations without adequate safeguards fulfilled in practice. Most of the equipment for the nuclear weapon programmes in Iraq came from the UK and Germany. The Scott Commission of Enquiry report from the UK when published will make interesting reading. South Africa also acquired its equipment and technology from Western nations. Very detailed documentation on the supply of equipment to Pakistan from Germany, France and Italy are available in public literature. According to the U.S. State Department report to Congress, China has helped Pakistan in both missile and nuclear technologies. It is also well known that China supplied enriched uranium to South Africa and Brazil. Twice, China was subjected to sanctions under the Missile Technology Control Regime by the U.S.. Only recently the two countries have signed an agreement according to which China has agreed to adhere to MTCR guidelines and the U.S. has lifted sanctions imposed on China. General Aslam Beg, former Chief of Army Staff of Pakistan, in his article in

DAWN of December 12, 1993, wrote that though Pakistan had reached full nuclear capability in 1987 "oblivious of restraints or principles and opportunistically propelled, the Bush Administration from 1987 to 1989 continuously for three years, certified that Pakistan did not possess any such nuclear capability." He confirms Mr. Seymour Hersh's account in an article "On the Nuclear Edge" in the *New Yorker* of April 1993 that the CIA analyst Mr. Richard Barlow got it right in his report. According to Mr. Hersh, Mr. Barlow was harassed in the CIA for his report until 1990.

North Korea is yet another country which, having signed the NPT, was believed to have embarked on a clandestine weapons programme. In the light of these developments, there appear to be enormous uncertainties in regard to nuclear weapon powers and non-nuclear weapon powers strictly adhering to their respective obligations under the NPT. The U.S. was prepared to downgrade its commitment to nonproliferation accepted both under the international Treaty and its domestic law and look away as Pakistan developed its nuclear weapons, giving a higher priority to get Pakistani support to sustain the war in Afghanistan than to non-proliferation. This could happen again under a different set of circumstances. Therefore, there is a strong feeling in India that the nuclear option should be sustained as an insurance against these multiple uncertainties.

The Nonproliferation Treaty is a mixture of success and failure. No nation in the world, except potential new proliferants, wants the end of the present non-proliferation regime with all its flaws and infirmities. At the same time, if the present flawed NPT is perpetuated unconditionally and indefinitely it would send a wrong message to the nations of the world. It would lead to the logical conclusion that the nuclear weapons powers desire to perpetuate the untenable division of the world into two categories—nuclear and non-nuclear weapons states. The charge of hegemonism against some of them will gain credibility. An international environment where nuclear weapons are legitimate for some powers only, will make it more difficult to deny the nonstate terrorist actors the legitimacy of terrorist use of weapons among their supporters at large. Resentful states prone to religious extremism will find more popular support within their own countries to pursue clandestine programmes. Societal verification in respect of clandestine activities will be easier if the weapon is illegitimate and very difficult if it is legitimate only for some nations. The unconditional and indefinite extension of the NPT is a clear negation of the spirit of the NPT, the goal of which is elimination of nuclear weapons. Such an extension at the end of twenty five years without a commitment to eliminate such weapons will be interpreted as giving up that goal. Further, such an extension will deny an opportunity to the international community to keep this vital issue on the international agenda. Such indefinite extension will reduce nonproliferation and counterproliferation strategies from a broad based international effort to limited national strategies of a few powers interested in upholding their nuclear hegemony. For these reasons, many Indians believe that the appropriate strategy is to have a limited extension of the NPT and for the international community to start negotiations for additional and supplementary agreements which would commit the world to the goal of elimination of nuclear weapons and to a non- discriminatory treaty to ban and eliminate them on the model of the Chemical Weapons Convention.

Situation in the Sub-Continent

The U.S. assessment appears to be that both India and Pakistan have the capability to assemble some nuclear weapons at short notice. While India has declared that it has no intention to assemble nuclear weapons and has offered proposals to Pakistan for an agreement that neither side use its nuclear capability first, from Pakistan there have been a series of nonofficial and semi-official statements on its possession of nuclear weapons. Pakistan has not responded to the Indian proposal on no first use. Dr. A.Q. Khan, the man who is reputed to have designed the Pakistani bomb, told a senior Indian journalist in January 1987 in the presence of a Pakistani editor, Mr. Mushahid Hussain who confirmed the interview and consequently lost his job, that Pakistan had the bomb. General Aslam Beg, the Chief of Army Staff during 1988-91, wrote an article in *Dawn* on December 12, 1993 that Pakistan reached full nuclear capability in 1987 and suspended weapon grade uranium enrichment on the basis of a decision unanimously taken by President Ishaq Khan, Prime Minister Benazir Bhutto and himself as the Army Chief in January 1989 since they felt Pakistan had adequate deterrent capability vis-a-vis India. In an interview with NBC TV on December 1, 1992, Ms. Benazir Bhutto, then leader of opposition, said that she came to know that bombs were assembled without her knowledge. General Beg has challenged her veracity in his article quoted above, and he has not been contradicted about his statements that Ms. Benazir Bhutto knew fully about the status of the programme, and the U.S. Administration issued misleading certificates on Pakistan not having an explosive device in 1987, 1988 and 1989. In February 1992, when Mr. Nawaz Sharif was Prime Minister of Pakistan, his Foreign Secretary, Shahryar Khan, gave an interview to the *Washington Post* to the effect that Pakistan had all components needed to assemble at least one nuclear weapon. He also said that he was making this statement to set right the problem of credibility that had persisted till then. Ambassador Robert Oakley told the *Pakistani Editors* in a speech in Lahore in August 1991 that Pakistan crashed through the red light of the Pressler amendment in the spring of 1990. Now Mr. Nawaz Sharif, the former Prime Minister of Pakistan, in his statement of August 23, 1994, has asserted Pakistan has the bomb.

The position in India is different. There have been no reports of militarization of its nuclear capability. Various retired Chiefs of Staff have been calling for India to exercise its nuclear option and General Sundarji has written a novel, *The Blind Men of Hindusthan*, describing the reluctance of the government to weaponise its capability. Mr. George Tanham of the RAND Corporation in his monograph on "Indian Strategic Thought" also refers to the non-involvement of the Indian military in the nuclear field. Things could have changed in the last few months, but no evidence of any such change is available.

The Pakistani disclosures have not led to any serious reaction in India. There appears to be general popular confidence that Pakistani sabre rattling can be handled by the Government of India. There is widespread consensus that Pakistan is inclined to focus attention on its nuclear capability and tries to raise fears in the international community on the possibility of escalation of war between the two countries to the nuclear level in order to bring to bear international pressure on India to settle the Kashmir issue on Pakistani terms. Pakistani strategy in this respect was foreseen and described by the American academic, Professor Stephen Cohen some fourteen years ago. In a paper titled "Nuclear issues and Security policy in Pakistan," presented at the annual meeting of the Association of Asian Studies, Washington D.C., in March 1980, he said that a Pakistani nuclear capability would, according to many Pakistanis, "neutralize an assumed Indian nuclear force. Others point out, however, that it would provide the umbrella under which Pakistan could reopen the Kashmir issue; a Pakistani nuclear capability paralyses not only the Indian nuclear decision but also Indian conventional forces and a brash, bold

Pakistani strike to liberate Kashmir might go unchallenged if the Indian leadership was weak or indecisive.

It would appear the Pakistani leadership, having achieved a nuclear capability, has been engaged in psychological warfare vis-a-vis India to test the strength of the Indian leadership's resolve on the Kashmir issue. Over the last five years, presumably they have not found the Indian leadership weak or indecisive since they did not try a bold Pakistani strike. It is to be noted that most of the talk about risks of a nuclear exchange emanate from Pakistan and not from India, which has offered Pakistan a no first use agreement.

There are no serious worries in the Indian leadership or military establishment about the risks of a nuclear exchange. India is already committed to a no first use policy. Therefore, risks can arise only as a result of Pakistani action. India is the status quo power and it is Pakistan which seeks revision of the status quo in Kashmir. Therefore, it is the risk taking proclivities of Pakistan that need to be studied. There is reasonable confidence in India that Pakistan is not likely to take undue risks. Pakistanis themselves have published extensively on the wars of 1947, 1965 and 1971, and it is to be said to the credit of the objectivity of many Pakistanis they now accept that all three wars were the result of Pakistani actions.

The defence capability of both India and Pakistan has declined in recent years. India has been steadily reducing its defence spending as a percentage of GDP and in real terms over the last five years, especially after it embarked upon its economic liberalization and reform programme. The Soviet Union is no longer present as a source of supply of defence equipment on favorable terms. Indian defence imports have declined. While Pakistan has not reduced its defence expenditures, it has ceased to have access to U.S. arms supplies consequent on the invocation of the Pressler amendment. Therefore, while both countries have suffered impairment of their respective capabilities, Pakistan would appear to have suffered relatively more. Having suffered three successive reverses, Pakistan is not likely to start yet another war. American authorities have been asserting that both India's conventional and nuclear capabilities are superior to Pakistan's. In India there is confidence that, in spite of nuclear sabre rattling, Pakistan would not start a war and there are no significant risks of a nuclear exchange.

Indian policy has been able to sustain peace with Pakistan for 23 years, the longest period of peace between the two countries since

Independence. Though Pakistan has extended extensive support to Sikh extremist terrorism, India has brought the situation in Punjab under control. Five years of transborder Pakistani support to the low intensity conflict in Kashmir has been contained without escalation and there are distinct signs the tide in turning and the excesses of the Pakistan-based mercenaries in Kashmir have alienated the valley population. It is this development that appears to have compelled Pakistan to focus on the nuclear issue to attract the attention of the international community and persuade it to intervene in the Kashmiri dispute. While continuing Pakistani support for terrorism in Kashmir must be contained, India feels that Pakistan has reached the peak of its verbal onslaught on the issue.

The Nuclear Issue in Pakistan

There appears to be general agreement in Pakistan that its weapons grade uranium enrichment programme was suspended in 1989. Whether this was a voluntary act as General Beg claims it to have been or an involuntary one due to technical reasons, as a section of the Indian scientific community suspects, is difficult to conclude. The U.S. government appears to subscribe to the view that the weapons grade enrichment programme has been suspended, and it wishes that suspension be made permanent under international verification. However, popular opinion in Pakistan would not permit such capping to be imposed unilaterally on Pakistan. There are estimates of the Pakistani nuclear arsenal ranging from two to seven or eight weapons. In the Indian view, Pakistan would not have kept its uranium enrichment programme suspended but for the fact of the tightened export controls and withdrawal of U.S. permissiveness extended to the Pakistani programme during the war in Afghanistan. This situation is not likely to change unless the industrialized countries and China extend technical help to Pakistan. One cannot rule out that possibility so long as the nuclear weapons powers try to maintain the legitimacy of nuclear weapons and vest them with prestige using them as currency of power in international relations. Therefore, over and above the uncertainties inherent in the nuclear policies of China and other nuclear weapon powers, this additional uncertainty about Pakistan compels India to keep its nuclear option open, although in the very restrained and non-provocative manner it has adopted over the years.

However, for Pakistan its nuclear arsenal appears to have an importance in its national psyche totally disproportionate to its operational significance. It gives them a sense of equality with India which has been an obsession since partition. As noted by General Beg, it endows Pakistan with a sense of deterrence vis-a-vis India and, consequently, gives Pakistan a sense of security. It also gives them status among the Islamic nations, which was the dream of Zulfikar Ali Bhutto who talked about the bomb in civilisational terms long before Professor Huntington came up with his thoughts on civilisational conflict. Without the bomb, the cut-off of U.S. military supplies would have created a paranoid sense of insecurity in Pakistan. In my view, the token Pakistani nuclear arsenal has contributed significantly to stability in the sub-continent and there are no advantages in disturbing it. The only problem posed by the Pakistani bomb is the talk by a section of the Pakistani military and political establishments about the Pakistani "strategy of defiance." This has nothing to do with India. This is an implied threat that unless Pakistan is accommodated in regard to its demands it will defy the West (the U.S.) and move closer towards Islamic countries with extremist proclivities. This strategy was unveiled by General Aslam Beg in support of Saddam Hussain in 1990 and continues to be propagated in Pakistan. In India, there is an impression that sections of the U.S. political and strategic establishments are worried about this contingency and, hence, attempt to placate Pakistan lest it should move closer to Islamic extremism. While that contingency cannot be ruled out, in India the assessment is that such a shift will create enormous tensions within Pakistan and will have an extremely negative impact on Pakistani territorial integrity and unity. That is a worrisome possibility. However, placating Pakistan on the nuclear issue by applying pressure on India on both the nuclear and Kashmir issues would be counterproductive.

Some analysts present the scenario of a "mad general" in Pakistan starting a war, as happened in 1965 and 1971, or using the bomb. While, again, though the possibility cannot be totally ruled out, the probability is extremely low. Pakistan has a way of dealing with its own generals. None of them exited from office with honour or died in bed while in office. Pakistanis now recognize that the past wars were ruinous and the next war, if started may have serious consequences to Pakistani unity and integrity. Pakistanis started the earlier wars under a mistaken perception about India's non-martial qualities, or international political alignments favouring them. They have no such illusions now. The Pakistani military has kept the past wars as copy book exercises. Within Pakistan, there is an awareness of the country's extreme geographic vulnerabilities should there be a nuclear exchange. While one encounters extremist views on political, social and economic policies, there is no extremist view in Pakistan on the nuclear issue.

India and Counterproliferation

India cannot have an adverse view on the concept of counterproliferation since India considers nuclear weapons as unusable in war and has been consistently in favour of elimination of nuclear weapons. India continues to keep its nuclear option open only because it has to interact and operate on the belief systems of the five nuclear weapons powers conditioned by four decades of nuclear theology, and India must counter the possibilities of political blackmail and misperceptions that a totally non-nuclear India might invite. However, there are serious doubts about the cost effectiveness of counter-proliferation strategy. It would appear future nuclear threats are likely to arise largely out of leakage of weapons, fissile materials and scientific and technological skills from existing nuclear weapons powers. The risks may not be confined to the former Soviet republics. There are possibilities of extremist leadership groups attempting to acquire such weapons, but that is not likely to be achieved unless there are large scale inputs from the industrialized countries with requisite technologies or from China. Secondly, the countries which are likely to have such ambitions are identifiable, and it would be better to focus on country specific strategies than indulge in grandiose global ones. Thirdly, whatever proliferation has taken place beyond the five declared nuclear weapons powers, is mostly because certain powers have consciously subordinated nonproliferation goals to political expediency.

The best counterproliferation strategy is to delegitimise nuclear weapons and start negotiating a treaty along the lines of the Chemical Weapons Convention to ban and eliminate them. Perhaps, unlike the chemical industry, the nuclear industry may lend itself to internationalized control as envisaged in the visionary Baruch plan at the dawn of the nuclear era. The world cannot talk of universal standards on trade and technological competition, democratic norms, human rights, and ecological concerns but continue to insist on having double standards on nuclear weapons. Any attempt at perpetuating such double standards is bound to fail.   The worry is at what cost to humanity.   Let not counterproliferation become a costly capability in the perpetual search for a nuclear weapons mission.

Proliferation of WMD and the Security Dimensions in South Asia: An Indian View

Krishnaswami Sundarji

THE PROLIFERATION OF WEAPONS OF MASS DESTRUCTION (WMD), or the already existing presence of WMD and their impact on security perceptions, cannot be examined strictly by region. For example, in South Asia, the circles of concern of India and Pakistan intersect. India's circle of concern intersects with China's. China's circle in turn, interacts with Russia, and for that matter, with the USA. Unless arms control initiatives take cognizance of such inter-relations, they will not succeed.

In this paper, I focus primarily on nuclear weapons, although I will cover chemical weapons as well. The concerns of any country are security or status or some mix of the two. Security consists of freedom from aggression or undue interference from others; first in the physical (military) and political sphere; and second, in the material and economic sphere. Status or prestige could also be a manifestation of a drive for worthy self-image. To assess the regional impact of the DOD's counter-proliferation policies, I have made certain judgments regarding the concerns of not only China, India and Pakistan, but also of the USA.

General Krishnaswami Sundarji is the former Chief of Staff of the Indian Army. He is a graduate of the U.S. Command and General Staff COllege and has commanded at the battalion, brigade, division, corp, and army levels. Gen. Sundarji is the author of *Blind Men of Hindustan: Indo-Pak Nuclear War*.

USA

I judge that the following are the primary U.S. aims:

- Avoid universal nuclear disarmament for as long as possible.
- Keep the U.S. nuclear stockpile level comfortably high, not only to ensure U.S. security, but to maintain a domestic consensus.
- Prevent any country other than Russia from obtaining a large force of missiles capable of reaching the continental United States (CONUS).
- Keep the numbers and sophistication of Chinese ICBMs as low as possible.
- Keep the numbers and sophistication of Chinese, French and British SSBNs as low as possible. Prevent new entrants to the SSBN club.
- Accept no international commitment that would hinder the maintenance and enhancement of U.S. technological preeminence.
- Prevent proliferation of WMD, local arms races and regional wars.

Retain U.S. freedom to use conventional forces to influence regional situations in order to safeguard U.S. interests, without any threat to forward deployed U.S. forces from WMD of regional powers: first, by preventing the emergence of new regional nuclear powers; second, by nuclear deterrence; third, by protecting forward deployed forces from regional nuclear attack by the deployment of an anti-theater ballistic missile system; fourth, by deterring chemical attacks from regional powers by retaining the right to retaliate with nuclear weapons (this last requirement requires that the USA not subscribe to a "no first use" doctrine).

China

China no longer sees Russia as its greatest threat. India was earlier seen as siding with the USSR against China, but is no longer seen in that light. This, coupled with the fact that India has explicitly accepted Chinese sovereignty over Tibet, places India in the category of potential friend and supporter, rather than in the category of potential enemy. China is therefore motivated, due to enlightened self-interest, to cultivate Indian friendship and support.   China has made a nuclear "no first use" declaration and has up to now not shown a penchant for nuclear blackmail. However in looking to the future, one must exercise caution.

The Chinese nuclear weapon capability and delivery means have thus far been vulnerable to possible Russian and American strikes. When their second strike capability improves, there may be a willingness to flex their nuclear muscle. This is speculative, and the Chinese may be serious in their claims that they will not use nuclear blackmail to achieve foreign policy goals. However, planners in other countries have to be cautious and not accept these statements at face value. As long as the capabilities remain, intentions can change overnight.

China had stated that it would not join any strategic arms reduction talks with the super powers till they first reduced their arsenals to fifty percent of the then existing levels. China now says that it would enter arms control talks when the big two reduce to the Chinese level of nuclear weapons, and in the meantime, it goes on defiantly with nuclear testing.

I judge that the following summarize China's aims:
• Be in the major league of world powers, by right and not accepted grudgingly as an "also ran."
• Become near-coequal in nuclear arsenals generally, if not yet in total military terms.

Keep the number of nuclear weapon powers in the world restricted to the present five, but not make common cause with the USA in this regard, if that country thwarts Chinese ambitions of becoming gradually coequal. The enlargement of the nuclear club might serve Chinese tactical aims of obtaining better leverage vis-a-vis the USA.

India

India has an unresolved border problem with China. Pakistan and India have fought three major wars and have yet to resolve the Kashmir problem. India's security problem is not limited to a bilateral Indo-Pakistan one. The threat from China has also to be taken into account. In the absence of credible international or big power guarantees, India judges that it needs both a nuclear and a conventional minimum capability to deter both China and Pakistan.

There might be some strengthening and restructuring of the United Nations. But, there is serious doubt in Indias to whether, in the next decade, it would be objective enough and reliable enough in maintaining international peace and order, and in effectively safeguarding the interests of all the members. Big power guarantees, such as they are, have very little credibility in India.

India and China have a border problem. Neither side has shown any intent of solving the border question by force of arms over the last three decades. However, Soviet constraints that operated in the past are no longer there. With the present balance of deployable conventional forces on the high Himalayan border, India can take care of any Chinese conventional threat (because of logistics on the Chinese side) as long as the Chinese do not have a one-sided nuclear advantage. Even if there is a strategic break through, terrain and climate will guarantee that unless the Chinese can totally capture the whole of India within the non-winter months—a virtual impossibility—they cannot make any deep foray into the plains of India and defend it successfully through the winter months. So, the strategic Chinese threat would more likely be nuclear blackmail. However, if the Chinese were to face a very adverse tactical situation in a border war and feel a threat to Tibet, there could be a nuclear threat to India. The targets could be tactical and strategic or only tactical, the latter being more likely. If the Chinese use only tactical nuclear weapons, India would do likewise on a *quid pro quo* basis. For the future, as long as both sides are aware that the other would be no pushover militarily and clear deterrent signals exist, the chances are that the border question would be resolved by negotiations involving give and take.

Pakistan

In Pakistan and India, there are broadly three schools of thought concerning mutual relations. The first believes the worst; that the other country is devious and untrustworthy besides being unreconciled to the very existence of the other. Hence, attempting to find peaceful and lasting solutions will be impossible; the only possible course will be to remain in a wary adversarial stand-off or undo the other country. Many in this group are misguided by propaganda, with some cynically pushing this line because of its value in domestic politics. This kind of thinking produced the three rounds of war between the two countries. Such wars in pursuit of policy might have appeared affordable in the past. However, today with both countries *de facto* nuclear, such wars have the potential of devastating India, and destroying Pakistan.

The second group consists of "do-gooders" who believe that if only we can side-line the wicked ruling elites, and enable large scale contacts between the two peoples, our countries can make up tomorrow morning! This group contains true idealists who abhor all and loathe nuclear weapons; some who are soft in the head; and a few who exploit this line cynically for their own purposes.

The third group is nascent in India and Pakistan. It consists of realists who have studied nuclear doctrine as enunciated by the big powers and believes that a fair, honorable and peaceful solution of all problems between the two countries is possible. It believes that even conventional war might lead to nuclear weapons use, and is no longer an option that can be lightly chosen by decision makers. This group feels that nuclear deterrence, in the interim, will add to stability and peace and that the only salvation is for both countries to follow policies of cooperation and not confrontation. I agree with this third school of thought.

At this juncture of UN efficacy (or, rather, the lack of it), only nuclear weapons would ensure the ability of Pakistan to live in security and with honor with an India seen as permanently hostile and with greater conventional power potential. Hence, that is its aim. Unless there are credible international and big power guarantees Pakistan quite rightly, in my opinion, would not give up a nuclear option.

Viability of a Doctrine of Nuclear Minimum Deterrence in South Asia

A mutual minimum nuclear deterrent will act as a stabilizing factor. Pakistan will see it as counteracting India's superior conventional power potential and providing a more level playing field. The chances of conventional war between the two will be less than before. As Kenneth N. Waltz puts it, "Conventional wars fought by countries that do not have nuclear weapons are likelier than conventional or nuclear wars fought by countries that have nuclear weapons."[1]

Assumed Indian Nuclear Doctrine[2]

India's nuclear doctrine is based on the following premises:

- Nuclear weapons can only be deterred by nuclear weapons.
- Minimum deterrence is adequate.

There is no need to match any adversary in the number of weapons, nor yields nor types of weapons, nor of achieving superiority as long as there is an assured capability of a second strike that can inflict *unacceptable damage*. Hence, a nuclear arms race is counterproductive.

At the tactical level also, the philosophy is nuclear deterrence. Tactical nuclear weapons are not regarded as automatically usable as the big powers used to think in the Fifties. The intention is to deter the adversary from making first use of tactical nuclear weapons, and thus gaining a battle-field advantage. In case this fails, the second strike will not be on tactical point targets but on area targets that abound in the combat zone. Most of these are optimally attacked by weapons of yields of 10 to 20 Kt fired as low air bursts (producing hardly any fall out). Hence, there is no need for unique tactical nuclear weapons to be produced. There is also no need for producing expensive, miniaturized sub-kiloton warheads to be fired, for example, from artillery. Such a requirement would only exist if they are to be used in war-fighting for giving close support to troops, whilst ensuring requisite safety.

Finally, I have also assumed that with no aim of changing the *status quo*, and with only deterrence that we are aiming for, Indian policy will be one of *no first use* of nuclear weapons. A declaration of *no first use* does not take away the fundamental right of a nation to defend itself by all means at its disposal when its very survival is in jeopardy. What it does do is to forswear brinkmanship in the very early stages of a conflict. This adds to stability and would be in the interests of all.

Western analysts have quite naturally been steeped in super- power nuclear doctrine, and most of them use scaled down versions of super power-doctrine for the developing world. Applying this, they assert that the spread of nuclear weapons to conflict prone areas like South Asia, will increase the likelihood of nuclear weapons use in war[3]. A few have articulated a contrary view, that the spread of nuclear weapons may indeed *increase stability*, rather than threaten international peace. Kenneth N. Waltz is the best known exponent of this theory of stable nuclear deterrence[4] and others have supported parts of his theories, if not the totality.[5]

Many weaknesses are attributed to SNP. The human ones are crazy or marginally competent political leaderships, a lack of knowledge leading to over-insurance and over-reaction, and teeming populations simmering with discontent tempting their rulers into popular but irresponsible acts. Structural weaknesses are poor political organization, a lack of checks and balances, a small nuclear force that may not survive a nuclear first strike against it, thereby encouraging a "use before you lose" attitude, likelihood of loss of nuclear weapons by theft or hijack to terrorists, and finally, weak safeguards against accidental explosions. Technological weaknesses are low levels of reliability, rudimentary Command, Control, Communications and Intelligence (C^3I), and weak controls leading to the "mad colonel" carrying out an unauthorized attack. Finally, there were so many false alarms in spite of the sophisticated surveillance systems in the West, that SNP systems put together with scotch tape and chewing gum invite disaster.

This listing appears formidable, but has never been argued against the background of a broad minimum deterrence doctrine. Discussions degenerate into theological harangues from the West, indignantly dubbed by the third world analyst as racist! Many young scholars, without cold war intellectual baggage, such as Devin T. Hagerty, argue that both the "proliferation is dangerous" school and the "more may be better" school, rest their arguments on "logics" that "...are ultimately inadequate, because neither yields compelling explanations of the consequences of nuclear proliferation."[6] He argues that, "The two countries continue to feel their usual assortment of imperatives toward conflict, like the insurgency in Kashmir, but nuclear weapon capabilities introduce a new set of incentives to cooperate. Among these are the desire to avoid mutual devastation....The fear of escalation is thus factored into political calculations: faced with this risk, states are more cautious and more prudent than they otherwise would be."[7] Having occupied a ring side seat for many years at the center of Indian decision making, I intuitively feel that Hagerty is right in his reading of the South Asian situation.

The Inner Ring—China, India and Pakistan

While some are prepared to concede for the purposes of discussion that minimum deterrence might be effective in the India-Pakistan relationship, most continue to be skeptical about its effectiveness in an India-China scenario. This skepticism is usually based on a few assumptions. First, that a comparatively minuscule nuclear arsenal that India might field can in no way survive a Chinese first strike and hence can be no deterrent.

Second, that even if some weapons survive, not much damage can be done by a few fission weapons when compared with the Chinese thermonuclear capability. Third, that in view of the foregoing, the fielding of such a puny nuclear force by India, far from adding to the security of India, would indeed increase its insecurity. An irate China may well *target* India, and hence India should desist. Targeting or retargeting can be done reasonably easily at any time; so whether one is *targeted* or not does not have much meaning *per se.* We are perhaps already *targeted* and have been so for quite some time. Why would the Chinese want to fire nuclear weapons at us; just because we are supposed to have deployed some nuclear weapons that have the range to reach China? That is absurd. There must be some strong reason to make the Chinese want to do so. If we are foolish enough to attack them first with nuclear weapons, they would certainly retaliate. If we attack them conventionally, in Tibet say, and create a situation so critical that they cannot handle it conventionally, they may use or threaten to use nuclear weapons. They may also threaten to use them as part of coercive diplomacy or nuclear blackmail, especially if we remain non-nuclear. Whatever the cause, are they more likely to use them if we are able to retaliate and do some damage to them subsequently, or if we are totally incapable of retaliating?

The survivability of an adequate Indian second strike is highly probable if we adopt rail mobile modes of deployment, with adequate dummies incorporated. In the event the Indians are content to remain in an "unweaponized" and "undeployed" state of *existential deterrence*, it is not just a question of needles in haystacks, but parts of many needles in many haystacks which might be brought together when required within hours to days, to form needles in yet many more different haystacks. Kenneth Waltz writes, that a preemptive first strike would be effective, "...only if the would-be attacker knows that the intended victim's warheads are few in number, knows their exact number and locations, and knows that they will not be moved or fired before they are struck. To know all of these things and to know that you know them for sure, is exceedingly difficult."[8] With any such deployment, an Indian planner may not have the degree of assurance that he would like about the survival of his second strike. However, with such a deployment no Chinese planner can be certain that no Indian second strike will survive to devastate a few major Chinese cities. There will be enormous reluctance to go for such a Chinese first strike. That is what deterrence is all about.

Doubts have been expressed regarding the efficacy of a few fission weapons against a more massive thermonuclear capability.[9] Writing about both these aspects, Waltz says, "Why compare weapons with weapons when they are not to be used against each other, but against cities that cannot counter them? China may need quite a bit to deter Russia, but India needs little to deter China. What issue between the latter two could justify the Chinese leadership risking a city or two? .... We know from experience or the Japanese do, how devastating small yield plutonium weapons of between 14 and 20 kilotons can be."[10]

The Outer Ring

The Geopolitical Threat

The nuclear weapon capable countries in the outer ring are Khazakstan, Israel and South Africa. Of these, South Africa claims to have dismantled its nuclear weapons, and Khazakstan has declared its intention to adhere to the NPT as a non-nuclear weapon power. India hopes that both these do happen. I do not think that India sees any threat in the Israeli possession of nuclear weapons, even though its missiles may have, or have in the future, the range to reach Indian targets.

The other potential candidates for proliferation in West Asia are Iraq and Iran. Saudi Arabia has nuclear capable missiles (sold by China) that can reach India, but as yet no nuclear weapon capabilities. In East Asia, the North Korean drive towards nuclear weapons, unless halted or capped, might lead to the following alternatives in the Korean peninsula: nuclear weapon armed North and a South with a nuclear weapon capability or at least an autonomous full nuclear fuel cycle, or a united Korea with nuclear weapons. This in part, and an unbridled vertical proliferation on the part of China, might more certainly propel Japan towards reexamining its nuclear weapon policy. On top of this, any weakening or perceived weakening of the USA's extended nuclear deterrence in defense of Japan will almost certainly push Japan towards producing its own nuclear weapons and ballistic missiles. It is true that Japan has been the only unfortunate target of nuclear weapons thus far, but faith in Japan's perpetual sainthood is not too strong in Asia. The memories of World

War II are still very vivid. In South East Asia, a possible proliferant is Indonesia. It might be driven by vertical proliferation by China, or horizontal proliferation in the Korean peninsula and Japan. If all this were to occur, India would be generally uneasy, but is still unlikely to feel any big threat geopolitically.

The Psychological Threat

Though clinically looked at, geopolitics may allay a sense of threat, psychological reasons may supervene and color threat perceptions. Indian allergy to fundamentalist Islam, reinforced by the Chinese sale of missiles to Saudi Arabia, Iran, Pakistan, etc., would play a part. It would almost appear that Professor Samuel P. Huntington's prophecy regarding the accommodation between the Confucian and the Islamic worlds is indeed being fulfilled.[11] The threat would appear to be most from rabid fundamentalist regimes with Iran leading the pack, and at the other extreme a non-fundamentalist Indonesia posing no threat for the present. However, the recent upsurge in fundamentalism in Indonesia is worrisome.

Effects of Proliferated Threats on Minimum Deterrence

If proliferation occurs, whether it is little or much, how would it affect SNP doctrines of minimum deterrence, with special reference to the Indian doctrine? Would a larger number of possible nuclear adversaries, severally or in varying combinations and alliances, compel or induce increases in nuclear stockpiles? If increases occur would they be modest or open-ended? In short would it lead to a spiraling Asian nuclear arms race? These are pertinent questions and have to be addressed. Not much literature exists on these subjects, and I will do my best to think them through.

Before analyzing this, let me ponder for a moment on the likelihood of alliances forming, and taking conjoint or orchestrated nuclear action against a nuclear adversary. We have all been used to the idea of alliances in the pre-nuclear era, fighting either powerful single countries or adversary alliances. In the post-nuclear era also alliances did face off, but did not fight. These post nuclear alliances were also qualitatively different. These alliances had two preeminent superpowers leading them. On the side of the Warsaw Pact, only the USSR had nuclear weapons and controlled their use. In the case of NATO too, this was essentially so with control resting with the United States, although the token British deterrent (and later the French *force-de-frappe*) did make a theoretical difference, although none in practical terms to the supreme control of the U.S.A. These were, therefore, not truly alliances of equal states, with equal states in an alliance defined thus—States all and each of which could undertake activity that might trigger adversary reaction that could cause exceedingly severe damage through nuclear weapons use to some or all the states of their own alliance. These cold war alliances were essentially two preeminently powerful states with adherents who were less than equal. This bitter pill was somewhat sugar coated in NATO without essentially changing the roles of supreme leader and camp follower. It was stark and without any attempt at camouflage in the Warsaw Pact. The question to be answered is: In a non super power milieu, can meaningful alliances of nuclear weapon powers form, against other nuclear weapon powers, given that any automatic inter-linking of the nuclear action-reaction sequence might very probably cause unacceptable damage to one's own country and people? Under these circumstances, any light hearted repetition of pre-nuclear formulas such as "an attack on country" A, "my ally, will automatically be considered an attack on my country" seem highly unlikely.

Even in pre-nuclear days when the scale of damage in conventional *total war* was rising, one saw the extreme reluctance of say, Neville Chamberlain's Britain to live up to professed obligations to some of the European powers at the cost of crossing swords with Hitler's Germany. As the damage potential of even conventional war rises still more with today's technologies, we see that the willingness to accept hurt for the sake of altruism is palpably decreasing; one can see national reluctance even on the part of the so called great powers to accept damage and hurt except possibly when their innermost core interests are threatened. Further, even the perceived extent of the innermost core interest is shrinking. For the present, tightly knit coalitions are most unlikely to form in a multipolar world of somewhat autonomous nuclear powers to confront other nuclear powers. There may be coalitions which form against non- nuclear weapons states that can be lectured, coerced, and if necessary militarily attacked without any danger of severe damage to the homeland of the "avengers." It is quite possible that loose groupings might form which avow common aims and generally make noises about consulting about the situation when any member is attacked, hoping vaguely to deter the aggressor (if it is a nuclear power) without committing themselves to any automatic nuclear action-reaction sequence in advance.

If this be so, there would be no need for any nuclear weapon power to assume that it needs a substantial addition to its nuclear stockpile to deter a multiple threat from more than one adversary. The multiple threat is most unlikely to take the form of a coordinated and premeditated nuclear first strike, so the size of the first strike against which survivability of the second strike has to be measured need not be inflated to the combined might of all potential adversaries. In war fighting, while more is generally better, in deterrence more is not better if less is adequate. Should deterrence unfortunately fail and a nuclear exchange takes place between two nuclear states, the theoretical possibility of a third nuclear state doing a hyena-act by threatening to use or using nuclear weapons on one of the stricken countries with whom it had a score to settle cannot be ruled out. However, such a brazen act in today's world is far-fetched. Even if this kind of contingency has to be catered for, I cannot imagine a steep increase in the level of nuclear stockpiles.

U.S. Policy on Counterproliferation

American policy has so far been dominated by attempts to tackle the supply side of proliferation without, in my opinion, conspicuous success. There are advocates for stronger punitive measures—political, technological, economic or even military against deviants to reinforce the present policy. Punitive actions have a high probability of success only in the case of nations that are below a critical size or level of key ingredients of national power. These ingredients include geographical spread, sizable population, natural resources, a technologically advanced industrial economy, military power, and competent political organization. If nations are above the critical level in these ingredients, punitive action may for a while appear to give results, but in the long haul will be decisively counter productive. India belongs to the latter category. Notwithstanding the disappearance of the Soviet Union and the USA being left as the lone super power, the state of the world is vastly different from the period when Great Britain produced such effective results from gun-boat diplomacy. Any U.S. attempts at emulation in today's world will be messy.

The demand side of the equation, the assuaging of the genuine security concerns of potential proliferants by credible international guarantees must get at least equal emphasis, if not priority over the supply side. This must be accompanied by such Confidence Building Measures (CBM) initiated by the "nuclear haves" led by the U.S., as:

• A genuine and credible effort on the part of the U.S.A. to reduce its own nuclear arsenals to drastically lower levels than presently contemplated, and to persuade the four other legalized nuclear weapon powers to follow suit.

• A non discriminatory universal comprehensive Test Ban Treaty (CTBT), with no loop-holes for the privileged.

• A universal cut off of weapon grade fissile material production, with non-discriminatory inspections.

• A *No First Use* declaration by all nuclear weapon powers. There are understandable reservations on this in the U.S.A. These could be overcome by ensuring that the declaration does not preclude nuclear retaliation against any country making proven first use of chemical weapons. In all other cases, the right to first use could be subject to prior UN approval.

I believe that India would fully support CTBT and fissile material cut off, if the regimes are non-discriminatory and leave no loop-holes for anyone. When these effective and non- discriminatory inspections are in place, India (and Pakistan) could agree to capping their nuclear weapon capability. This does not mean a *roll back* or dismantling of the capability to deploy and use nuclear weapons at short notice. A roll back and dismantling will have to wait for universal nuclear disarmament. It could mean capping the future production of weapons grade fissile material, that would, in turn, limit the size of potential nuclear arsenals of both India and Pakistan, and thus prevent a nuclear arms race.

The Indian short range *Prithvi* missile is undoubtedly dual capable, as are many fighter-bombers in the inventory of both India and Pakistan are. I do not see any pressures to decommission these fighter-bombers in South Asia! The conventional warheads of the *Prithvi* include top attack anti-tank munitions, for example. Non-deployment of this missile, in which India has invested resources over many years, would seriously compromise India's anti-tank capabilities, because this system had an allotted role in the total anti-tank function. Similar imbalances would occur in other conventional functions as well. Hence non-deployment of the *Prithvi* would not be acceptable to India. I believe that neither India nor for that matter the U.S.A. should make heavy weather of Pakistan obtaining, developing or deploying short range missiles. This would only make the undeclared minimum nuclear deterrence that is present in South Asia more stable.

The *Agni* (IRBM), on the other hand, only makes sense with a nuclear warhead. It will have the reach to cover much of mainland China, and without it India would have no minimum deterrence vis-a-vis China, as Indian fighter-bombers can only reach Tibet. India would never accept limitations to *Agni* development now. Waiting to do so *after* being hit by a Chinese first strike would be too late. Non-*deployment* may be negotiable, but not non-*development*. I also believe that India would desist from developing an ICBM that would have the range to reach CONUS.

Chemical Warfare (CW)

I intend to address here a hoary and much touted belief that CW is a poor man's answer to an adversary's nuclear capability. The assumption is that the non-nuclear country is either technologically, industrially or economically incapable of producing nuclear weapons, or that the threat has come upon it so suddenly that there is inadequate time to produce nuclear weapons. If the non-nuclear power uses its CW capability before the other side uses its nuclear capability, there has to be the presumption of almost certain nuclear retaliation. It can be argued that this fear of escalation into nuclear response was what deterred Saddam Hussein from making first use of CW either against Israeli strategic targets or on tactical targets in the combat zone during the gulf war.

Let us assume that minimum nuclear deterrence is operating mutually in the South Asian context. This might be *unweaponized* and *undeployed* by Western definition. However, as long as all parties are understood to be capable of retaliation within a matter of hours, the first use of CW by any country seems most unlikely since the recipient of chemical attack is almost certain to retaliate by making a second strike with WMD. If it possesses both a CW and a nuclear capability, the retaliation might use either, depending upon a number of variables. The initiator of the first strike will have to assume the worst. Therefore, it would be most unlikely that CW would be initiated. In case the recipient of the CW strike is either without or believed to be without a CW capability, it would be almost axiomatic that nuclear retaliation would ensue. Deterrence would be stronger still. When minimum nuclear deterrence is in place, therefore, it is my view that creating or deploying a CW capability would be an exercise in futility.

Conclusion

In the event of nuclear proliferation in Asia (or for that matter, anywhere else), India would be sad indeed that the world continues to fail to leash the nuclear menace, even if it cannot in reality be expected to banish nuclear weapons in the immediate future. The onus for this failure should rest squarely with the five permanent members of the security council, with the U.S.A., the only super power taking the major blame. These countries claim the privileges and rights of being the premier nations of the world, but cannot see their way to setting an adequately worthwhile example by truly drastic reduction of their stockpiles and concurrently organizing a credible enough system of international security guarantees. Till this is done, to claim that no other nation that feels threatened has the right to do anything about it, and to continue to crusade for discriminatory non- proliferation is not only perverse but guaranteed to fail in the long haul.

Notes

1. Kenneth N. Waltz, "What Will Nuclear Weapons Do to the World?" in John Kerry King, ed., *International Political Effects of the Spread of Nuclear Weapons* Washington, D.C.: U.S. Government Printing Office, 1979 p.194.

2. See General K. Sundarji, "Nuclear Deterrence: Doctrine for India," published in two parts; Part 1 in *Trishul*, Vol. V, Issue No 2 December 1992, Defense Services Staff College, Wellington India; and Part 2 in the July 93 issue of the same journal.

3. This position almost amounting to theology, is an enduring and predominant one in Western literature; to give a decade-wise sampling: Kathleen C. Bailey, "Doomsday Weapons in the Hands of Many: The Arms Control Challenge of the '90s" (Urbana: University of Illinois Press, 1991); Lewis A. Dunn, "Controlling the Bomb" (New Haven: Yale University Press, 1982); Ted

Greenwood, Harold Feiveson, and Theodore B. Taylor, "Nuclear Proliferation: Motivations, Capabilities and Strategies for Control" (New York: McGraw-Hill, 1977); Leonard Beaton and John Maddox, "The Spread of Nuclear Weapons" (New York: Praeger, 1962).

4. Kenneth N. Waltz, "The Spread of Nuclear Weapons: More May Be Better," *Adelphi Paper No. 171* (London: International Institute of Strategic Studies, 1981).

5. Bruce Bueno de Mequita and William H. Riker, "An Assessment of the Merits of Selective Nuclear Proliferation" in *Journal of Conflict Resolution 26*, No. 2 (June 1982) pp. 283-306; Steven J. Rosen, "A Stable System of Mutual Nuclear Deterrence in the Middle East" in *American Political Science Review 71*, No. 4 (December 1977) pp. 1367-83; John J. Weltman, "Managing Nuclear Multipolarity" in *International Security 6*, No. 3 (Winter 1981/82) pp. 182-94; John J. Weltman, "Nuclear Devolution and World Order" in *World Politics 32*, No. 2 (January 1980) pp. 169-93.

6. Devin T. Hagerty, "The Power of Suggestion: Opaque Proliferation, Existential Deterrence, and the South Asian Nuclear Arms Competition," in *Security Studies*, Volume 2, Numbers 3/4, Spring/Summer 1993, Frank Cass, London.

7. Op. cit. 6, pp. 258-9.*

8. Kenneth N. Waltz, "The Spread of Nuclear Weapons: More May Be Better," *Adelphi Papers No. 171* (London: International Institute of Strategic Studies, 1981) p. 16.

9. "Nuclear Politics in India" by Bray and Moodie in *Survival*, IISS London, May/June 1977, p. 175.

10. Op cit. 1 "International Political Effects of the Spread of Nuclear Weapons" p.188.

11. Samuel P. Huntington, "The Clash of Civilizations?" (Harvard University, John M. Olin Institute for Strategic Studies: *Project on The Changing Security Environment and American National Interests: Working Paper No. 4*, January 1993).

Security Implications of Nuclear Proliferation in South Asia

Munir Ahmad Khan

THE U.S. HAS BEEN PURSUING A POLICY TO PREVENT THE spread of nuclear weapons since 1945 when the awesome destructive power of these weapons became apparent. It offered a number of proposals including the Baruch Plan to control the spread of nuclear weapons but the Soviet Union rejected them. The U.S. proceeded to develop nuclear weapons leading to an arms race joined later by the U.K., France and China. After the 1964 nuclear explosion by China, the Soviet Union realized the serious consequences of nuclear proliferation and joined hands with the U.S. in sponsoring the Non-Proliferation Treaty to arrest further proliferation. The U.S. has steadfastly espoused the cause of nonproliferation to prevent threshold nations from joining the "Nuclear Club." In spite of these efforts, a number of near-nuclear countries have emerged and attempts by others to acquire similar capability have emerged. A proliferated world would be a dangerous world. Therefore, the U.S. has apparently decided to make a more determined effort to curb proliferation, both by pursuing nuclear disarmament and by discouraging threshold nations from going nuclear.

The U.S. policy is shifting from nonproliferation to counterproliferation which implies more aggressive measures to pre-empt, resist and counter emerging threats of nuclear proliferation and other weapons of mass destruction. The success of this new policy will depend not only how determinedly the U.S. pursues new counterproliferation

---

Dr. Munir A. Khan, a nuclear engineer, was Chairman of Pakistan Atomic Energy Commission from 1972 to 1991. He is a member of Sigma Xi and was elected as fellow of the American Nuclear Society in 1993. Dr. Khan did graduate work at Raleigh, North Carolina, as a Rotary Scholar and postgraduate studies at the Illinois Institute of Technology, Chicago.

measures but on how well one understands the underlying motives which propel nations to acquire nuclear weapons and provide incentives for foregoing the nuclear option.

Nuclear weapons are almost 50 years old. The technology associated with these weapons has spread widely and cannot be retrieved. Technical fixes, embargoes and restrictions on materials, technology and equipment acquisition can delay but not prevent a nation with modest industrial infrastructure and strong political will from acquiring nuclear weapons capabilities. This has been amply demonstrated in Latin America, the Middle East, South Asia and the Far East. It would, therefore, be unwise to rely heavily on technical fixes. Moreover, human ingenuity cannot be prevented from devising and discovering innovative methods and techniques for acquiring nuclear capability and developing new types of deadly chemical and biological weapons. Therefore, it is necessary to go to the root of the problem and understand why nations wish to go nuclear.

Basic motivations for acquiring nuclear or other weapons of mass destruction are essentially political. They stem from security perceptions, in particular, the felt need to meet threats—real or imaginary—to their survival, territorial integrity and vital national interests. In certain cases, nations may also seek to acquire these weapons to extend and project their power at the regional or global levels. Others may consider such weapons as symbols of power and prestige or to intimidate their neighbors. A comprehensive and effective non-proliferation regime should address the underlying political and moral causes besides invoking technical, legal and institutional fixes.

South Asia contains one-fifth of the world's population, including a majority of the human beings living below the poverty line. It forces with serious economic, social, ethnic and political problems. The region is smoldering with tensions between neighboring states and armed hostilities on their borders. In this environment of mistrust the to main adversaries in the region, namely India and Pakistan, have acquired a nuclear weapons capability. Should another war break out between these two countries, there is serious danger of a nuclear confrontation which could lead to a great human tragedy, as well as massive destruction of the economic, industrial and political structure of both countries. While the threat of a global nuclear war between the major nuclear powers, the U.S. and Russia, has receded the possibility of a nuclear flare up in this sub-continent has heightened creating an alarming situation. The problem facing the people of the sub-continent and the international community is how to contain, reduce and eliminate the hovering nuclear threat emerging in South Asia. With unresolved problems, increasing tensions, deepening suspicion, worsening nuclear rhetoric, growing nuclear capability, lack of a command and control system, we have a recipe for a potential nuclear catastrophe.

Emergence of the Nuclear Race in South Asia

Before suggesting ways and means for eliminating nuclear proliferation in South Asia, it is necessary to understand the history of introduction of nuclear technology into the subcontinent and the motives which led India and Pakistan towards acquiring and retaining a nuclear option.

The history of development of nuclear technology in South Asia goes back to the early 1950's when India launched its programme. Looking back, it is now clear that right from the beginning the in tent and direction of India's nuclear research a programme was towards acquisition of a nuclear weapons capability. Its technical and political leadership made no secret of this objective. India made full use of the ready availability of nuclear technology in the 1950s and 1960s when there was no effective bilateral or international safeguard systems to control the transfer of nuclear materials, equipment and technology. The two superpowers were engaged in developing their nuclear arsenals and believed that the enormous technical difficulties and financial costs of developing nuclear weapons, together with the secrecy that surrounded their programs, would constitute sufficient barriers against proliferation by lesser powers (notably the developing countries). Cold war rivalry prevented the two superpowers from reaching agreement on the question of proliferation. India made full use of the available opportunity to obtain nuclear technology, facilities and plants at a minimum cost and sometimes as a gift as exemplified by the 40 MW plutonium production reactor called the Canada-India reactor (CIR). The latter was made available without formal safeguards, except for an understanding that the reactor would not be used for military purposes. In 1964, India completed a reprocessing plant with the assistance of British and American suppliers. With CIR and the reprocessing plant in place India could by 1964 extract 13 Kg of weapons grade plutonium equivalent to two bombs per year without any safeguards. It is clear that India's pursuits of a nuclear capability and acquisition of essential facilities preceded China's nuclear explosion of October 1964.

India's nuclear programme was not a reaction to China's but was in fact conceived and instituted well before anything was known about China's nuclear efforts.   However, after the Chinese test explosion, India accelerated its programme and started stockpiling unsafeguarded weapons grade plutonium.

The rapid development and direction of India's programme proved worrisome to Pakistan in the early 1960's.   At that time, there were repeated reports about the claims made by Indian leaders, including Nehru and Bhabha, that India could go nuclear in one or two years.   Pakistan's concerns were not shared by Canada or the U.S. Pakistan was repeatedly assured by these countries that India would not go nuclear but this did not allay Pakistan's fears.   In the mid-1960's, when the two superpowers launched efforts leading to the Non-Proliferation Treaty,   Pakistan supported their efforts.   Pakistan was concerned about a nuclear threat emanating not primarily from the acknowledged nuclear states, but from the potential and undeclared nuclear countries such as India.   Therefore, it co-operated in cosponsoring a UN Conference in Geneva in 1968 with the object of eliciting security guarantees from non-nuclear weapons states (NNWS) against nuclear attack, threat or blackmail from any quarter. The nuclear weapons states (NWS) were unable to offer any credible positive guarantees and could not assuage the fears of NNWS. The NPT text was approved in 1968 without addressing this matter in a satisfactory manner.

In 1971, during the fourth UN Conference on Peaceful Uses of Atomic Energy held in Geneva, India publicly announced its intentions of conducting a peaceful nuclear explosion (PNE). The major powers took no official notice, while Pakistan protested both to the U.S. and Canada. The Canadian Prime Minister traveled to India to urge the Indian Prime Minister to honor the undertaking given to Canada that the CIR facility would not be used for military purposes or to manufacture a nuclear explosive device. But it was of no avail. With the gathering of nuclear clouds over the subcontinent, Pakistan faced a very grim situation. It had a very rudimentary nuclear infrastructure and all its facilities were under IAEA safeguards. At the inauguration of the Karachi Nuclear Power Plant in November 1972, the President of Pakistan made a major policy declaration. He said that India and Pakistan were too poor to engage in military applications of atomic energy and proposed that South Asia should be made a nuclear-weapons-free-zone (NWFZ). This proposal has remained a cornerstone of Pakistan's declared nuclear policy.

In 1974, India exploded a nuclear device.   This action did not surprise Pakistan but nevertheless it shook the country. The world media expressed indignation, but no major power condemned it. France dispatched a letter of congratulations; the USSR seemed to acquiesce; the U.S. government was restrained; China kept official silence. In response to Pakistan's protests, the government was told that what had been learned could not be unlearned. The U.S. Secretary of State visited India in October 1974 and avowed that India and the USA now shared another "tradition."

These developments shocked Pakistan. With the cut off of all Western military aid after 1965, forcible break up of the country in 1971 and a nuclearised neighbor, Pakistan felt increasingly insecure. Pakistan placed the matter before the United Nations in 1974 and formally presented a proposal for the establishment of a nuclear free zone in South Asia. Although this proposal was adopted by a large majority of the General Assembly members, the major nuclear weapons states and industrialized countries abstained. The message that Pakistan received was that, sooner or later, India would be admitted to the "Nuclear Club" as a "defacto" if not "dejure" member. The political leadership of Pakistan realized that Pakistan had to face a nuclear India alone, and had no choice but to acquire nuclear technology under safeguards, if possible, in order to neutralize India's nuclear edge.

In April 1979, the U.S. cut off all aid to Pakistan because of its alleged nuclear programme. After the Soviet invasion of Afghanistan in December 1979, the U.S. reviewed its strategic interests in the region and resumed economic and military co-operation with Pakistan to force the Soviet forces out of Afghanistan.

During the 1980's, the United States continued to place pressure on Pakistan with regard to the nuclear issue asking it to sign the NPT. Pakistan, on the other hand, contended that nuclear proliferation in South Asia was a regional issue and could not be resolved by singling out Pakistan because it also involved India, which had already exploded a nuclear device. Pakistan emphasized that both countries should be asked to adhere to the Non-Proliferation Regime simultaneously.   Pakistan sought to initiate a dialogue with India on the nuclear issue and made a number of concrete proposals to India which would require both countries to:

- sign the NPT simultaneously;
- accept fullscope safeguards;

- allow reciprocal inspection of each others nuclear facilities;
- agree to a bilateral treaty banning nuclear tests;
- establish a Nuclear Free Zone in South Asia;
- make a joint declaration of non-acquisition or manufacture of nuclear weapons;
- convene a UN-sponsored conference to discuss nuclear issues in South Asia.

India rejected all these suggestions and refused to put forward any proposals of its own to strengthen the non-proliferation regime in South Asia. Pakistan kept the U.S. informed of all these initiatives and the negative responses from India. Gradually, the United States began to realize that the nuclear issue in South Asia was, indeed, a regional issue and could not be resolved by forcing Pakistan to sign the NPT unilaterally.

India for its part, insists that the nuclear issue in South Asia is not a regional matter but is an extra-regional and a global one. India expresses its concern about nuclear weapons in China and the nuclear arsenals of other nuclear powers. It is willing to adhere to the Non-Proliferation Regime only within the framework of global nuclear disarmament.

To respond to the security concerns expressed by India and at the suggestion of the U.S., Pakistan, in June 1991, proposed a five nation conference embracing India, Pakistan, China, the U.S. and the former Soviet Union to discuss the nuclear issue in South Asia. India refused and proposed instead bilateral negotiations with major nuclear powers. During U.S.-India discussions held in September 1993, India accepted in principle the proposal for holding of a multilateral conference of nine nations including the U.K., France, Germany and Japan, in addition to the original five, to discuss nuclear and security issues in South Asia. However, India reversed its position and declined to go along with this proposal.

From Pakistan's perspective, India faces no military threat from Pakistan, neither nuclear nor conventional. If India agrees to sign the NPT, Pakistan will automatically do the same. India with 8 times the population of Pakistan will continue to retain an overwhelming conventional military superiority over Pakistan. It would appear that it is Pakistan that needs a nuclear deterrent against a far stronger neighbor than vice versa. It seems that India has other objectives in pursuing its nuclear option. India visualizes itself as a great power in the making for the 21st century with a legitimate sphere of influence extending from the Gulf to the Straits of Malacca and encompassing the Indian Ocean. It not only wants to be accepted as a dominant regional power but an extra regional and a global power. If this is true, then even if Pakistan were to succumb to India or sign the NPT it would not make the nuclear issue in South Asia go away. The possession of nuclear weapons is regarded by India as essential for asserting its power beyond its frontiers including a global role.

Coming to the other weapons of mass destruction, the situation is different. Both India and Pakistan have signed the recently concluded international Chemical Weapons Convention banning the production, possession and use of chemical weapons. It is a non-discriminatory treaty with universal application. As for biological weapons, India and Pakistan have supported the Biological Weapons Convention which is currently under negotiation in Geneva. This represents a welcome development because chemical weapons are much less expensive to produce and easier to deliver than are nuclear weapons. They can cause real havoc in the densely populated region of South Asia. It is hoped that India and Pakistan will ratify the Chemical Weapons Convention as well as the Biological Weapons Convention when it is concluded.

The most disturbing development emerging in the sub-continent is the introduction of ballistic missiles. As offensive weapons, such missiles are virtually unstoppable; and defence against them is beyond the technical and financial resources of the two countries. They are also force multipliers and enhance the range and effectiveness of weapons of mass destruction. They can generate terror as has been evident in the recent conflicts in the Middle East. Ballistic missiles are inherently destabilising and have added a grave new dimension to threat perceptions in South Asia.

India has taken the lead in developing, testing, producing and deploying ballistic missiles. Its arsenal includes Nag-anti-tank missiles; Trishul-low range anti-aircraft and Akash-high range anti-aircraft missiles; and Prithvi-ground-to-ground missiles with a range of 250 Kms. All these missiles are of immediate concern to Pakistan. Prithvi is being mass produced and reported to have been deployed against Pakistan's eastern borders, as well as in Kashmir. It can reach almost all the population centers, as well as economic, commercial and military targets in Pakistan. It can carry conventional, chemical, biological and nuclear war-heads, which poses a most serious threat to Pakistan.

India has also successfully tested the Agni IRBM with a range of 2500 Kms. It can be upgraded to cover a greater distance. This missile has no other use but to carry nuclear war-heads. In addition, India is developing Suriya which is an ICBM with a range exceeding 6000 Kms.

These developments have led to a dangerous missile race in the sub-continent. Pakistan has been forced to react by initiating its own missile development programme. It is alleged Pakistan has purchased components and technology for M-11 missiles with a range of 300 Kms from China and is trying to develop a Hataf missile with a range of 500 Kms. The missile race does not bode well for military stability and can make any new conflict in the region most destructive.

The current situation in the subcontinent is militarily and politically exceedingly dangerous. Both India and Pakistan are regarded as nuclear capable. India exploded a nuclear device 20 years ago demonstrating its nuclear capability. It is believed that Pakistan could also do so on short notice. India has a large nuclear programme and has already accumulated 500 Kgs of unsafeguarded weapons grade plutonium using its two plutonium production reactors and associated reprocessing plants. This is sufficient for 60 to 100 weapons. India is adding about 45 Kgs per year of weapon-grade plutonium (plus an unknown quantity of highly enriched uranium from a plant in the South) which is equivalent to more than 10 weapons per year. In addition, India has over 1 ton of unsafeguarded reactor grade plutonium which can also be used for military purposes. India has already tested the nuclear-capable Agni missile with a range of 4000 Kms. It also has demonstrated the ability to launch satellites capable of military reconnaissance missions over vast areas of the globe.

Pakistan is known to have facilities for producing highly enriched weapons-grade uranium (HEU) which have been in operation for the past few years. Pakistan also possesses the technical know-how to manufacture or test a nuclear device even though it has not yet done so. However, Pakistan's nuclear infrastructure and inventory of HEU is much smaller when compared to that of India. But the very fact that Pakistan has a nuclear capability appears to have acted as a deterrent; no open hostilities have erupted between the two countries over the past 22 years. Both India and Pakistan have denied that they have converted their nuclear capability to nuclear weapons use. But nuclear rhetoric on both sides is increasingly strident and certain elements in both countries are proposing an open declaration of their nuclear status instead of pursuing their current policy of official ambiguity. This heated rhetoric is linked with domestic politics and both governments have continued to disavow the possession of nuclear weapons. Nevertheless, pressures are building up in both countries which would indicate that they could be heading towards acknowledged military nuclearization. Even though the existing nuclear capability of these two countries has served as a symbolic deterrent, the situation could change through miscalculation or pre-emption. The disturbing thing is that both countries do not appear to have a sound control, command and communication system or enough know-how to install necessary safety measures, which leaves open the possibility of a nuclear mishap having grave consequences.

The nuclearisation of South Asia will have an impact extending beyond the region, altering security perceptions in neighboring countries and those well beyond South Asia. The introduction of ballistic missiles has exacerbated the situation. The testing of Agni by India has sent a disturbing message to many countries. Fired from the north-east of India, Agni can cover all of South China. Launched from Nicobar Island in the Indian Ocean (which lies only 250 miles off Sumatra), it can reach most of the ASEAN countries. From its west coast, it can cover the whole of the Gulf, as well as most of Iran and Saudi Arabia. From the south, it can reach Diego Garcia and challenge sea traffic between Europe and the Far East. Starting from the northern tip of India, it can cover most of the Central Asian Republics.

Thus, nuclearization of South Asia could have a spill over effect in a number of countries. It might revive interest in nuclear weapons in Kazakhistan and encourage Iran to acquire its own nuclear capability and threaten U.S. and European interests in the Gulf. It may also make ASEAN suspicious of India's military build up. Japan may find its crucial shipping lanes threatened, particularly if India also acquires nuclear armed submarines.

It appears that India is on a collision course not only with its smaller neighbors but with major powers including China and Japan in Asia and the U.S. and Russia outside. In this way India's nuclear and missile capability is not only a potential threat to peace and security in the region but a global problem in the making.

India insists that the nuclear issue in South Asia is not a regional but a global one and it is prepared to give up the nuclear option when all the nuclear weapons states of the world agree to destroy their respective nuclear arsenals and accept a non-discriminatory non-proliferation regime. There is no doubt that a moral case for the early elimination of nuclear weapons is a strong one. Some concrete moves have been made to reduce the nuclear arsenals of Russia and the U.S. by a factor of 10 by the year

2003, and even further cut-backs are envisaged in the future. We should all work towards delegitimisation of all weapons of mass destruction including nuclear weapons and their ultimate elimination. But this does not mean that, pending the achievement of these goals, proliferation at the regional level should continue or that the presence of nuclear weapons in declared nuclear weapon states can be used as an excuse for starting a nuclear race in a highly volatile conflict-ridden region.

If India has any intention of becoming a nuclear power at this time then it has to compete with other nuclear weapons states on building a credible nuclear arsenal. This will require inviting a back-breaking burden on its limited resources which are sorely needed for its economic and industrial development. It will necessitate extensive nuclear testing which will trigger testing by others. It will also have to confront a strong current of unfavorable world public opinion. Even if India chooses, at great expense, to become a full-fledged nuclear weapon state at the cost of its economic development, it would be susceptible to the same fate that befell the Soviet Union. India has certain legitimate national interests and security concerns which should be duly addressed. This is why the proposal for a multilateral conference of nine nations, including India and Pakistan along with five nuclear powers as well as Japan and Germany, offers an excellent opportunity for conducting a meaningful dialogue to deal with various security issues in South Asia.

Kashmir

The most important issue, which threatens peace and security in South Asia and has led to three wars in the subcontinent over the last 40 years, is the still unresolved Kashmir problem. Kashmir can yet spark another war with dire consequences for both countries. It is no exaggeration to say that the key to peace in the subcontinent and its denuclearization lies in the peaceful resolution of the Kashmir issue. Pakistan believes that it should be resolved in accordance with the principle of self-determination as agreed by India and Pakistan and reflected in the UN resolutions giving the people of the area the right to join India or Pakistan through a free and fair plebiscite. India insists that the problem does not exist because its annexation of Kashmir is final and irrevocable. The fact is that India is facing serious insurgency in Kashmir which has cost thousands of lives. It keeps over 400,000 troops in the state of Jammu and Kashmir incurring an expenditure of over two billion dollars per year, clear indication that the problem does exist and remains to be resolved. As long as the Kashmir issue persists, there can be no real improvement in Indo-Pakistan relations and, therefore, little prospect for peace and security in the region. Both sides continue to spend large sums on defence and a dangerous arms race with a nuclear dimension is accelerating. The Kashmir problem is sapping the energies of both countries, not only adversely affecting economic development, but arresting the growth of the entire subcontinent. While the other Asian countries are galloping ahead economically, South Asia is lagging behind. It is astonishing that the GNP of all the South Asian countries is less than the GNP of South Korea. The exports of India and Pakistan are less than the exports of Malaysia.

India contends that a compromise on Kashmir would have serious repercussions and could encourage centrifugal tendencies among other states of India. Pakistan believes that Kashmir is the unfinished agenda of partition and should be resolved through negotiations and not by force. It appears that India is ignoring the experience of big powers like the former Soviet Union in Afghanistan and the U.S. in Vietnam by holding on to Kashmir by force. Actually India would gain in stature and strength if it disengages militarily in Kashmir and finds an honorable way out as France did in Algeria. It is about time that these two countries resolved their outstanding problems and retreated from the brink of nuclear confrontation, devoting their energies to economic development, which holds the key to their survival as independent and united countries.

Conclusion

Judging from existing trends, the security situation in South Asia is worsening. India, which is the dominant military power in the region, has uneasy relationships with all its neighbors. It views China with suspicion. Despite the fact that Bangladesh has achieved its independence from Pakistan, relations between New Delhi and Dhaka are far from satisfactory. India's police action in Sri Lanka has left deep scars of suspicion there. Nepal has a number of problems with India. Thus, it is not simply Pakistan that has differences with its big neighbor; India has problems with all its neighbors. Even if Pakistan is wrong, in some ways all the neighbors of India can not be wrong at the same time. It is important that India adopt a more conciliatory, less confrontational stance, vis-a-vis its neighbors, if it is to create an environment arguing for peace and security in South Asia. As far as Pakistan is concerned, its security problems have deepened over the last four years. It had enjoyed a mutually beneficial and constructive security relationship with the U.S., which has evaporated after the withdrawal of Soviet forces from Afghanistan. This relationship had provided a certain equilibrium in the region and afforded Pakistan a sense of security, vis-a-vis its powerful neighbor India. Since 1990, with the application of the Pressler Amendment, all economic, military and strategic co-operation has been terminated. Political relations between Islamabad and Washington have suffered a serious setback. Pakistan has relied heavily on U.S.-made military equipment and hardware for its defence. Under the Pressler law, the U.S. can not supply military equipment or other forms of security assistance to Pakistan. This has seriously undermined the defence preparedness of Pakistan because most of its weapons systems have been sidelined for want of spare parts and technical support.

By contrast, India has continued to upgrade its military hardware with ongoing supplies from Russia and other former Soviet Republics, as well as Western Europe. India also has a strong defence industry of its own which meets 80 percent of its needs. While Indian military might is increasing, Pakistan's defensive capability has eroded. This has caused a serious imbalance of power in the region. This can only serve to facilitate aggression. Therefore, it is important that U.S.-Pakistan relations be normalized and ways and means be found so that a military balance in the region, which has become dangerously lopsided, is restored. Unless this is done, Pakistan will continue to feel increasingly insecure and those in the country who favor resort to the nuclear option will gain ascendancy. It is not in the interest of peace to drive Pakistan into a nuclear corner.

In spite of all the intractable problems between India and Pakistan, certain measures can be taken for reducing tensions between the two countries and improving the overall security climate to gain more time for resolution of key issues, including the nuclear issue. These measures may include:

i) A first step, a dialogue between India and Pakistan to discuss all outstanding problems. The fact that no constructive and meaningful dialogue has been held between the two sides in recent years is itself an indication of deep-seated mistrust and lack of communications. The two countries must be brought to the negotiating table, and external help is needed in settling the differences and finding a lasting solution to their problems.

ii) To facilitate such a dialogue, the outside friendly powers, particularly the United States, can play a vital role. The U.S. has succeeded in initiating the peace process in the Middle East. Perhaps similar behind the scene efforts could be launched regarding Indo-Pakistan problems.

iii) On the nuclear issue, the U.S. has already presented several proposals. The idea of a nine nation conference should be pursued more vigorously. India has agreed to it in principle and Pakistan has also accepted. India should be persuaded now to agree to convening the conference at an early date.

iv) India and Pakistan should be engaged more intensively in discussions regarding a ban on nuclear testing, capping of nuclear programs, a freeze on fissile material production, and non-testing or development and deployment of ballistic missiles.

v) Although official negotiations and discussions between India and Pakistan have been difficult and non-productive, unofficial, informal meetings between scholars, experts and opinion makers of the two countries have provided excellent opportunities for free and frank exchanges of views at various levels. This is, indeed, a very valuable communication channel and should be both strengthened and broadened. In the long run, unofficial dialogue may provide some hope of an official breakthrough. On the nuclear side, informal contacts have already played a significant role in paving the way for an agreement on "No attack on each others' nuclear facilities." This idea was officially endorsed in 1985, but negotiations on the final text and ratification required an additional six years. It might be extremely productive if a dialogue was held between the two countries at an unofficial level to identify areas of possible further agreement.

All in all, the security environment in South Asia is extremely disturbing. Relations between India and Pakistan have been exceedingly tense over the past several years. The problem in Kashmir has taken an ominous turn. Bilateral discussions are at a stand still. If hostilities break out, the possibility of nuclear confrontation can not be ruled out. Therefore, it is essential that efforts be made to defuse the situation and address the root cause of the outstanding problems between India and Pakistan. The basic issues are political and, unless they are resolved, there will be only limited progress in the nuclear domain.

The U.S. can play a very constructive role by ensuring that the military balance in South Asia does not become too lop-sided. It can also use its good offices to initiate a negotiating process in the region to resolve the Kashmir problem, which holds the key to peace and security in South Asia.

Three Models for Nuclear Policy in South Asia: The Case for Nonweaponized Deterrence

George Perkovich

INDIANS, PAKISTANIS AND CHINESE—NOT AMERICANS—WILL decide the future of nuclear weapons programs in South Asia. Optimally, these decisions will derive from deliberate, far-sighted calculations of national, regional and global interests. Americans and other outsiders can only facilitate and cajole in this process, providing analyses of the various regional and global interests involved. Where appropriate, the international community should go further and affect the local national and regional calculations of interest by providing incentives for considering broader global interests. Among these interests are the avoidance of escalation-prone conflict, the non-diversion of resources which could otherwise enhance economic development, and the buttressing of democracy and economic reform in India and Pakistan. Satisfying each of these global interests clearly augments the national interests of India, Pakistan and China.

It should be unquestioned that Indians, Pakistanis and Chinese will retain ultimate sovereignty over nuclear decisionmaking. Yet, often, Indian, Pakistani and, less so Chinese elites feel that their sovereignty over these matters is questioned by the United States and other powers,

Mr. George Perkovich is director of the Secure World Program of the W. Alton Jones Foundation in Charlottesville, VA. His writings on nonproliferation have appeared in *Foreign Affairs, Foreign Policy,* the *Atlantic Monthly,* the *Bulletin of Atomic Scientists, The New York Times, The Washington Post, The Los Angeles Times,* and *The Christian Science Monitor.* He received an M.A. from Harvard University and a B.A. from the University of California at Santa Cruz.

implicitly if not explicitly. Consciously or not, Americans as representatives of the widely proclaimed sole remaining super power sometimes act arrogantly. Complex psychological, cultural and political factors make these relationships unusually demanding for all parties. These relational impediments must be recognized and overcome.

It does not diminish or underestimate Indian and Pakistani sovereignty when Americans or others urge these nations to refrain from pursuing nuclear weaponry. Preventing and reversing the spread of nuclear weaponry is in the world's interest and that of the United States precisely because this weaponry poses unique and far-reaching threats to all states' security. While American diplomacy and non-proliferation policy often seem meddlesome or designed to protect an American strategic advantage, these negative impressions should not obscure the more fundamental reality that common regional and global weapons interests are shared. It is precisely these interests which incline many analysts and officials from non-nuclear states also to urge regional and global disarmament. This reflects the underlying danger of nuclear weapons and related technologies which gives every citizen in every state an interest in preventing the spread and potential use of these weapons.

Fortunately, where nuclear weapons policies are concerned, circumstances should increase the likelihood that diverse states will recognize these shared interests in denuclearization. Globally, the declared nuclear powers have reversed their arms race. The United States and Russia have undertaken previously unimaginable reductions. While leaders have failed to articulate a vision of the future role of nuclear weapons in global security and the steps by which elimination of the nuclear threat can be achieved, a general devaluation of nuclear weapons has occurred. This devaluation brings the position of the nuclear "haves" towards the position of the "have nots." It has heightened global pressures against those who would seek to deploy or use nuclear weapons in this new context.

The Cold War's end has deepened the awareness that non-military strength is increasingly the key to security and national fulfillment. The Soviet Union is seen as a colossal failure precisely because it so overemphasized military strength at the expense of economic development and the political processes necessary to encourage it. The power and vitality of economic prowess will become starker when the expected realignment of the UN Security Council occurs, giving permanent seats to non-nuclear Germany and Japan. The growing desire for international trade boosts the interests of all parties—developed countries as well as developing—in establishing conditions where commerce, not military competition absorb the creative energies of governments and people.

In addition, states will lose convenient pretexts for nuclear weapons programs as nuclear power continues to wane as a cost-effective source of electricity. In the past, civil nuclear programs have served as cover under which certain states have conducted undeclared nuclear weapons work. Yet, as plutonium fuels prove especially non-competitive, and the declared nuclear weapons states move to ban further unsafeguarded production of this material, the capacity of other states.to conduct clandestine nuclear weapons programs will diminish.

Trends to devalue nuclear weaponry have been most dramatic where reversal was most needed—in the United States and Russia. Fortunately, in many ways, remediation has been less necessary in India and Pakistan. There decision-makers and opinion-shapers approach nuclear weapons issues very differently than have the United States, the former Soviet Union and other declared nuclear powers. Most Indian and Pakistani elites show little interest in postulating how nuclear war could be managed, how deterrence could be extended across a range of conventional and nuclear scenarios, or whether worst-case analyses require an ambitious program to deploy nuclear weapons and elaborate command and control systems. Instead, at least for now, they wisely seem to accept the basic and mutual deterrent effects of one country's capability to drop a nuclear weapon on another.

Building on this favorable ground, this paper will discuss three leading models of future nuclear policy regimes in South Asia—the "NPT" model; the "Managing Proliferation" or "Nuclear Weapons Safe Zone" model; and the "Non-Weaponised Deterrence" model. While I unavoidably reflect American perspectives, the aim of the paper is to articulate shared Indian, Pakistani, Chinese and global interests which argue for and against each of the three potential nuclear regimes.

Ultimately, the paper recommends a policy of nonweaponized deterrence as a significantly more feasible alternative than either Indian and Pakistani deployment of nuclear weapons or accession to the Nuclear NonProliferation Treaty (NPT) as non-nuclear weapons states. In essence, non-weaponised deterrence entails verified agreements that a country will not assemble and deploy nuclear weapons or ballistic missiles, but could retain the material and know-how required to construct a nuclear weapon if an imminent threat of aggression arises from an adversary with nuclear weapons capability. A nonweaponized deterrence regime, with subsidiary confidence-building measures and agreements, would provide the deterrence of the nuclear "genie" without the costs and instabilities of deployed nuclear arsenals.

The logic of non-weaponized deterrence can be seen in recent American and Russian decisions to eliminate medium-range missiles, sharply reduce their strategic nuclear forces, reduce the alert status of their nuclear arsenals, halt explosive testing of nuclear weapons, etc. These moves reflect a gradual dismantlement of the hair-triggered doomsday machine created in the Cold War. As political relations improve, the logic of recent denuclearization steps point toward a time when states or the international community would retain only blueprints and materials from which nuclear weapons could be quickly reconstructed should the need ever arise. India and Pakistan can leapfrog the costly and misbegotten process of nuclear arms racing and instead settle today on a structured regime of non weaponised deterrence. This is in their interests whether or not the established nuclear powers join them. Yet by adopting this self-interested position, India and Pakistan would enhance their capacity to press the rest of the international community to expedite the denuclearization of the long-standing nuclear weapons states. Conversely, by going against the grain of denuclearization, India and Pakistan would reduce their political standing, their economic viability and their security.

The NPT Model

The traditional position, with many advocates in the broader community of non-proliferation specialists, is to insist that both countries sign the NPT as non-nuclear weapons states and eliminate their nuclear weapons capabilities accordingly. This policy, while reflecting an optimal objective, is deeply flawed at the present time. First, an NPT-centred policy fails to recognize how thoroughly opposed Indian officials and citizens are to signing a document that divides the world into two classes of power the few with nuclear weapons, and the many without. For many Pakistanis and Indians, whose societies are long-time victims of European colonialism, nuclear capability gives their nations sovereignty on par with the greatest world powers. The politics encasing this symbol of sovereignty are difficult to crack. By acting as if these politics are not of genuinely great significance, Western policy appears cynical. Furthermore, many Pakistanis view a nuclear weapons capability as a necessary "last ditch" deterrent against a more powerful India which has not thoroughly accepted the viability, or even the legitimacy, of an independent Pakistan. A similar though less compelling logic influences India's position toward China.

The NPT-centred policy suffers a further flaw insofar as its proponents rarely offer serious measures to redress the discrimination of the treaty. American interlocutors often act as if this discrimination should be accepted as a fact of life; Indians and Pakistanis, they say, should skip the rhetoric and move on to more serious issues like the danger and pointlessness of their nuclear programs. But for Indians, especially, discrimination is precisely the fact of life that animates or justifies much their interest in nuclear capability. Saying "no" to the NPT reflects national power; it conveys equality of status and sovereignty.

Of course, now that the Cold War has waned, American officials and analysts frequently seek to deflect discrimination-oriented criticism of the NPT by arguing that Article VI, with its call on the nuclear weapons states to pursue disarmament, can satisfy countries like India's and Pakistan's demand for equity. Proponents of this approach argue that the established nuclear powers are now fulfilling Article VI through the INF Treaty, START, START II and a comprehensive test ban. This should make it fair and persuasive to continue to center a near-term nonproliferation policy on the NPT.

However, while recent arms reductions are profoundly constructive, the heart of the discrimination case is that some states—the recognized nuclear powers—uncompromisingly reserve the right to possess the deterrent power of nuclear weapons while denying it to others. Strategic threats to the United States may be uncertain, but the United States insists on having nuclear weapons to deal with them. Meanwhile, Pakistan and India have identifiable threats to their security—Pakistan is conventionally overmatched by India, while India borders not only Pakistan but larger and nuclear-armed China. Still, the U.S. blithely insists they must abjure nuclear deterrence. (That the U.S. has been more accommodating to Israel on this point further undermines diplomacy with Pakistan and India.) Nothing in the current and prospective nuclear arms reduction agenda indicates that the nuclear powers are willing to do without nuclear deterrence. The position is still discriminatory. (Of course, discrimination *per se* does not then generate an Indian or Pakistani national interest in assembling and deploying nuclear arsenals.) One way to overcome the discrimination flaw would be to offer alternate means and assurances to protect the legitimate security interests of countries like India and Pakistan. Another more immediate step would be to broaden the U.S.-Russian arms reduction process to include the strategic forces of China, the United Kingdom and France. Until this is done, India and Pakistan will resist abandoning their nuclear options.

Finally, in nuclear diplomacy with India and Pakistan, tone and attitude matter greatly. Unfortunately the discriminatory structure of the NPT and the sovereignty-laden attributes of nuclear weapons heighten the passion and moralism of the discussants. One cannot escape the possibility that race complicates nuclear diplomacy with South Asians. An eminent Indian strategist revealed much in a recent discussion when he said, "What the world needs is for blacks in America to become 51 percent of the population. Then you will get rid of your nuclear weapons the next day, as South Africa has prepared to do." The feeling exists among some Indian and Pakistani elites that Western non-proliferation policy in the Third World reflects a "white man's" view that "black and brown" people are peculiarly unfit to have such weapons. The tolerance of the Israeli nuclear program is seen as the nonproliferation exception that proves the racial rule. Of course, race and cultural prejudices affect relations within South Asia as well; the point is to bring these insidious issues into the light where they can be recognized and dealt with directly.

The Managing Proliferation Model

A second "school" of U.S. and South Asian nonproliferation specialists seeks to "manage" overt proliferation. Recognizing that security interests may impel Pakistan and India to seek-nuclear weapons capability, these specialists—who in the U.S. can be found in assorted think-tanks and lower levels in the Department of Defense—argue that India and Pakistan should be declared as nuclear weapons states. If proliferation is bound to occur anyway, according to this school, the objective should be to help manage it by assisting them in achieving stable, survivable and safely configured small arsenals with centralized and efficient command and control systems. This basic "regime" has been described by some Indian analysts under the rubric of a Nuclear-Weapons-Safe Zone or "minimal deterrence." It has been endorsed by some Pakistani analysts such as General Arif as well.

Unfortunately, numerous unintended effects would bedevil the "managing" proliferation strategy in South Asia. In particular, much harm would be done to the domestic well-being of the newly nuclear states. The domestic dangers of nuclear weapons programs tend to be overlooked in the field of security studies. However, American and Soviet experiences in nuclear weapons production reveal the systemic harm the nuclear establishments have caused to their host countries. Although what little we know about the workings of nuclear weapons establishments has come recently from American and Russian sources, there is evidence that Indian and Pakistani societies will also suffer economic, environmental, political, and security ills if their nuclear weapons establishments continue to grow and become more entrenched and resistant to political oversight and control.

Nuclear weapons programs visit great economic costs on their sponsors. This runs against the canard that "nukes give you the most bang for the bucks." That claim rests on dubious and incomplete accounting.

The "nukes are cheap" argument tends not to count the costs of maintaining scientific and engineering cadres and research and design facilities required to produce fissile materials, and design and assemble nuclear weapons. These costs are often hidden in budgets of civil nuclear programs which themselves are often obscured from public view. Every highly trained scientist and engineer working on weapons could alternatively be applying his or her talents to economically productive tasks. On the materials ledger, uranium enrichment and/or plutonium separation and manufacture are so costly that a number of highly-developed countries have opted not to pursue these technologies on economic grounds. Germany, for example, is reversing earlier plans to contract for plutonium reprocessing. The "more bang for the buck" argument also tends to overlook the development costs of ballistic missiles which can be hidden in civil space program budgets. The expense of military units which would be assigned to secure, maintain and operate these weapons is generally not included in the nuclear "bill". Furthermore, reliable command and control of deployed nuclear arsenals requires an expensive? highly technical apparatus of communications technology, hardened facilities, sophisticated components within weaponry, and elaborate intelligence gathering and information processing technology. Such command and control systems are enormously costly and often can be spread across a variety of "departments" and programs thereby diminishing the apparent costs of nuclear weapons *per se.*

On the other end of the nuclear weapons "life cycle," no state currently accounts for the enormous expense of decommissioning obsolete nuclear facilities. No state has established or paid for facilities and procedures to permanently dispose of radioactive waste which results from producing these weapons. Indeed, these costs are so great that politicians and industrial leaders in the United States, Russia, France, and the United Kingdom choose simply to postpone reckoning with them. Finally, were nuclear weapons actually used in South Asia, the victors, if there were any, would face an unprecedented burden of refugees, lost agricultural output if the Punjab were contaminated, and a host of other economic pains like those besetting the victims of Chernobyl today.

All of the financial costs of nuclear capability would grow if India or Pakistan chose to "go nuclear" and openly assemble and deploy nuclear weapons. Once the bomb is out of the basement, both countries, and perhaps China, would be pressed into an action-reaction cycle of deployments, modernization and counter-deployments and counter-modernization. Indian analysts wisely speak of capping a potential arsenal at a minimal deterrent level. Yet, even if such self-control were to occur, a minimal deterrent arsenal would be vastly larger and more elaborate and costly than the current nonweaponized deterrent.

The forces envisioned here as a minimal deterrent. including submarine-launched missile capability, would consume a major fraction of India's yearly defence expenditures which the International Institute of Strategic Studies estimates was more than $8 billion in 1991. (This figure itself does not account for hidden costs associated with the ongoing development of nuclear weapons capability and of delivery systems work conducted through the civilian space program). Even without submarine-based forces, such an arsenal would probably require a large increase in the costs now paid to maintain India's nuclear option. An arsenal of this size and nature would require much more extensive testing, including probably over time, explosive testing of nuclear warheads. These activities are costly in budgetary terms and, as the U.S. and Russia have discovered, in the toll taken on the environment. The additional command and control capabilities required to manage an arsenal that includes mobile land-based launchers and submarines would also be technically and financially demanding. The logic of creeping sophistication and expense is apparent.

A major additional domestic "cost" of nuclear weapons production is the environmental and human health damage associated with these activities. In the United States, for example, the estimated 30-year cost of "cleaning up" contaminated earth, waterways and buildings associated with nuclear weapons production will be $300 billion, or roughly an additional $5 million for each warhead produced by the United States. Walls of secrecy make it difficult to assess environmental and human health damage done by India's (or China's, or France's or Israel's) nuclear weapons production activities. Yet, press accounts of accidents and the general operational inefficiency of the Indian nuclear establishment suggest that significant environmental and health damage has already been done. The "costs" of accidents and unsafe conditions may never actually be paid by the government, but they are nonetheless visited on the nation.

Another major domestic ill-effect of nuclear weapons production is the tendency of nuclear establishments to form a secretive, unaccountable state within a state. Obviously some technical and military information associated with nuclear weapons must remain secret, but in every existing nuclear establishment "national security" privileges have resulted in wildly excessive secrecy and restrictions on political liberties and accountability. This is most debilitating and ironic in democracies. Here governments are obligated to provide their people and their elected representatives with enough accurate data and analysis to enable informed debate over the costs and merits of particular nuclear policies. Such debate should consider whether producing and deploying nuclear weapons (or, in the case of the declared nuclear states, seeking nuclear reductions) is in the societies' overall interests. When the public and/or its elected representatives are not allowed the information needed for informed debate, democracy erodes. Typically, secrecy hides over-expenditures, incompetence, and minor and major disasters. This benefits (seemingly) the narrow interests of the nuclear establishment at the expense of society.

Citing the state-within-the-state problem is not to condemn those who manage nuclear weapons complexes. Often these are responsible people who believe they are operating in their nation's interest. Yet, objectively, in every society that contains a nuclear weapons establishment, the record of oversight has been poor, and democratic principles and procedures have been undermined at the expense of the societies at large. Ultimately, as in Russia and the United States, the tension between popular aspirations for democratic accountability and the weapons establishments' appetites for resources and autonomy weakens the legitimacy of the government and calls into question its national security policies.

Nuclear weapons programs also can profoundly affect the character of partisan politics within a state, making it difficult to keep political debate on a rational, balanced keel. All states which have developed nuclear weapons capability face adversaries. Political leaders in these states, therefore, compete over how best to deal with these adversaries. In this competition, a leader's or party's position on nuclear weapons can become a high-profile, emotional issue. Nuclear weapons become entwined with a nation's sense of sovereignty—"the bomb" becomes a symbol of sovereignty. Irresponsible political forces find it easy to manipulate the potent nuclear symbol for their own narrow and ephemeral purposes. The "bomb" becomes equated with sovereignty, national pride, status, toughness, etc. Those who question the utility of the "bomb" can be cast on the losing side of emotional political contests. Historically, across a wide range of societies, the politics of the "bomb" has worked to the advantage of political forces which arguably are less dedicated to democracy, tolerance of diversity, economic development, and to the peaceful resolution of conflict.

For example, in the United States, presidential candidate Ronald Reagan exploited the symbolic value of nuclear weaponry by campaigning for a massive build up and modernization of American nuclear forces. This "tough minded" approach buttressed a chauvinistic nationalism and a professed willingness to flex American military muscles around the world. Of course, the issues were more complicated than this. Much of the 1980s force modernization had been initiated by President Carter as his position weakened in 1979 and detente collapsed. President Reagan himself, according to Secretary of State George Shultz's persuasive memoir, deeply desired to rid the world of nuclear weapons. Yet political campaign expediency, the unrelenting hawkishness of some of his ideological appointees, and a belief that only American military superiority would compel Soviet reductions resulted in an Administration which heightened the currency of nuclear weapons. On balance, the Reagan experience shows that politicians who seek to shroud themselves in the shadow of nuclear weaponry tend to conduct more bellicose foreign and military policies.

Similar tendencies appear in India. Whatever one thinks of the Bhartiya Janata Party's (BJP) economic policies, the party's advocacy of assembling and deploying nuclear weapons symbolizes a general bellicosity and toughness. The BJP says it will be tougher on Pakistan, tougher on Muslims in India—India will become a more forceful and tightly controlled state. The nuclear weapons establishment, by its very existence, serves as a symbolic and substantive tool for the BJP or other parties to use in their quest for power. In return, if the BJP wins power, the establishment could enjoy greater budgetary and political prerogatives, far from democratic checks and balances. It remains for Indians to decide whether in fact the BJP represents the public's best interests. I merely suggest that something profound and exemplary in the character of the Indian society and state has, thus far, caused the country to forego deploying nuclear weapons; a decision now to "go nuclear" would change that very character of the Indian polity.

The "bomb" works for certain political forces in Pakistan, too. General (retd.) Mirza Aslam Beg, the former army chief of staff, and a man with political ambitions, gave a series of interviews in July 1993 wherein he boasted (ambiguously) that Pakistan had "tested" a nuclear device, presumably in a laboratory. He also rattled the nuclear sabre, speaking of his willingness to use nuclear weapons to save the state in a conventional conflict. It is no accident that Gen Beg made these pronouncements shortly after Pakistan's president announced his resignation, opening the campaign for his successor. Gen Beg clearly sees the nuclear "card" as an ace which may help him or his allies affect the national political game. Is this in the interest of the Pakistani people, the region or the world?

To be sure, in Pakistan as well as in India, the U.S., Russia and elsewhere, hardline political forces would find other useful symbols if nuclear weapons were not available. The point is that when nuclear weapons establishments are present, the "bomb" becomes the highest symbol to be grasped by a certain kind of politician. The "bomb's" power on the popular imagination is so great that it can deform political competition and impede the functioning of society, allowing uninformed fears or uninformed delusions of omnipotence to distort decision-making. Whether this is good or bad depends on the beholder; the phenomenon, however, is important to recognize.

Turning to the more commonly recognized international repercussions of deployed nuclear arsenals, several stand out.

Deployments of ballistic missiles will cause both India and Pakistan (and China) to presume that these weapons can carry nuclear warheads, which in turn would be likely to lead to destabilizing competition. Tremendous pressures would mount to counter each other's deployments, and to enhance arsenals qualitatively and quantitatively. Scenarios for pre-emption will emerge, requiring expensive protective measures in the form of mobile or submarine-based launchers and more sophisticated command and control provisions. Nuclear doctrinal problems will emerge and confront both sides with the dangers of nuclear escalation and the impossibility that nuclear exchanges could be limited. In short, India and Pakistan would find it hard to resist adopting the technological and doctrinal patterns of the other declared nuclear powers. To their credit, Indians and Pakistanis (and Chinese to some extent as well), have heretofore avoided this infection of nuclear logic. Of course, some Indians and Pakistanis believe that they can deploy nuclear weapons and avoid unstable competition. But the major prior case of an adversarial dyad "going nuclear"—the U.S. and the USSR—resulted in decades of instability which lasted until massive redundancy in second strike capability had been achieved. The price was terribly severe. A belief that India and Pakistan could manage nuclear deployments in a stable manner seems to be based on an underlying mutuality of interest and understanding. Yet, such shared interests and understanding should make nuclear deployments unnecessary in the first place.

Indian and Pakistani interests would also suffer from the international backlash which would occur following nuclear deployments. The U.S. and major non-nuclear powers such as Japan and Germany would be the most likely nations to react negatively. This could take the form of political ill-will and lessened inclination to cooperate with India and Pakistan on a variety of global issues and in a variety of fora. Most ominously, international financial institutions such as the International Monetary Fund (IMF) and World Bank, as well as major aid donors, could become less disposed to assist India's economic development. International business could also view a nuclear competition in South Asia as a sign of broader political uncertainty and unsound fiscal priorities. This degrades the investment environment.

Ultimately, the case can be made that no sound strategic rationale for India's or Pakistan's assembling and deploying nuclear weapons has been offered.

China is the true target of Indians' pro-nuclear arguments. Here, given the apparently serious concern over China's threat to Indian security, one would expect a well-developed, comprehensive Indian strategy for reducing the threat or protecting against it. Such a strategy would clearly define "the problem" which China poses to Indian security and the objectives which must be met to redress it. An array of means would then be outlined to pursue these objectives: bilateral diplomatic initiatives; regional or international diplomatic campaigns; arms control and confidence-building measure proposals; and, as a negative inducement, military programs which could in theory heighten Chinese incentives to engage forthrightly in the diplomatic and arms control realm. Anyone seriously trying to solve a major bilateral security challenge would come up with these elements of strategy.

Yet, the Government of India does not appear to have a comprehensive strategy toward China. The former Indian Foreign Secretary, Muchkund Dubey, said as much on All India Radio in August 1993, when he acknowledged that India was "not in a planned way, not wholeheartedly" pursuing Chinese arms reductions and global progress toward disarmament.[1] Indian analysts have still not made a clear case about how India's security in relation to China will be enhanced by assembling nuclear weapons and deploying them on ballistic missiles oriented toward China. Missiles appear to be the answer, but what is the question? No case will be compelling until it evaluates the "going nuclear" strategy against other competing or complementary strategies for pursuing India's security objectives with China.

The outstanding contention between India and China, in General Sundarji's view, is the "unresolved border problem"—China's occupation of the Aksai Chin plateau adjacent to Ladakh, Kashmir in northwest India and India's occupation of the North-East Frontier Agency, which China claims. And here progress is being made by diplomats. According to an August 25, 1993, Reuters report, India and China have agreed "substantially to reduce the number of troops along their Himalayan border" as part of proposed confidence-building measures between the two countries. Regarding other security issues,

The nuclear threat to India from China can be assessed as of medium possibility. The Chinese have a declared policy of "no first use." The Chinese possess a fairly large nuclear inventory and in theory can mount a strong disarming-cum-decapitating first strike against India. However, even this cannot give any assurance of total success; a residual capability of taking out a few Chinese cities is almost certain (after India deploys Agni). Even if they break their declared policy and are prepared to launch a first strike against India, what could trigger such action? The border dispute leading to border clashes would not be reason enough. An Indian attempt to detach the Tibet Region from China might be adequate reason; but then this is not an Indian aim.[2]

From this analysis it appears that China, like India, is a status quo power, at least in South Asia. Nothing in the threat equation here necessarily warrants missile deployments and nuclear weaponization.

The border dispute aside, it is apparent that Indian production and deployment of ballistic missiles intended primarily toward China could worsen the security relationship. Longer range Indian missiles could compel Chinese military and political leaders to pay more attention to possible threat scenarios from India. Conceivably, but by no means certainly, this could induce Chinese leaders to seek more formal strategic accommodation with India. However, for this to happen, India would first have to clearly state what feasible steps it wants China to take in the security realm. In the absence of an overriding diplomatic strategy, the unadorned deployment of longer range Indian missiles would most likely result in negative Chinese attention. China's guard would be raised, relations would become more tense and militarized. China might or might not compensate for Indian deployments with additional Chinese conventional or nuclear deployments, but in any case, a greater premium would be placed on competitive, balance-of-power policies rather than on more cooperative approaches to security. India's relations with China would most likely worsen. In a strategic competition, China's burgeoning economy gives it a preponderance of power. Taking the path of military competition with an inferior economy is a dead end for India, as it proved to be for the Soviet Union.[3]

Fortunately, India has less risky alternatives for pursuing its security vis-a-vis China. A strong case can be made that India would augment its security more by avoiding arousal of Chinese military concerns and a hardening of American, European, Japanese and other bilateral relations toward India, which would follow overt Indian weaponization. By rejecting weaponization, India would be better placed to build cooperative security relations with China, the United States and Japan. And with better relations with Beijing, Washington and Tokyo, India would find itself with important strategic options. In balance of power terms, were China to become threatening, India could turn to Washington for augmentation, at first in the form of international pressure on China to abandon a threatening stance. Were Washington to become bellicose which is extremely difficult to conceive in the post-Cold War era as long as India is working with and not against the grain of devaluing weapons of mass destruction—India could turn to China. In short, India has the potential to play a classic balancing role in Asia. With longstanding healthy ties with Russia, and the potential for still more positive relations with Japan, India's position appears still stronger.

This is not to dismiss the particular military threats some Indians perceive from China. The point is to thoroughly evaluate and debate the best means for India alone and with international partners to reduce these threats. A diplomacy-first strategy may yield better results than exercising the capability to produce and deploy nuclear weapons and ballistic missiles. India is in a good position to rally the U.S., Russia and Japan to support diplomatic pressure on China to enter nuclear arms reduction talks, and to create a missile-free zone in southwest China where India has concerns. But these strategic diplomatic options become harder to pursue if India becomes a nuclear weapons state armed with ballistic missiles.

Of course, no Indian security strategy will succeed if the Indian economy does not become more potent and the polity more stable and efficiently managed. This challenge—economic development and governmental effectiveness—is the greatest threat to Indian security. By acting as if military hardware is the key to power, status and security, India appears to be following a Soviet strategy. The result of that strategy is apparent: inadequate economic development, isolation from the global economy, technology embargoes and increased social and political restiveness. India's interest would be much better served when the full potential of India's possibilities in Asia would be realized through "further progress on the road towards economic liberalization; the revitalization of India's federal polity; India's ability to liberate itself from the current quagmire of Indo-Pak relations; a faster pace of Sino-Indian normalization; and the injection of significant political and strategic content in India's relations with the United States and Japan."[4]

Nonweaponized Deterrence

Unlike both the NPT-centred policy and the managing proliferation school, a realistic near-term policy seeking to construct a nonweaponized deterrence regime can bridge the valid interests of India and Pakistan and the international strategic community. The foundation of a non-weaponised deterrence regime would be a declared policy by both India and Pakistan not to assemble and deploy nuclear weapons. Once this clear declaration of intent is registered, both countries could undertake detailed, largely verifiable steps to demonstrate that they are abiding by this declared policy and not assembling or deploying nuclear weapons. Attendant bilateral, regional and global arms control and confidence-building measures would heighten confidence that an underground arms race is not continuing, while the process of implementing this regime would buttress regional and global security relations. Deterrence would not be sacrificed: the capability would remain to quickly construct and deploy by air nuclear weapons in the event that either state was unambiguously threatened by strategic aggression from the other or from third parties.

A non-weaponized deterrence policy draws on the advantages of the current ambiguity in Indian and Pakistani capabilities. It recognizes the domestic and international liabilities of weaponization and missile deployment, and the opposite political and strategic liabilities of completely abandoning nuclear capabilities. At the same time, it seeks to build confidence that could ultimately lead both countries to decide it is in their interest to move down the nuclear ladder as regional and global conditions warrant. This policy may require, for the sake of mutual reassurance, both countries to reduce the ambiguity of their status by soon taking some steps down from where they now stand. Yet these steps can be taken discreetly without requiring either country to risk the public upheaval of repudiating declared policy or relinquishing national sovereignty.

By advocating a policy of non-weaponised deterrence—as opposed to immediate accession to the NPT—and by pointedly offering with other nuclear weapons states positive and negative security assurances, the United States could demonstrate respect for both countries' legitimate security interests as well as their demands for equity.   U.S. acknowledgment of India's and Pakistan's security concerns and technical achievements would greatly improve the tone and substance of nuclear diplomacy with both countries. In return, the international community would benefit from India's and Pakistan's actionable declaration that they need not construct or deploy nuclear weapons to achieve deterrence or prove their prowess. India and Pakistan would signify awareness that their security would actually be threatened by construction and deployment of nuclear weapons.

The long-term objective of India and Pakistan and the international community should be to improve their security environment to the point where these countries can sign binding, universal non-proliferation commitments. (India is pivotal here; if it can be reassured regarding China, its steps toward denuclearization will in all likelihood be followed by Pakistan.) But unlike the NPT-centred policy, the nonweaponized deterrence approach does not sacrifice attainable progress for remote perfection.

Operationally How Nonweaponized Deterrence Could Work

Inspired technical and diplomatic feats must be performed to structure and verify a non-weaponised deterrence relationship between India and Pakistan and to solidify the Indo-Chinese security relationship. Yet this task is much easier than would exist if India and Pakistan signed the NPT or an analogous regional agreement to abandon completely their nuclear weapons capabilities. Leonard Spector, in the Fall 1992 issue of *Foreign Policy,* succinctly described the extraordinarily detailed and intrusive measures which would have to be taken into account for all the research and development facilities, the non-nuclear components and the fissile materials produced or acquired in the denuclearizing state. Ultimately, some uncertainty would still remain even if these measures were agreed upon and implemented.

This is not an argument against the NPT, but rather an argument that puts the feasibility of nonweaponized deterrence in perspective. A strong nonweaponized deterrence regime does not have to be as "perfect" an arrangement whereby the parties are to relinquish all nuclear weapons resources, as in the NPT. Under non-weaponised deterrence, some capacity to construct a nuclear weapon upon strategic warning is assumed. None of the parties is left vulnerable, completely denuded of its nuclear protection. This in itself should deter cheating in a strategic environment in which the parties have engendered enough mutual confidence to engage in building this regime in the first place. (The counter argument is that the ready potential to weaponize makes such a relationship perpetually unstable. Yet, if underlying relations are so uncooperative that cheating is a high probability, the two countries would not be likely to reach the agreements necessary to formalize the non--weaponization regime in the first place).

In general terms, a non-weaponized deterrence regime would have three components. Starting with the easiest and most immediate step, both sides must agree on measures to verify the agreed non-deployment of nuclear weapons. This focusses on delivery systems—particularly ballistic missiles and modified aircraft. Affirming nondeployment is intrinsically valuable, and it is also vital because it is technically achievable, whereas verifying the actual non-possession of assembled nuclear bombs or warheads is extremely difficult. The size of missiles and their production and test facilities and the observability of modifications on aircraft allow high confidence that non-deployment could be verified with a modicum of on-site inspection. The U.S. and others, particularly Russia and Japan, could usefully offer to assist with monitoring and verification requirements.

Second, India and Pakistan must define what level of nuclear weapons preparation is permissible and then verify as well as possible that both sides do not cross that line(s). For the foreseeable future, it is assumed that both countries will retain weapons grade fissile materials and non-nuclear components, along with research and development facilities. Ideally, both countries would not maintain finished nuclear weapon cores; currently, each is believed to possess a small number of these components. In any case, the relevant components are small enough that neither country could have high confidence that the other had dismantled and no longer possessed their cores (this would also be true if both signed the NPT in its current form). The best that can be achieved are binding agreements not to maintain finished cores and acceptance of intrusive verification measures which would put a "cheater" at some risk of being detected. In the near-term, the most feasible approach would be to build on the openness already achieved in the 1988 agreement by India and Pakistan not to attack each other's nuclear facilities. This agreement requires the two countries to exchange lists detailing the location of their "nuclear facilities and installations" and updating the information each year or when a new facility is built. The data exchange began in 1991. A next step would be to begin detailing what activities occur in these facilities. Eventually,mutual inspections could be negotiated.

The third and broadest objective of a nonweaponized deterrence regime is to buttress crisis stability and escalation control. This can most readily be done by injecting buffers of time into the entire process from weaponization to possible use of nuclear weapons. Many momentous activities occur along this band of activity: a precipitating crisis; decision to weaponize; assembly of a weapon; deployment; target selection; launch decision; execution of launch and actual detonation over target; retaliation decision, etc. Regional and global security can be enhanced by adding time between each of these and other relevant stages of the process. The more demanding the nonweaponization regime and its verification measures, the greater the time India and Pakistan and the international community would have to process information, clarify facts and intentions, mediate and resolve a confrontation short of nuclear warfare.

Importantly, the required arms control and confidence-building measures can be accomplished without either side having to surrender completely the current ambiguity of their nuclear policies. The declaration of commitments not to weaponize and the corresponding steps described above which reduce ambiguity of intentions—and below, could be undertaken today with as much verification as politics allows. If this entails some disassembly of weapons components, such steps are no more difficult to agree to and verify under a non-weaponized deterrence regime than they would be if both countries openly declared that they had "gone nuclear." Indeed, politically the task would be simpler because neither side would be "giving up" something which it had proclaimed to its citizens and the world that it possessed. In short, there is no basis for the contention that arms control and confidence-building measures are "impossible" without prior declarations that weaponisation has occurred.

Two other measures would greatly buttress confidence in the non-weaponisation regime. They could be pursued immediately, in tandem with early discussions of formalizing a non-weaponization regime. First, both India and Pakistan could bind themselves to long-standing statements that neither will conduct an explosive test of a nuclear device. Such an agreement, however, will probably require first some significant progress in comprehensive test ban negotiations by the five established nuclear powers. This seems likely. India and Pakistan are unequivocally committed to joining and adhering to a comprehensive test ban. The stakes are high: a nuclear weapons test by either Pakistan or India would prompt the other to respond with some escalation of its own nuclear weapons program, initiating a major crisis.

Second, India and Pakistan could agree unilaterally, bilaterally or as part of a global regime to cease production and acquisition of weapons-grade fissile materials highly enriched uranium and plutonium. Such a cut off would cap the weapons potential of both countries and add confidence in each other's intentions not to weaponise. It would also give political leaders additional leverage over the nuclear bureaucracies.

Pakistan has already frozen uranium enrichment and declared its willingness to agree formally to cease future fissile material production if India will follow suit. For its part, India wants at least the three established "Asian" nuclear powers to stop first: the U.S., Russia and particularly China. This may happen. The Clinton Administration's anticipated proposal for a verifiable global convention to cease production of fissile materials for weapons purposes should be achievable given the end of the Cold War. The U.S. has already ceased production, and Russia has consistently said it would stop by the year 2000. China reportedly has enough separated plutonium on hand to fulfill its weapons requirements. The absence of valid military requirements for fissile materials, paired with the economic, environmental and security pressures against using plutonium for civil purposes, vastly improve the chances that regional and global bans or severe limitations on the production and use of weapons-usable materials can be achieved.

Even without China or a global ban, the recalcitrant Indian position could be opened by a package deal whereby India stops producing and separating weapons-usable materials and accepts International Atomic Energy Agency (IAEA) safeguards on the facilities required to verify it. Allowance could be made for a small plutonium breeder research and development facility which would be safeguarded. In return, India would receive Western cooperation in supplying and modernizing its troubled civilian nuclear complex. For instance, India's Tarapur reactor, which the U.S., and more recently France, stopped supplying due to the Indian refusal to accept safeguards, will run out of fuel shortly. The U.S. could consider supplying this fuel in return for a verified cut-off in uranium enrichment and plutonium separation, although this would require waiving or amending the Nuclear NonProliferation Act of 1978 which bars U.S. exports of nuclear fuel to countries not accepting IAEA safeguards on all their facilities. The U.S., along with Russia,and more ambitiously, China, would be subject to the same verification requirements as India and Pakistan. Such a package does not require India to cave in to long-rejected demands to sign the NPT or to accept blanket international safeguards on its entire nuclear complex. Only facilities relevant to uranium enrichment and plutonium reprocessing would be safeguarded.

The reciprocal verification with the nuclear weapons states would give India the equity it has passionately sought. On the energy side, Indian officials would gain new economic and technical assistance.

Additionally, as part of the non-weaponised deterrence regime, India and Pakistan could mutually pledge not to be the first to use nuclear weapons and not to transfer nuclear weapons-relevant materials to other countries or actors. Representatives of both countries' nuclear program could be invited to participate in meetings of the Nuclear Suppliers Group and other nuclear export control fora. This would augment an important overall effort to increase transparency in both programs, and greater civilian authority in the case of Pakistan.

In sum, the international security field has developed a broad range of feasible arms control and confidence-building measures which could be used to construct a strong non-weaponised deterrence regime in South Asia. If the proper incentives can be created, building such a regime can spare India, Pakistan and the international community the expense and danger of a nuclear arms race on the subcontinent.

Missiles As Key:
A Critique of U.S. Policy

A missile race on the subcontinent would arguably constitute the greatest threat to stability there and the strongest drive to nuclear weaponisation. Either country's deployment of a tried and true ballistic missile system could threaten the other's nuclear capability—weaponized or non-weaponized—in a bolt-from-the-blue scenario. The compression of time would weaken the targeted country's confidence that it could maintain a non-weaponised deterrent capability. Both countries would then be pressured to engage in the kind of hair-triggered, first-strike competition that unsettled and exhausted the United States and the Soviet Union from the 1950s on.

Hence, achieving over time a regional or global ban on ballistic missiles is imperative. To expedite this process, India should be joined by the U.S., Japan, and Russia in encouraging China to relocate missiles which may be located in southwest China. While Indian and Pakistani interests to forego missile deployments are strong, without a change in China's posture, such a change would heighten India's incentive—and,therefore, Pakistan's—not to deploy missiles capable of delivering nuclear weapons. The mid-term objective could be a South Asian ballistic missile-free zone, covering the subcontinent and southwest China. China should also be pressed to reiterate its no-first-use pledge and to undertake confidence-building measures to assure India that this pledge is serious.

Politically, however, it may first be necessary to sort out basic principles and interests. The United States, India and Pakistan need to determine whether and how the ambiguities between missile and civilian space launch capabilities can be sorted out, and whether and how the United States and other technology leaders could construct a bargain with countries like India which would in effect trade ballistic missile programs for economic and technical assistance in gaining access to space. This requires grater clarity of purpose and interest within each country.

For its part, the United States must recognize the problems posed by its non-proliferation approach. The cryogenic rocket dispute involving India and Russia stands as the most controversial case. In simple terms, the United States and other countries must become more creative and forthright in facilitating India's and other nations' access to space-launch vehicles share so many technical features that the challenge is enormous. Yet, to date, the United States has developed and applied a tough, restrictive policy to prevent missile program development without a complementary policy on space access. This one-sided approach derives in part from the way the U.S. government is organized: one set of individuals and bureaucracies is in charge of non-proliferation, while another set is in charge of civilian space policies. These elements of the U.S. bureaucracies follow divergent imperatives and do not integrate their approaches well. Moreover, governmental and industrial interests defending U.S. space-launch enterprises jealously protect their "markets." Hence, positive space-access incentives which could be provided to compensate for negative non-proliferation policies tend not to be forthcoming.

A no-incentives, tough-control policy is bureaucratically simple and politically appealing. And it will yield important delays in other countries' acquisition of ballistic missiles. Yet, over the medium and long tem it seems that a supply-side, technology-denial strategy is inadequate. Nor can this weakness be fully redressed by counter-proliferation activities to preempt or weaken other states' capabilities. A comprehensive strategy requires efforts to eliminate the demands that states like India and Pakistan have for ballistic missiles. Providing important benefits in return for forgoing ballistic missiles may be a way to enter the political process of reducing demand.

For its part, India could find that non-weaponised deterrence offers a strategic concept which satisfies political and military interests in retaining the nuclear option, but does not require constructing or deploying ballistic missiles. Were India and Pakistan to adhere to a nonweaponized deterrent strategy and undertake verifiable measures to heighten each other's confidence in non-weaponisation, they would be more disposed to relinquish ballistic missile capability in return for economically beneficial assistance in developing and deploying civil space technology. The United States and others could be encouraged by the regional actors' adherence to non-weaponised deterrence, and attendant verification, to be more forthcoming with such assistance.

As a starting point, the parties need to sit down and earnestly discuss whether under any conditions a trade-off could be made between missile programs and cooperation in gaining access to space, including cooperative work on sophisticated satellites. If India, for example, would under no condition halt its plans to produce and deploy ballistic missiles, then the United States and others would stand firm on their export controls. Conversely, if in principle India (and Pakistan) would be willing to forgo testing, production and deployment of ballistic missiles, then a dialogue over conditions is possible. Those in the United States who seek to enhance high-technology trade and cooperation with India would be given a much improved chance of prevailing in American political and economic struggles over this issue. In such a dialogue with India, the United States and the international community must be better prepared to offer meaningful cooperation. In the near term, the priority should be to determine whether any agreement on the broader principles is possible.

Responding To A Few Possible Critiques

Naturally, advocating something like non-weaponised deterrence for India and Pakistan risks legitimizing other actors' quests for nuclear know-how and materials. "If India and Pakistan can openly have weapons materials and facilities, why can't we?" Also, nonweaponized deterrence acknowledges—temporarily—a third tier in the non-proliferation regime, which may be seen as discriminating against the noble non-nuclear adherents to the NPT.

Several responses to this argument seem fitting. First, although nonweaponized deterrence falls short of complete denuclearization, it still yields a better result for non-nuclear states than the current situation of unchecked nuclear programs in India and Pakistan. It does not preclude eventual accession to the NPT when additional global progress on security and disarmament is attained. By drawing India and Pakistan (and perhaps some day Israel) into the non-proliferation regime through nonweaponized deterrence, the international community is enhancing non-proliferation, not legitimizing proliferation. The principle of both the global non-proliferation regime and of nonweaponized deterrence is to create conditions whereby states find it not in their interests to acquire, deploy or use nuclear weapons.

Second, the rest of the world has signed the NPT, or in the case of Argentina and Brazil, the functional equivalent. These countries have found it in their interests not to seek nuclear weapons capability. India's, Pakistan's or, more speculatively, Israel's settling on a nonweaponized deterrence regime unequivocally does not worsen the security interests of NPT signatories. This offers no legitimate pretext for them to hedge or renege on that treaty's obligations. in any case, the most severe measures are warranted to maintain adherence to the NPT by its signatories and those such as Belarus, Kazakhstan and Ukraine which have committed to sign.

Third, regarding the risk of legitimizing other countries' quests for nuclear capability, it is important to note the truly special security predicaments of India, Pakistan and Israel. Each of these countries faces militarily superior adversaries with weapons of mass destruction on their borders. Each has found itself unable to sign the NPT from the beginning. In the absence of robust security guarantees from the international community, which each of these countries has sought without satisfaction, their quest for the nuclear option has made sense. Yet, so has their decision not to exercise this option.

Universalizing Nonweaponized
Deterrence to Square
The Nonproliferation Circle

India and Pakistan have much to gain and little to lose by forgoing the assembly and deployment of nuclear weapons. Nonweaponized deterrence is in their interest even if the established nuclear weapons states achieve little further progress in disarmament. Yet, the prospects for the global non-proliferation regime would improve greatly if the established nuclear powers were to offer a vision in which they, too, move toward nonweaponized deterrence.

Nonweaponized deterrence for the established nuclear powers seems far-fetched at first glance. Indeed, when Jonathan Schell proposed the basic notion in the midst of the mid-1980s' Cold War, the strategic community ignored it, calloused by the unchanging rivalry with Soviet-led Communism and the unending march of nuclear technology. Schell arrived at "weaponless deterrence" deductively, from the premise that nuclear weapons must be abolished if humanity is to survive, but nuclear know-how, many believe, cannot be "uninvented." His arguments, focussed primarily on the super powers, were brilliantly marshalled, but the circumstances of the world deflected them. Today, however, nonweaponized deterrence emerges through induction. Listening and reading how Indian and Pakistani elites understand nuclear capability and deterrence in the context of South Asia, it becomes evident that they can derive more benefit from their nuclear know-how by not assembling and deploying weapons than if they openly cross the threshold to nuclear weapons status. Moreover, the logic of nonweaponized deterrence can be seen now in the nuclear arms reduction and control measures ratified and proposed by the United States and Russia in the last several years.

The 1987 INF Treaty eliminated a whole class of nuclear weapons. The START I Treaty and the tentative START II agreement achieve significant disarmament, especially in types of weapons—vulnerable, multiple-warhead missiles—which quicken the time between crises and decisions to launch nuclear attacks and counter-attacks. In January 1992, President Bush decided to take American strategic bombers off alert. The next month, Russian Foreign Minister Kozyrev proposed to take all nuclear weapons off alert, possibly removing the warheads from the missiles that carry them. Influential arms controllers in Washington are reviving President Reagan's 1986 Reykjavik proposal to eliminate all ballistic missiles, as proposed by Alton Frye in *Foreign Policy*. The Russian, French and American nuclear test moratoria, which point toward an eventual comprehensive test ban, would cap the qualitative arms race, and over decades hint at a gradual withering of nuclear weapons establishments. The much-discussed fissile-material production cut-off would similarly cap established nuclear weapons programs and, over time, signify the diminished value of nuclear arsenals.

Other recent shifts in strategic thought reinforce the feasibility of nonweaponized deterrence. Limited ballistic missile defenses, as well as theater air defenses such as Patriot follow-ons, could provide political confidence that the risks of a break out from a nonweaponized deterrence regime can be minimized. Additionally, a growing number of security analysts have begun to explore the technical and strategic feasibility of a small, invulnerably deployed and internationally-controlled nuclear force which would exist solely for the purpose of retaliating against nuclear attacks on non-nuclear states. While American strategists have led these early explorations, several Indian commentators have publicly endorsed them in India. Such a force could bolster the confidence of states such as India and Pakistan as well as faithful adherents to the NPT.

Each of these enacted and prospective measures contribute to the dismantlement of the hair-triggered doomsday machine built for the peculiar global stand-off of the Cold War. They point toward a situation where what is left are blueprints and disassembled pieces of nuclear weaponry which could be reconstituted if needed. In an age where proliferation becomes a dominant security concern, global strategies are required. Nonweaponized deterrence must be considered a serious part of this strategic mix, and South Asia is a place to begin.

Notes

1. FBIS, NES, 93-153, August 11, 1993, transcript of August 8, 1993, broadcast. On the broader point, Indian interlocutors—doves and hawks alike—have agreed vigorously when this absence of strategic thinking is pointed out. "This is exactly the problem," one Indian analyst said recently, "our government, our leaders do not think strategically. There is no strategy!" Outside observers such as the RAND Corporation's George Tanham have also written on the absence of strategic thinking in India. "Indian strategic culture," *The Washington Quarterly*, Winter 1992, pp. 129-142.

2. K. Sundarji., "Regional arms reduction and limitation in the post-Cold War era: South Asia," paper presented at the U.S. Defense Nuclear Agency Conference, June 10, 1993.

3. While most Indian elites, including in key articles K. Subrahmanyam, wisely avoid the slippery slope of the nuclear targeting doctrine, India would fare badly by deploying missiles capable of reaching major Chinese cities or military forces only makes sense if India is prepared to plan for first use of these weapons. This follows the common assumption that China enjoys marginal conventional superiority and, in warfare, could present India with defeat without having to use its own nuclear weapons. Faced with defeat, Indian leaders would presumably contemplate first-use of nuclear weapons, near the battlefield, either for tactical reasons or because of range limitations on delivery vehicles. General Sundarji emphatically dismisses the notion of Indian first-use in "the tactical sphere" by saying that India's battle field use of nuclear weapons "would be credible only after China has made first use." This needs more explanation. Why is only a second-strike battlefield attack credible? I assume that General Sundarji in his military analysis does not reject first-use primarily on moral grounds, but rather from concern that first-use would lead to escalation up the nuclear ladder. Yet, the risks of escalation are enormous even for the side that "goes second." The very fallacies of escalation control in nuclear warfighting, which General Sundarji and others rightly identify, would obtain for a party that contemplates retaliation at the tactical level. If India deploys nuclear weapons capable of hitting Chinese targets and India faces defeat at the hands of Chinese conventional forces, the second use of nuclear weapons would be too late. The choice will be whether to seek to escape defeat by unleashing nuclear weapons first, bearing the huge risk of escalation. On the other hand, if China is not conventional aggression. In this case, an Indian missile arsenal could make sense as a second strike deterrent (but an air-delivery capability would also suffice in the region of actual conflict). Yet there is no conceivable scenario wherein China would find a national interest in such a risky nuclear-backed aggression which world result in global economic, political and perhaps military recriminations of historic proportions. Nothing in Sino-Indian relations or in the global balance of power makes this seem plausible.

4. C. Raja Mohan, "Real threat perceptions in Asia: An Indian perspective," unpublished manuscript, 1993.

Dealing With North Korea:
Speak Softly and Carry a Bigger Stick

Leonard S. Spector

THE PROSPECT OF HIGH-LEVEL U.S.-NORTH KOREAN nuclear talks has raised hopes that Pyongyang and Washington may soon resolve the confrontation over the North Korean nuclear program. Agreement on the new talks followed President Jimmy Carter's June 1994 meeting with North Korean leader Kim Il Sung.

As a basis for the new talks, Pyongyang agreed to "freeze" its nuclear program. Specifically, it pledged that it would not refuel the key, 5-megawatt reactor at its Yongbyon nuclear complex, would not "reprocess" fuel it had recently removed from that reactor to separate the fuel's weapons-usable plutonium, and would not prevent International Atomic Energy Agency (IAEA) inspectors from continuing their monitoring all of the country's declared nuclear facilities and materials to make sure that none were used for nuclear arms.

No one can argue against proceeding with the talks, which may, indeed, lead to an end of the North Korean nuclear crisis. But while hoping for the best, it is essential that the Clinton Administration simultaneously plan for the worst. All too often North Korea's past promises of cooperation have proven ephemeral, and all too often it has used the time gained by bogus bargaining tactics to enhance its nuclear capabilities. This time, the stakes are higher than ever before. If Pyongyang again reverts to its "talk and fight" strategy, its next nuclear advance could make it a de facto nuclear power.

Leonard S. Spector is a Senior Associate at the Carnegie Endowment for International Peace and Director of the Endowment's Nuclear Non-Proliferation Project.

North Korea's most glaring failure to make good on its pledges of cooperation has been its unwillingness to implement the Declaration on the Denuclearization of the Korean Peninsula, which it signed with South Korea in December 1991. Under the pact, the North agreed to mutual nuclear inspections with South Korea to augment those by the IAEA. It also agreed that it would not possess uranium enrichment or plutonium reprocessing plants—the key technologies for producing material for nuclear weapons. Not only has the North failed to implement the bilateral nuclear inspections with the South, but far from dismantling the reprocessing plant at the Yongbyon complex, it has actually worked to increase its capacity at least two-fold.

Similarly after agreeing to inspections by the IAEA, which began in May 1992—and after pledging that the agency could visit any location in North Korea whether or not declared as a nuclear site—Pyongyang has prevented the agency from undertaking "special inspections" at two undeclared nuclear waste sites. The agency has demanded access to the facilities in order to resolve discrepancies in the North's initial declarations regarding its past production of plutonium.[1]

Most recently, after repeated warnings by Washington and the IAEA, North Korea deliberately destroyed key evidence about its past plutonium production by refueling the 5-megawatt reactor at Yongbyon without permitting the IAEA to segregate selected fuel rods for future examination. Indeed, the North secretly built a new, high-speed refueling machine apparently so that it could accelerate the unloading process and present with world with a *fait accompli*. As part of the stratagem, North Korean nuclear aides had previously told their IAEA counterparts that the refueling would take two months or more; as a result, when the procedure began, the agency incorrectly assumed it had ample time to resolve the controversy before key evidence would be destroyed.

In response to refueling, the agency's Board of Governors on June 10 terminated all technical assistance to North Korea and referred the matter to the UN Security Council, where the Clinton Administration sought, with some difficulty, to build a consensus for sanctions against the North. The first phase of these sanctions, intended to punish Pyongyang for destroying evidence about its nuclear past, would have been relatively mild, and would have included the termination of all UN development assistance to Pyongyang and a ban on arms transfers to and from North Korea.[2] Washington suspended the sanctions effort once it reached agreement with Pyongyang on the new round of talks.[3]

In his meeting with Jimmy Carter, Kim Il Sung declared that the entire nuclear dispute could be resolved through a high-level U.S.-North Korean dialogue. This statement and the North's willingness to freeze aspects of its nuclear program and permit continued IAEA inspection as the talks proceed appear to be promising developments.

There is, however, reason to question the North Korean leader's sincerity in seeking a resolution of the conflict through wide-ranging negotiations, since as recently as mid-May Pyongyang deliberately thwarted an opportunity to begin the very talks Kim told Carter he was seeking. At that time, Washington and Seoul had removed all preconditions for "broad and thorough" discussions on the nuclear issue. Rather than begin the talks, however, the North sabotaged them with its accelerated defueling of the Yongbyon reactor.

Moreover, with its deliberate—and apparently premeditated—destruction of evidence about its nuclear past, Pyongyang's challenge to restraints on its nuclear program has become so brazen that even more serious challenges must be anticipated.

Thus, the failure to resolve North Korea's nuclear history in the face of its wilful destruction of key evidence could be a precedent that undercuts the agency's authority in a number of other important cases.

Thus, while the Clinton Administration pursues the new round of talks, it must simultaneously take steps to prepare for the next crisis.

What form will the crisis take? Predictions are dangerous, but one scenario stands out as most likely: in September or October 1994, during the U.S. Congressional elections, the North will declare that it intends to begin separating the plutonium from the recently discharged spent fuel, *with inspectors present,* arguing that the magnesium-oxide sheathed fuel would otherwise deteriorate.

This action, although it would breach an understanding with the United States, would not violate any IAEA rules or the Nuclear Non-Proliferation Treaty (NPT). Within several months, however, it would provide the North with enough plutonium for four or five nuclear weapons. The material would be under IAEA monitoring for the moment, but at any time the North could complete its now suspended withdrawal from the NPT or find some other pretext for ousting the IAEA inspectors—and within weeks, or even less, have a small nuclear arsenal.

Moreover, even with inspectors present, it could legally export some of the material to Iran or Libya—under IAEA monitoring—and give these countries similar de facto nuclear weapon capabilities. And if inspections cease, clandestine transfers would be impossible to monitor.

How can Washington avert such a scenario? Diplomatic threats are not likely to influence the North. Washington was having difficulty mustering international support for weak sanctions against Pyongyang following its outright violation of IAEA rules; obtaining support for more severe sanctions to punish the North for actions that are entirely legal would be even more difficult. The task would be all the more difficult, since the North would be arguing that processing the fuel was essential to avoid an unmanageable radioactive waste situation caused by the disintegration of its corroding spent fuel.[4] It would also undoubtedly point to the fact that Japan is currently engaging in IAEA-monitored plutonium extraction without U.S. objection.

Moreover, even if a consensus for harsh sanctions could be obtained, by the time such sanctions might ultimately take effect, Pyongyang would have its plutonium in hand.

Two other scenarios would be almost equally disturbing. Before reprocessing the spent fuel, the North could make good on the threat it made prior to Jimmy Carter's visit to oust the IAEA in retaliation for the sanctions that body imposed. This would leave the North free to extract the plutonium from the spent fuel at its leisure—with the disturbing consequences outlined above. Or, in violation of IAEA monitoring rules, it could remove and hide away the recently discharged spent fuel rods, leaving the world to wonder whether they might be reprocessed in a still-clandestine facility.[5]

These latter scenarios would require the North to transgress its IAEA monitoring agreement, but even if the international community were to react vigorously, the North still could have its plutonium by the time any sanctions might start to take effect.

In the end, unless the pending talks are successful, the only way for the United States to dissuade the North from taking such steps is through the threat of military action, in particular through the threat to destroy the Yongbyon reprocessing plant.

No final decision need be made by the United States beforehand as to whether to go through with such an obviously dangerous action. But to deter the North from further adventurism, preparations to carry out such an attack are needed, together with a privately communicated warning to North Korea that any reprocessing—with or without IAEA inspections—or any attempt to remove the spent fuel would be taken as a threat to vital U.S. interests and would be met with a very harsh, but unspecified response.

To make a credible threat, however, it is not only necessary for the United States to have the basic resources on hand to bomb the installation; it must also have enough military force in the region to deter the North from starting a war in the aftermath of the bombing or from taking other highly destructive retaliatory actions.

As it turns out, the Clinton Administration is already augmenting U.S. military capabilities in the area, along with those of South Korea, in order to counter the North's declaration that it would consider the imposition of sanctions to be an act of war. The U.S. sanctions effort is suspended for the moment, but the Administration can still take advantage of its military build-up to buttress a warning to North Korea not to move any further towards producing separated plutonium. Obviously, Washington must take care to avoid turning the military expansion into a provocation that the North could use to scuttle the new round of talks. So far, the Clinton team has done much to bolster U.S. and South Korean capabilities without crossing this line, and it should be able to extend this effort further.

Even if Washington and Seoul were convinced that war could be avoided, an actual military strike against the Yongbyon reprocessing plant would have many drawbacks. It would surely intensify North Korean interest in nuclear arms and, at best, would only delay, not eliminate, Pyongyang's bid to acquire them. And, if the North had removed the spent fuel, it would still have the wherewithal for a mini-nuclear arsenal, if it already possessed or could later build a secret plutonium separation plant to process the material.

There is also some risk that bombing the facility would result in the release of radiation. The spent fuel's overall radioactivity will decline significantly in coming weeks, however, reducing this danger. Moreover, in the 1991 Gulf War, U.S. pilots used techniques that minimized radioactive contamination when they destroyed two operating reactors at Tuwaitha, techniques that presumably could be used against Yongbyon.

Thus, on balance, if the North takes steps to reprocess the spent fuel, with or without IAEA monitoring, or if it attempts to remove the material, the Clinton Administration might ultimately decide that military action against Yongbyon was unwise and choose instead to accept a nuclear-capable North Korea, relying on traditional deterrence to contain this new threat. What is important now, however, is that Washington attempt to deter the North from making such further nuclear advances in the first place, by demonstrating that the United States and its allies are in a position to carry out a military strike and by creating the perception in Pyongyang that they might, indeed, take such action.[6]

Kim Il Sung suggested to Jimmy Carter that the nuclear confrontation with Washington has been exacerbated in part by unauthorized actions by more junior North Korean officials. Perhaps Kim is sincere about ending the nuclear impasse and perhaps a new spirit of cooperation will emerge now that he is personally taking charge. Some U.S. officials also believe that the prospect of a vote on sanctions at the Security Council was so unpalatable to China—which would have had to choose between acquiescing in the punishment of an another Communist state and exercising its first veto in many years—that in late May Beijing pressured Kim into adopting a more conciliatory stance.

Two years of increasingly audacious North Korean challenges to restraints on its nuclear program, however, provide strong grounds for skepticism that a major shift in the country's posture is at hand. Washington has tolerated a number of Pyongyang's nuclear trespasses, hoping to correct them at a later stage in the negotiating process. The next trespass, however, could net Pyongyang a de facto nuclear arsenal. While time still remains, Washington needs to implement a credible strategy to deter the North from taking this fateful step.

Notes

1. The agency's late-1991 decision to begin using its longdormant special inspection authority was well publicized in the months before North Korea ratified its inspection agreement with the IAEA in April 1992. Thus there can be no question that the North was aware that the agency would be prepared to employ this tool as necessary, when it began inspections in North Korea the following month. The IAEA decision to revitalize its special inspection authority, it may be noted, was taken after it became clear that the agency's traditional inspections limited to declared nuclear sites had completely failed to detect Iraq's clandestine nuclear weapons program.

2. A second and, possibly, third phase of increasingly harsh measures to be adopted in the event of further North Korean provocations were also part of the U.S. sanctions proposal.

3. The Clinton Administration may have had little choice but to defer its bid to punish North Korea for its bald violation of IAEA rules, but it is important that Washington ultimately seek to vindicate the agency. The ability to probe the

past to verify the initial nuclear inventory that a state presents as the basis for future inspections is crucial to the effectiveness of the IAEA system. The IAEA's right to scrutinize the past has been critically important, for example, in the case of South Africa, a country that acknowledged building nuclear arms—as the IAEA has attempted to ensure that Pretoria has indeed placed all of its weapons-grade nuclear materials under agency inspection. Moreover, in coming months, the agency will also be seeking to establish comprehensive inspections in other countries with complex nuclear histories, including, Argentina, Belarus, Brazil, Kazakhstan, and—if it joins the Nuclear Non-Proliferation Treaty (NPT) as it has promised—Ukraine.

4. Although the North Koreans have told one U.S. specialist that they must begin reprocessing by late-summer 1994 because the fuel will otherwise deteriorate, a number of technical fixes could alleviate this situation. One would be to adjust the chemistry of the water in the cooling pond housing the spent fuel, an approach used by Great Britain. Another option would be to store the fuel dry, in specially shielded casks that are available commercially in the West.

5. See, Philip Zelikow, "Can Talks with North Korea Succeed?" *New York Times*, June 24, 1994.

6. This approach is akin to the decades-long U.S. effort to deter Soviet aggression by the threat of initiating nuclear war, a step that could have had the most devastating consequences not only for the Soviet Union but also for the United States. While many doubted that an American president would have "pushed the button" had Soviet forces began to advance through West Germany, the credible *threat* to use nuclear arms is believed to have contributed significantly to checking Soviet adventurism in Europe.

The United States and WMD: Missile Proliferation in the Middle East

Zalmay Khalilzad

American Interests

As a general policy, the U.S. opposes the proliferation of Weapons of Mass Destruction (WMD) and ballistic and cruise missiles. The spread of such capabilities to some states or regions is particularly consequential to its effect on other U.S. interests. In the Middle East, the acquisition of WMD and missiles by hostile states is particularly threatening to the U.S. interests. The reason for the special importance of proliferation in this region is the growth in the relative importance of the Middle East in post-Cold War U.S. national security strategy. With the end of the Cold War, some regions have become less important and the United States can be more selective with respect to involvement in them. However, the opposite is the case with regard to the Middle East.

Major Regional Contingency, Middle East. First and foremost, the West's dependence on Persian Gulf oil is increasing and is likely to continue to increase throughout the decade. This is an interest that we share with many other states especially our more wealthy allies in Europe and East Asia. As demonstrated in the Gulf, the U.S. opposed the domination of this region by a hostile power and is willing to go to war to prevent hostile regional hegemony. Long-standing U.S. ties to Israeli and some of the Gulf Cooperation Council (GCC) states also contribute to the region's critical importance.

Dr. Zalmay Khalilzad is the Program Director for Strategy, Doctrine, and Force Structure of RAND's Project AIR FORCE, and Director of the Greater Middle East Studies Center. Prior to his present position, he was Assistant Deputy Under Secretary of Defense for Policy Planning from January 1991 and December 1992. He holds a Ph.D. from the University of Chicago.

In addition to these political and economic factors, the Middle East is important because developments there can directly affect the military security of Western Europe. With long range missiles and WMD, hostile states in the Middle East will be able to threaten Western Europe.

Thus, the region has become a central focus of the post-Cold War american national defense planning. With the end of the global threat, the U.S. has a regional defense strategy that incorporates an understanding of U.S. vital national security interests in the Middle East.[1]

The U.S. forces are being sized to deal nearly-simultaneously with two major regional conflicts (MRC). From a Central European front we have moved towards two probable regional fronts: the Middle East and the Korean Peninsula.

In the aftermath of the Cold War and the Gulf War, the United States is the preeminent outside power in the Middle East. The U.S. has more forces and prepositioned equipment in the Middle East than it did prior to the Iraqi invasion of Kuwait. America has also entered cooperative security agreements with several GCC states over the last three years. American forces are the backbone of the coalition which enforces the security zone in northern Iraq, the no-fly zone in southern Iraq and the embargo regime against Baghdad. Our forces participates in monitoring the Egyptian-Israeli agreement in Sinai and in monitoring Libyan compliance with UN resolutions. A peace agreement between Syria and Israel is likely to further increase America's role in this region.

Given that most of the reasons for which the U.S. is concerned with the region apply equally or with even greater force to its allies and friends in Europe and East Asia, it is reasonable for the U.S. to expect that they will share the burden of dealing with the security challenges of this region.

The Proliferation Problem

United States interests in the region make the proliferation of WMD and missiles to the Middle East particularly important. What is the status of proliferation in this region? What are the prospects for reduction in existing capability? What about further spread? What would be a prudent approach for dealing with the problem by the United States?

WMD and Missile Capabilities in the Middle East

The level of capability varies a great deal across the region.

Iraq. The Gulf war and the defeat of Iraq had a major impact on the Iraqi WMD and long-range missile programs. Iraq had established an immense capability for producing WMD and long range missiles. According to some estimates, Iraq had invested more than ten billion dollars in its the nuclear program alone.[2]

In addition to a declared civilian program subject to IAEA safeguards and inspections, Iraq, starting in 1981, proceeded on a second covert path for producing nuclear weapons-grade material. It sought a number of different methods for enriching uranium: calutron, chemical enrichment and centrifuge enrichment. Further, Iraq employed some 20,000 people in its nuclear program. At the time of its invasion of Kuwait, Baghdad was less than one year from producing one or two nuclear devices with more to follow in several years. Prior to and during the Gulf war, U.S. information on Iraq's nuclear capability was very limited. Iraq had carried out a massive deception operation to protect its program. However, Iraq's defeat produced the circumstances which allowed the UN Special Commission on Iraq (UNSCOM), relying on various sources, to uncover significant details about the program and to destroy some key elements.

At the time of its invasion of Kuwait, Iraq had a massive chemical weapons capability and had used chemical weapons against Iran and its own Kurdish population. UNSCOM inspectors report that they had, by October 1991, found 100,000 chemical bombs and shells. Iraq also possessed biological weapons, in violation of the 1972 Biological and Toxin Weapons Convention. Baghdad had concentrated on the botulinum toxin and anthrax bacteria. UNSCOM found evidence of both of these agents as well as clostridium perfingens.[3]

Iraq also had a number of long range missiles—SCUD-Bs, Al-Hussein—with a range of 600 km—and Al-Hijarah—with a range of 750 km. In December 1990, Iraq launched an experimental space launch vehicle.

The Iraqi program was motivated by two regional factors. First, Iraq sought regional hegemony in the Gulf and ultimately in Middle East. It appears Saddam Hussein saw WMD and missiles as important in Iraq's competition with Iran—a country with greater size and population. Second, the Iraqi program appears to have also been motivated by the

Israeli WMD and missiles capabilities. The Israeli attack on Osirak in 1981, was followed by a major covert nuclear program. Further, Israel's success in placing a satellite in orbit in September 1988 was followed by the launch of the Iraqi space vehicle.

The Gulf war and its aftermath set back the Iraqi WMD and missile programs significantly. According to the UN commission, all weapons grade nuclear material has been taken out of Iraq. All known enrichment facilities have been destroyed. The same is true of Iraq's chemical weapons. The UN is placing a monitoring system for observing WMD-related facilities. The UN has also destroyed all longer range missiles it has discovered. However, according to the CIA, Iraq might well be hiding SCUD missiles with ranges longer than allowed by the UN, as well as, chemical munitions and its BW program.[4]

Although Iraqi capabilities have received a severe setback, its incentives for acquiring WMD and missiles probably persist. It might well try to reconstitute WMD and missile capabilities after the embargo is lifted. Already there have been reports indicating efforts by Iraqi front organizations to buy components for missiles. Iraq has thousands of nuclear experts and technicians who could support a possible restart of the country's program in the future. It is possible that the new monitoring system would be more effective than the old one in detecting Iraqi WMD activities; however, this task will become considerably harder once sanctions are removed.

Iran. While the Iraqi programs have received a severe setback, the Iranian WMD and missiles programs are expanding and pose a serious long-term challenge for regional security. Iranian motives are also regional and include competition with Iraq for regional domination and a broader role in the Middle East. Iran might also be influenced by the nuclear and missile developments in the adjacent South Asian region.

There is little doubt that Iran aspires to acquire a nuclear capability. Like Iraq before its invasion of Kuwait, it has pursued a two-pronged approach: a covert program and an overt civilian one.

Iran, under the fundamentalist regime, became interested in nuclear weapons in the mid-1980s because of its war with Iraq. However, based on what is known, it has not been successful in acquiring significant quantities of fissile materials. Iran has explored both the plutonium and highly enriched uranium routes.

Under the Shah, Iran had started an ambitious nuclear power program. It was stopped in the aftermath of the fundamentalist takeover of Tehran. However, during the Iran-Iraq war, some reactors under construction were bombed by the Iraqis. To-date, Iran has been seeking the completion of two 1100MW(e) reactors, which were started by the Germans. It has also been interested in buying new reactors. Under pressure from Washington, the Germans refused to complete the reactors. However, the Russians apparently have agreed to complete the German plants. The U.S. is discouraging the Russians from going ahead with the project. But, given the recent U.S.-North Korean agreement, which includes the construction of two power reactors in North Korea, the Russians are unlikely to change their mind. However, it is possible that, given the poor state of the Iranian economy, Tehran might not be able to finance further work on the project in the near future. Iran has also agreed to purchase smaller power reactors from China. As far as Iran's covert program is concerned, it has been active in seeking to buy parts for critical components in the West. It has also sought help from Pakistan, China, North Korea.

According to the CIA, Iran is 8-10 years away from producing nuclear weapons. This is not a very long time. The time might be shortened if Iran succeeds in purchasing fissile materials from the outside; again, according to the CIA, Iran has been actively pursuing this possibility in Russia. Iran can accelerate the timetable even more if it can purchase fully fabricated nuclear weapons.

Iran already has chemical weapons and is suspected of possessing a covert BW program as well. It has ballistic missiles—SCUD Cs and Bs—and is seeking systems with increasing range—including mobile missiles—from North Korea and China. To that end, Tehran has been interested in the North Korean No-Dong missile with the possible range to target Israel.

Some of its missile launchers are mobile. It is also building its own missiles. It has produced one called Oqab with a range of 30-40 km. It is planning to build a much longer range version and might do so by the end of this decade.

Israel. Israel is the dominant military power in the Middle East. It has the region's most advanced nuclear and missile capabilities, and these capabilities are growing. Israel sought its nuclear and missile capabilities for the most fundamental reason—survival. It lacked strategic depth, was surrounded by hostile states with larger size, population and potentially conventional capabilities. Therefore, it developed—by regional standards—a very advanced WMD program. It refused to sign the

Nuclear Non-Proliferation Treaty (NPT). Besides WMD, Israel has a number of different missiles. It has the capability to deliver WMD, including nuclear weapons, by missile to any country in the region, from Morocco to Iran.

With U.S. assistance, Israel also has the most capable conventional military capability in the Middle East. The quality of its equipment, its military personnel and its capability for battle management is not equaled by any other state in the region.

The collapse of the Soviet Union removed a major source of military support for Israel's Arab rival, Syria. The defeat of Iraq limited Baghdad's ability to threaten Israel. Unless Iraq and Syria gain access to major new military equipment, because of the continuing obsolescence of their conventional systems, the conventional balance is likely to become even more favorable to Israel in the coming several years.

Historically, the Israeli nuclear and missile programs have been an incentive for the acquisition of nuclear capability by some of the other Middle Eastern states. To compensate for their current strategic inferiority, Israel's most likely adversaries might become more energetic in seeking increased WMD and missile capabilities.

Israelis worry that over time their nuclear monopoly in the region will come to an end and their population centers will be placed at greater potential risk. This potential, combined with the appreciation of its current superiority and the fear that more hostile regimes might come to power, have helped produce the Israeli push for a peaceful settlement of the Middle East conflict.

Other Arab States. Several other Middle Eastern states also have some WMD and missile capability. Egypt has chemical weapons and ballistic missiles. Algeria has a 15 MW thermal Chinese research reactor. Saudi Arabia has long-range missiles. Libya is suspected of working on both chemical and biological weapons and it already has ballistic missiles. It is working on its own al-Fatah missile. It has been interested in purchasing complete nuclear weapons and fissile materials. Syria has ballistic missiles—250-300 km range SCUD Bs—and chemical weapons. It is also suspected of working on BW.

Prospects

There are conflicting trends affecting prospects for the spread of WMD and missiles. Arms limitations are widely recognized as a necessary part and product of the resolution of the Arab-Israeli conflict. Israel has been more willing to discuss arms control issues. The successes in the Arab-Israeli peace process will have positive effects in building the foundations for significant agreements on WMD and missiles—especially in the longer term. Even in the short-term, it will provide important opportunities for small steps in terms of confidence and security building measures (CSBMs). Some progress has already been made in the multilateral working group on regional security and arms control.

However, bigger steps such as limitation on WMD and missiles, face major hurdles. There are significant differences in the approaches of the regional parties. Israel believes that major arms control talk—especially one dealing with its nuclear program—should not take place until peace treaties are implemented and tested. It should also include all major states of the region—Iraq, Iran, Syria, and Libya. Besides an end of the threat to its national survival, Israel also wants a regional verification system based on mutual inspection. It would probably also insist on adequate capability for responding to a breakout or abrogation of any agreement. The Arabs, especially Egypt. would like the issue of WMD—including the Israeli nuclear issue—to be dealt with earlier and have raised this in connection with the question of the indefinite extension of the NPT.

Several key Middle Eastern states—such as Iran and Libya—oppose the peace process, and the prospects for bringing them into the fold are not promising in the foreseeable future. Getting agreement between the Middle Eastern states on the relationship between the various stages of the peace process and different arms control measures will be a major challenge for American diplomacy in the coming years.

While progress in the Arab-Israeli peace process will have a positive effect, there are several other factors that can have the opposite effect. As the impact of the Arab-Israeli conflict on the security calculations of the region's states weakens, others sources of rivalry and conflict—including some new ones—might well become more important and act as incentives for the acquisition of additional WMD and missile capabilities. These issues may include: a) polarization between those who continue to oppose peace with Israel and those who have made peace with Israel; b) increased Arab-Arab rivalries concerning other issues; c) Iranian-Arab rivalry and d) the rise of new threats from outside the region, such as threats from South Asia.

Some states in the region might also seek increased WMD capability because of hostility towards the United States. Iran and Iraq are opposed to the U.S. presence in the region and see U.S. strategy and policy as the major obstacle to achieving their goals. Based on the Desert Storm experience, these states probably would not want a direct conventional confrontation with the U.S. as long as they are certain about U.S. will and capabilities. To deter the U.S. from getting involved in the conflicts against them, or to neutralize U.S. conventional superiority, states such as Iran might well see asymmetrical military strategies as their best option. An emphasis on WMD—especially nuclear capability—may be one lesson that some may have learned from the Gulf war.

Another factor which will contribute to further spread is that access to relevant technology is likely to become easier. The technologies for producing WMD and missiles are relatively old. More and more states will be able to master them. The number of suppliers is increasing. And even the U.S. is weakening its controls on the export of relevant technologies because of the end of the Cold War and economic considerations.

Implications

The spread of WMD—especially BW and nuclear weapons—and missiles to hostile states in this critical region can have several negative implications for U.S. interests. Even in a regional confrontation involving nuclear weapons, the U.S. would have enormous advantages—the U.S. homeland will not be vulnerable to direct attack for some time to come and the U.S. would have clear escalation dominance over regional powers armed with WMD and missiles. However, the acquisition of nuclear and biological weapons, and missiles may cause potential aggressors to act more assertively. It would make it more difficult and costly for the U.S. to defend its interests. For example, had Iraq possessed mobile missile armed with nuclear weapons, the Saudis might have been more reluctant to invite the U.S. forces into the country and the U.S. and its partners might have:

- Been reluctant to go to war to liberate Kuwait.
- Postponed initiating hostilities.
- Terminated the war earlier—and on different terms.
- Avoided attacks on sensitive targets such as the Iraqi NCA.

The spread of WMD and missiles can increase the threat to our forces, our allies in the region and adjacent areas. It can also increase another kind of threat: the risk that terrorists might gain access to and use WMD in the region or even in the U.S.. Although terrorists have not used WMD so far, that could change.

What to do?

To deal with the potential threats from the spread of WMD and missiles to the Middle East and other critical regions, the United States needs to move on four fronts:

Continue Technology Denial. Limitations on providing key technologies to hostile regional states still can play an important role. To succeed the U.S. needs cooperation from others who also possess these technologies. In addition to the denial of technology, it is also important to improve the security of fissile material, technologists and actual weapons on the territory of the former Soviet Union. The denial of technology can delay a country's program and make it more costly; more time may allow for the emergence of a government less interested in WMD and missiles, increased costs can deter some countries from pursuing the program, and more time can be used to affect the incentives of potential acquisition of WMD and missiles. But technology denial is unlikely to succeed in preventing determined countries from eventually acquiring WMD and missiles. But even if proliferation is inevitable, the later, the better.

Reduce Incentives. The success of the peace process will affect some of the incentives and will have a positive impact. Other regional approaches and carrots and sticks designed for specific countries will be vital. In the case of the Middle East, designing such tailored approaches for Iran and Iraq should be a primary focus of U.S. policy and strategy. The U.S. willingness and ability to protect allies will also play an important role in discouraging countries such as Saudi Arabia from seeking WMD.

Increase Military Capabilities to Deal with the Proliferation Problem. Since it is possible that some hostile states may acquire WMD and missiles, the U.S. needs to increased counter-proliferation capabilities in several areas:

- <u>Intelligence</u>: we missed the boat on Iraq. The focus of collection should range from technicians to fine-grained intelligence for targeting.
- <u>Deterrence</u>: the requirements for deterring acquisition and use of WMD and missiles might be different from state to state. The U.S. needs to tailor its approaches. We also need to examine what type of American nuclear declaratory policy might be appropriate for deterrence in regional contexts.
- <u>Counterforce Requirements</u>: the capabilities developed should be informed by consideration of a full range of options to seize, disable, destroy, or otherwise deny the use of WMD. The U.S. needs the capability to attack all time-urgent targets simultaneously. We have significant short-falls in several of these areas.
- <u>Defense</u>: offense is unlikely to be 100 percent effective in at least some cases. Therefore, to be effective in counter-proliferation, the U.S. needs to increase its capability for active and passive defense. Increase defense capability—against both ballistic and cruise missiles—is particularly important for securing cooperation from regional friends in confronting a regional adversary armed with nuclear or biological weapons and missiles capable of reaching their territory.

Prevent WMD Terrorism. Although historically terrorists have not used WMD, this might change in the coming years. To hedge against this possible danger, the United States needs an increased capability for detecting and defeating attempts to introduce WMD into the United States.

Conclusion

WMD and missile proliferation is a central global security issue of the coming era. Given the special importance of the Middle East to the United States, the proliferation of WMD and missiles in this region is particularly threatening. This is unlikely to change for the foreseeable future.

The proliferation problem is a permanent one. And there are no quick fixes for dealing with it. The challenges are multiple. The threat posed by nuclear, biological and chemical weapons are different from one another. The same applies with regard to cruise and ballistic missiles. For the coming several years, the challenges we face are likely to be regional. Technological change is likely to blur regional and global lines.

Several countries which have only regional reach now could, over the longer term, acquire globally capable systems perhaps threatening the U.S. itself. To protect itself, its interests and its allies, the U.S. needs a comprehensive and flexible counterproliferation strategy.

Notes

1. Dick Cheney, *Defense Strategy for the 1990s: The Regional Defense Strategy,* Washington D.C., the Department of Defense, January 1993. Also see, William J. Clinton, A National Security Strategy of Engagement and Enlargement, Washington D.C., the White House, July 1994.

2. David Kay, *Denial and Deception: Iraq and Beyond*, Washington D.C., Working Group on Intelligence Reform, 1994.

3. Department of Defense, Conduct of the Persian Gulf War, Washington DC, Department of Defense, April 1992, p. 15.

4. James Woolsey, Speech to the Washington Institute's 9th annual Policy Conference, Wye plantation, September, 1994.

WMD Proliferation in Asia:
A Chinese Perspective

Wenguang Shao

MOST OBSERVERS SEEM TO AGREE THAT THE ASIAN security environment is going through a transition from the Cold War structure to a new phase of pluralism. Certainly the security landscape is vastly different and much improved from what it was even ten years ago. In the past forty years or so, the region saw two hot wars involving the United States and other outside powers, a spread of U.S. military bases and bilateral alliances, a massive deployment of Soviet forces on the Chinese border, heightened tension in a divided Korean peninsula, and skirmishes and conflicts across ethnical, religious, territorial and ideological lines. All these happened against the backdrop of a global rivalry between the two super powers that inevitably spilled over to the region.

Today, the political and security atmosphere among the Asia-Pacific members is much relaxed, and the danger of war has visibly diminished. American bases at Clark and Subic are closed, Chinese-Russian borders are more noted for their barter-trade markets than stationed troops, Cambodia is well on its way to recovery from its destructive war, and the two Koreas are admitted into the United Nations. As we speak today, Chinese President Jiang Zemin is visiting Vietnam. In clear contrast to what is happening elsewhere, East Asia is widely recognized as a region

Dr. Wenguang Shao is currently Counselor at the Embassy of the People's Republic of China in Washington, DC, and Assistant to the Ambassador. Prior, he was Deputy Division Chief for U.S. Affairs, Chinese Foreign Ministry. Dr. Shao graduated from Beijing University of Foreign Studies and received an M.A. from the Fletcher School of Law and Diplomacy, Tufts University, and a Ph.D. in political science from the University of Oxford.

with the fastest and most dynamic economic growth, and its vast market potential has drawn direct foreign investment from Europe and North America. The new-found wealth and heightened expectations for things to come in turn provide a demonstrable stake in peace and stability for the entire region.

While the strength of Asia lies in its diversity—diverse cultural traditions, religious faiths, ways of life, and social systems—its success underscores the similar historical experiences, traditional values and ideals shared by Asian countries. The upsurge of Asian confidence brings with it a new sense of Asian identity, and efforts are underway to enhance collective peace and prosperity through cooperation among themselves and with other countries and regions. It is true that there are still potential sources of instability such as territorial disputes, historical grievances and ill-founded suspicions. There are also concerns about possible defense spending increases in some Southeast Asian nations that may conceivably lead to an escalated arms race.

However, in this post-Cold War era a general relaxation of tension appears to be the main trend in the region, and opportunities for peace continue to arise. The collective interests and popular demands in Asia are not for interstate rivalries but for dialogues and mutual trust, not for resort of force or threat of force but for peaceful settlement of disputes, not for artificial barriers and exclusive trade blocks but for free trade and open market. Above all, the Asian countries want to be free from the scourge of weapons of mass destruction and, like all other countries, they hope to see genuine efforts made in the disarmament and arms control area for the ultimate removal of such weapons from the face of the earth. Now that the world situation has drastically changed, it is a widely shared desire in Asia that not only can we create a peaceful international environment for a sustained period of time, but that chances will increase for mankind to ultimately eliminate the threat of a nuclear war.

China's Role

Of the five declared nuclear-weapon states in the world, China is the only one in Asia, and it is keenly aware of its inevasible responsibility toward international arms control and disarmament. China identifies itself with other Asian nations in pursuit of common objectives of peace, stability and development in the region. It shares the major concern of the world community over the danger of the spread of weapons of mass destruction, and wants to work with other nuclear-weapon states toward WMD non-proliferation. Preventing the spread of nuclear, chemical, biological and other types of WMD has long been the goal of China's policy which, together with its national defense efforts, serves the fundamental interest of its national security. As non-proliferation has evolved over the years to encompass a wide range of activities, China has become an important player in this field, and today it is widely regarded as an indispensable member in the United Nations disarmament effort to strengthen dialogue and cooperation worldwide for the common objective of peace and security.

To fulfill its legitimate self-defense needs, China develops and possesses nuclear weapons. Contrary to the fallacy of a "China nuclear threat," which is sometimes used by others to justify their own nuclear-weapon programs, China's nuclear arsenal is very small, and its technological sophistication is such that it is no comparison to those held by other nuclear-weapon states. According to one estimate, the nuclear inventories of Russia and the United States are each 20 times as large as China's. And even after START II is fully implemented, the United States and Russia will each deploy about 10 times more nuclear weapons than China.[1]

China is also different from the others in that it adopts a long-standing no-first-use policy. On the very day it became a nuclear-weapon state in 1964, the Chinese Government declared that at no time and under no circumstances would China be the first to use nuclear weapons. It has also undertaken not to use or threaten to use nuclear weapons against non-nuclear-weapon states or nuclear-free zones. In keeping with this policy, China has signed and ratified the relevant additional protocols of the Treaty for the Prohibition of Nuclear Weapons in Latin America and the South Pacific Nuclear-Free-Zone Treaty. It formally acceded to the Treaty on the Non-Proliferation of Nuclear Weapons (NPT) on March 1992.

China takes the most radical approach towards complete prohibition and thorough destruction of all weapons of mass destruction, something that not everyone may be aware of. Chinese Vice Premier and Foreign Minister Qian Qichen proposed at the 1994 session of the UN General Assembly that a convention be concluded on the complete prohibition of nuclear weapons in the same way as the conventions banning all biological and chemical weapons. Under this convention, all nuclear-weapon states should undertake the obligation to destroy their nuclear weapons under effective international supervision. This, China believes, will enable the international community to harness nuclear energy only to the service of peace and development for the benefit of mankind.

No First-Use

On September 3, 1994, President Jiang Zemin of China and President Boris Yelsin of Russia signed a joint statement on detargeting from each other the nuclear weapons under their control. The statement, *inter alia,* reiterates their obligation not to be the first to use nuclear weapons against the other side. Chinese leaders also discussed the possibility of a no-first-use treaty among the nuclear powers with the other four countries, including at the meeting between President Jiang Zemin and President Clinton in Seattle last November.

A pledge by all nuclear-weapon states not to use nuclear weapons at all is a crucial element in the international effort to prevent the proliferation of nuclear weapons. It will not only make their testing, development, production or deployment of nuclear weapons lose any meaning, but it will be a more effective step towards the non-proliferation goal underscored by NPT and the proposed comprehensive test ban treaty (CTBT) simply because it will take away any incentive to spread such weapons. For this reason, all the nuclear-weapon states should undertake the same no-first-use commitment, and conclude a treaty among themselves to this purpose. Parallel negotiations should also be conducted with the aim of concluding an international convention on unconditional non-first-use of nuclear weapons and non-use and non-threat of use of nuclear weapons against non-nuclear states and nuclear-free zones.

As China sees it, recent developments have provided favorable conditions for a no-first-use international convention. With the end of the Cold War and East-West confrontation, the danger of a world war has greatly diminished. Under START I and START II, both the United States and Russia have undertaken to reduce drastically their nuclear arsenals and moved to detarget their nuclear weapons from each other. Detargeting has also taken place between China and Russia. With the conclusion and implementation of CFE, the level of military confrontation in Europe has come down and the imbalance in conventional forces in Europe removed. Furthermore, relations between any pair of the nuclear-weapon states have made positive progress, and as is demonstrated by China's agreement with Russia, a mutual no-first-use pledge can only solidify their commitment to friendly relations rather than increase the possibility of hostility. Especially in this post-Cold War era, strengthened cooperation among the Perm Five in the UN Security Council requires mutual confidence among them. Threat of use of nuclear weapons among them not only is detrimental to building such confidence but is woefully behind the times.

Nuclear Nonproliferation

As 1995 is drawing near, attention is increasingly focused on issues concerning NPT review and extension. China supports a smooth extension of the treaty. The preparatory committee for the 1995 conference of the States Parties to NPT has held three sessions, and China's attitude is fairly flexible on various issues, including the issue of whether there should be indefinite extension or one for a fixed term of years. However, NPT extension can be greatly facilitated if progress can be made in a number of areas:

• Acceleration of the nuclear disarmament process by the major nuclear powers, including implementation of the nuclear disarmament treaties according to their planned timetable, and further reduction of their nuclear arms on a large scale;

• A no-first-use commitment by the nuclear-weapon states, and an unconditional commitment not to use or threaten to use nuclear weapons against non-nuclear-weapon states or nuclear free zones, leading to the conclusion of an international convention;

• Strengthened cooperation on peaceful uses of nuclear energy, especially for the purpose of economic and social development of developing countries;

• Joint efforts toward improvement of world non-proliferation mechanisms, with full participation of all countries.

In the context of NPT extension, there is the related question of how to provide security assurances to non-nuclear-weapon states. Given their security concern about external nuclear threat, it is understandable that countries without nuclear weapons want to obtain security assurances from nuclear-weapon states in return for their pledge not to develop their own nuclear-weapon program. On this issue, China's approach may be more reasonable to the non-nuclear-weapon states in that it calls for unconditionality for such assurances as a genuine way to allay their security concerns. Some nuclear-weapon states, on the other hand, appear to want to attach conditions to their negative security assurances plan, leaving out in particular countries which are not party to NPT. It is also noted that while the Nuclear Posture Review undertaken by the United States department of defense re-examined the issue of negative security assurances and their implications for nuclear proliferation, it did not call for any changes or any other major U.S. strategic policies.[2]

With regard to testing of nuclear weapons, China has made it clear that it always exercises great restraint on nuclear testing although it is not part of the moratorium observed by the other nuclear powers. It is widely recognized that the number of nuclear tests China has conducted is extremely limited. China argues that the countries that possess the largest nuclear arsenals were the first to develop nuclear weapons, have conducted the largest numbers of nuclear tests and are the most advanced in nuclear weapon technology. Nothing would serve better China's policy of peace and its own national security interests than to see all nuclear weapons prohibited, the existing arsenals destroyed and a comprehensive test ban concluded in this context. China supports the early conclusion of a comprehensive, effective and universal test ban treaty, and will take an active part in the negotiating process together with other countries to conclude this treaty no later than 1996. China has made the pledge that after a comprehensive test ban treaty is concluded and comes into effect, it will abide by it and carry out no more nuclear tests.

On October 4, 1994, China and the United States signed a joint statement on stopping the production of fissile materials for nuclear weapons. In support of their shared interest in preventing the proliferation of nuclear weapons, both countries agreed to work together to promote the earliest possible achievement of a multilateral, non-discriminatory and effectively verifiable convention banning the production of fissile materials for nuclear weapons or other nuclear explosive devices. It is now up to the Conference on Disarmament in Geneva to build up a consensus on a negotiating mandate for talks on the fissile cutoff treaty and on the establishment of a committee for that purpose.

According to some reports, the Clinton administration recently proposed to Russia that the ABM Treaty be modified and that new agreed definitions be adopted to "clarify" how to interpret the treaty. The U.S. administration's stated objective is to allow the United States and Russia to develop and deploy anti-tactical ballistic missile defenses capable of engaging theater ballistic missiles with ranges of up to 3,500 km.[3] Many countries follow this development with grave concern for fear that, under the current international situation, attempts by the United States and Russia to develop theater missile defense (TMD) systems may trigger off a new round of nuclear arms race as well as arms race in the outer space.

Export Controls

In carrying out its obligation under NPT, China is guided by the principle of never advocating, engaging in or encouraging nuclear-weapon proliferation, nor helping other countries develop nuclear weapons. Its track record clearly indicates that it has taken an extremely prudent and sensitive approach to the matter of nuclear exports, and has confined such exports strictly to the purpose of peaceful uses of nuclear energy. All potential recipient countries must comply with three conditions set forth by China: (1) a guaranteed use for peaceful purposes; (2) acceptance of IAEA safeguards; and (3) no transfer to third countries without China's permission. Under China's export control system, only specially designated Chinese companies are allowed to engage in exports of nuclear equipment and technology for peaceful uses, and export applications are reviewed on a case-by-case basis. Although China is not a member of the Nuclear Suppliers Group or the Zangger Committee, its nuclear exports review process seeks guidance by referring to the general international norms and practices embraced by such entities. However, China does not export to non-nuclear states any equipment and technologies for reprocessing, heavy-water production or enriched uranium.

Another aspect of export control relates to chemical and biological weapons, which are also weapons of mass destruction. China opposes any use or proliferation of chemical weapons and signed the Convention on Prohibition of the Development, Production, stockpiling and Use of Chemical Weapons in January 1993. China is well on its way to ratifying the convention and hopes the major CW countries in the world will do so expiditiously. China does not produce or possess chemical weapons, nor allow exports of chemicals, technologies and equipment for making chemical weapons. To this end, the Chinese government formulated its export administration procedures in this area in 1990 on the basis of the chemicals control lists discussed during the negotiations on the chemical weapons convention, and it has enforced the control very strictly. There have been occasions where China challenged charges made by other countries that it deliberately exported chemical weapon precursors, and it questioned the intelligence on which such charges were based. One recent case was the *Yin He* incident in July 1993.[4]

With regard to biological weapons, China consistently stands for the complete prohibition and thorough destruction of such weapons and upholds the policy of not developing, producing or storing such weapons. In 1984, China acceded to the Convention on the Prohibition of Biological Weapons. Since then, China has taken seriously its obligations in all aspects.

On October 1994, China and the United States signed a joint statement on missile proliferation. Under the agreement, the United States will lift the sanctions imposed on China in August 1993, and once the sanctions are lifted China will not export ground-to-ground missiles featuring the primary parameters of the Missile Technology Control Regime (MTCR)—that is, inherently capable of reaching a range of at least 300 km with a payload of at least 500 kg. Both sides also reaffirm their respective commitments to the Guidelines and parameters of the MTCR, and have agreed to hold in-depth discussions on the MTCR.[5]

This agreement has removed a thorny issue from the agenda of Sino-U.S. relations and paved the way for closer cooperation between the two countries in non-proliferation efforts. The sentiment was echoed by MTCR members in their joint statement at their three-day plenary meeting in Stockholm in October where they "expressed hope for a deepened dialogue" between China and the MTCR.[6] China is not a member of MTCR and has not participated in its work to design and revise the regime's provisions in this increasingly complicated area. One has reason to believe that there will be more discussions between China and MTCR members so as to enable China to understand better its rules and parameters for a more effective enforcement in the future.

Furthermore, there is a need for countries both in and outside the MTCR regime to adopt a consistent position on non-proliferation of missiles and other types of advanced weapons, matching words with deeds, balancing rights with obligations and avoiding double standards. In this connection, the question of American sales of advanced weapons to Taiwan has threatened to disrupt the prospects of China-U.S. cooperation in the non-proliferation area. China regards such sales as another form of proliferation in a geographical area sensitive to the security interests the Chinese mainland, and urges the United States to resolve the issue strictly in accordance with the principles set forth in the three Sino-U.S. joint communiqués, particularly the joint communiqué of August 17, 1982.[7]

In general, China holds that no country should seek armaments exceeding its legitimate defense needs, nor should advanced conventional weapons of high destructiveness be transferred in the world without control. Accordingly China treats its very limited program of conventional weapon transfers with utmost prudence and responsibility, making sure that such export should be conducive to the enhancement of the just defense capability of the recipient countries, produce no adverse effect on peace, security and stability in the regions concerned, and not be used to interfere in other countries' internal affairs. China has expressed its favorable attitude toward openness and transparency in the field of armament and international arms transfer (TIAT), and it takes part in the United nations Register on Conventional Arms Transfers. At the same time, China holds that an expanded transparency regime should be based on equal consultations among all the countries concerned and should not undermine or diminish the countries' national security.

The Korean Nuclear Issue

Following their agreement in August 1994, after two years of protracted negotiations, North Korea and the United States signed a framework document in Geneva on October 21 aimed at resolving the issue of North Korea's nuclear program and paving the way for normalized political and economic relations between them. The immediate effects are the defusing of the mounting tension surrounding the dispute and the evaporation of imminent prospects of confrontation between North and South Korea as well as the United States. To Asian countries, how the Korean nuclear program dispute is resolved may have direct security implications for the entire region. Others may also see the issue in the context of non-proliferation of weapons of mass destruction.

China supports the denuclearization of the Korean peninsula and opposes the existence of any nuclear weapons no matter who possesses them. China deems it essential to preserve peace and stability in the peninsula, which may not be helped either by a deterioration in the political situation or fear of nuclear weapons. Nor will the neighboring countries be immune from the ramifications. Mindful of historical lessons from failure in peaceful settlement of disputes resulting in armed conflicts, China has all along called for talks to be conducted between the DPRK and the U.S., the DPRK and the Republic of Korea, and the DPRK and the IAEA—parties directly involved in this issue. Facts have shown that this is the only feasible approach. China has cooperated with the parties concerned and helped sustain the negotiations that finally came to fruition. It shares the relief and satisfaction over the progress made toward a negotiated settlement.

All countries both in Asia and in other parts of the world share the desire to see the agreement implemented fully by the parties directly involved or associated with it, and their differences resolved on the related issues. Consultations are underway to tackle the specifics in the agreement, including the proposal for setting up a Korea Energy Development Organization (KEDO). China has been working quietly and in its own way to facilitate the settlement process, and its role is generally viewed as very positive and effective. In addition to the immediate concern of IAEA inspection, spent fuel rods and supply of light-water reactors to North Korea, both North and South Korea should be encouraged to continue their dialogue so as to iron out their differences, implement their reconciliation agreement and joint declaration on denuclearization, and work toward improved relations and national reconciliation.

Nonproliferation and Security in Asia

One area regarded by observers as a potential hotbed of dangerous arms race is South Asia. Some people may suspect that India and Pakistan are engaged in a continued expansion of nuclear weapons capabilities, which, coupled with the ongoing conflict between them, raises the probability of nuclear war in South Asia.[8] China, on its part, shares the interest in preserving peace, security and stability in South Asia, and supports any voluntary efforts by countries in South Asia toward denuclearization and establishing a ballistic-missile-free zone on the sub-continent. Moreover, China states that its unconditional commitment not to use or threaten to use nuclear weapons against non-nuclear-weapon states or nuclear weapon free zones applies to all countries in South Asia, and this may very well give strong tangible support for the establishment of a nuclear-weapon-free-zone in South Asia. Also, China has indicated that it would have no difficulty in participating in the proposed conference among China, Russia, the U.S., India and Pakistan on the nuclear issues of the region as long as the other parties agree to do so. It is in everyone's interest for such a conference to achieve its desired results, and China says it is prepared to make its own contributions to peace, security and stability in this region.

As a developing country in the Asia-Pacific region, China attaches great importance to the maintenance of peace and stability in its surrounding areas. Its declared policy is never to seek hegemony or spheres of influence, nor establish military bases abroad. It is also of the view that among the Asian countries, territorial or boundary disputes and other contentious issues should be solved peacefully through negotiations. The use or threat of force in the region cannot be accepted. It is in this spirit that China has conducted negotiations with the Russian Federation, Kazakhstan, Kyrgyzstan and Tajikistan on the reduction of military forces in the border areas and on confidence-building measures in the military field, with considerable progress made. In 1993, the Chinese and Indian governments signed significant agreements on the maintenance of peace and tranquillity along the line of actual control in their border areas as well as on other measures. Border talks are also ongoing between China and Vietnam.

With regard to efforts toward a security arrangement in the Asia-Pacific Region, China believes that any such arrangement should adapt to the diversity and complexity of the region, and should be based on the special characteristics of the region. China is prepared to continue to pursue dialogues with parties concerned in bilateral and regional settings in the belief that such dialogues can only be practical and effective if conducted at different levels, through different channels and in various forms, serving the ultimate purpose of strengthening peace and security in the region.

In July 1994, China joined seventeen other countries in the first meeting of the ASEAN Regional Forum in Bangkok. China holds identical or similar views with ASEAN countries on many international and regional issues of common concern and wants to work with them to develop regional dialogues on political, economic and security issues. The same is true with regard to efforts to develop security dialogues in Northeast Asia. All these undertakings may help enhance understanding and mutual trust among the countries in the region, and can certainly contribute to our collective search for ways to preserve regional peace and security. There are indications that China will gradually increase transparency of its defense capabilities.

Notes

1. *The New York Times,* October 26, 1994; Dunbar Lockwood, "The Status of U.S., Russian and Chinese Nuclear Forces in Northeast Asia," *Arms Control Today,* November 1994, p.23.

2. Dunbar Lockwood, *Ibid.,* p. 21. The negative security assurance formula of the U.S. is, "the United States will not use nuclear weapons against any non-nuclear-weapon state party to the nuclear Non-Proliferation Treaty (NPT) or any comparable internationally binding commitment not to acquire nuclear explosive devices, except in the case of an attack on the United States, or its territories or armed forces, or its allies, by such a state allied to a nuclear-weapon state or associated with a nuclear-weapon state in carrying out or sustaining the attack."

3. Lisbeth Gronlund, George Lewis, Theodore Postol and David Wright, "Highly Capable Theater Missile Defenses And the ABM Treaty," *Arms Control Today,* April 1994, p.3.

4. In July 1993 the United States accused the Chinese cargo ship *Yin He* of carrying chemical weapon precursors, thiodiglycol and thionyl chloride, bound for Iran. After exhaustive inspections, including those conducted by the representatives of Saudi Arabia as the third party and participation by technical experts dispatched by the U.S. government, it was indisputably established that the ship did not carry the above-mentioned chemicals, to the great embarrassment of the U.S. government.

5. China is not a party to the MTCR. Following U.S. Secretary of State James Baker's visit to China in November 1991, the Chinese Government announced on 22 February 1992 its intention to act in accordance with the existing MTCR guidelines and parameters in this area. This commitment was predicated upon U.S. removal of its June 1991 sanctions on China, which took effect on March 23 and thereby triggered off China's commitment concerning MTCR. In August 1993, the U.S. government decided to impose new sanctions against China, with the unfounded accusation that China had made an M-11 missile related transfer to Pakistan. In strongly protesting against the U.S. decision to resume sanctions, the Chinese foreign ministry then stated that it was left with no alternative but to reconsider its commitment to MTCR.

6. Jon b. Wolfsthal, "U.S., China Reach New Accords on MTCR, Fissile Cutoff Issues," *Arms Control Today,* November 1994, p.28.

7. In the Sino-U.S. Joint Communiqué of August 17, 1982, the U.S. Government "states that it does not seek to carry out a long-term policy of arms sales to Taiwan, that its arms sales to Taiwan will not exceed, either in

qualitative or in quantitative terms, the level of those supplied in recent years since the establishment of diplomatic relations between China and the United States, and that it intends gradually to reduce its sale of arms to Taiwan, leading, over a period of time, to a final resolution."

8. Zachary S. Davis, *Nuclear Nonproliferation Strategies for South Asia*, A CRS Report for Congress, May 3, 1994, p. 1.

Nonproliferation and Counterproliferation: A Russian Perspective

Sergei Kortunov

THE MAJOR CHALLENGE OF THE 90'S IS NOT THE POSSIBILITY of a global war, generated by the weapons of mass destruction accumulated in the U.S. and former Soviet Union, but rather the possibility of spreading associated technologies, goods and human expertise from the storage facilities, defense industries and research centers located on the territories of the former two centers of power. It has become clear that mankind is entering a perhaps less dangerous but at the same time less stable world.

This worrisome trend has provoked debate in the world security community over the need to strengthen nonproliferation regimes, *inter alia*, by putting in place effective national export control systems. Clearly, the problem of non-proliferation has emerged as one of the priority challenges facing the world community. Its urgency has been also confirmed recently by the discovery of a clandestine nuclear weapon development programme in Iraq, the dissolution of the Soviet Union which has left nuclear arms deployed in several ex-Soviet republics, the actions of North Korea, which announced its intention of leaving the Nuclear Non-proliferation Treaty (NPT), and the continuing ambivalent position of Ukraine with respect to nuclear weapons on its territory.

Dr. Sergei Kortunov is the Head of the Department of the Russian Foreign Ministry, dealing with the issues of the Russian defence-industries conversion and persecuting political control over arms, military technology and services transfers in Russia as well as nonproliferation of nuclear weapons and missile technologies. From 1987 to 1990 he was an active participant in the INF, CFE and START negotiating and implementation process. Dr. Kortunov graduated from the Moscow Institute of International Relations and acquired a Ph.D. in 1982.

Although the problem applies to the post-Cold War world at large, the matter of particular concern in this respect is the situation in the former Soviet Union or, to put it another way, in the geopolitical space that used to be the Soviet Union. The break-up of the Soviet Union destroyed completely the export control system that proved to be effective in the past. At the same time, incentives to export arms, high technologies and sensitive products, have been growing in Russia and other former Soviet republics.

Basic Principles

Turning now to Russia, one can see that its principled adherence to the task of non-proliferation has been expressed in one of the first announcements made by President B.N. Yeltsin on 29 January 1992, and the many subsequent statements made by the Russian leadership.

All those statements are based on a fundamental national interest of Russia to strengthen the non-proliferation regime and to build up an effective national export control system. One should underline that Russia is carrying out non-proliferation tasks and putting its national export control system in place not as a favor to the Western countries but for its own national sake. The reason is simple: Russia has inherited from the Cold War perhaps the worst periphery in terms of its boundaries. All the would-be proliferators are there. That is why in case of failure of non-proliferation and export controls, Russia would be the first and the major victim of potential proliferation. That is also why strengthening NPT regime and setting up the effective export control system is a strategic imperative for this country, a matter of vital importance and even national survival.

The basic principles of Russian policy in the sphere of nuclear non-proliferation can be summarized in the following way:

First, Russia insisted from the very beginning that the disintegration of the USSR should not lead to an increase in the number of nuclear powers, as they are defined in the 1968 NPT. Accordingly, Russia proceeded from the view that all the former republics of the USSR, except Russia *per se*, which is the successor to the Soviet Union in terms of this Treaty, should adhere to it as non-nuclear states and conclude with the IAEA essential control agreements. Consequently, Russia stipulated that the temporary deployment of nuclear weapons on the territories on

Ukraine, Belarus, and Kazakhstan was not an obstacle to such adherence, considering their commitment to become nuclear free states.

It should be noted that this approach was in full accordance with the position of other state signatories to the Treaty, including its depositories. It flowed from the understandings between the countries of the Commonwealth of Independent States (CIS), reached in Alma-Ata and Minsk, and also from the Lisbon Protocol.

At the same time, the position of some signatories of those documents, especially of Ukraine, on the status of nuclear weapons deployed on their territories, remained unclear. That it why Russia stated on several occasions that she counted on support for increasing pressure on Kiev for rapid adoption by Ukraine of nuclear weapon free status, barring from receipt, under any circumstances, of operational control over nuclear weapons.

Secondly, as with other major players of world politics, Russia insisted that the existing international non-proliferation regimes, the foundation of which lies the 1968 Treaty, should be strengthened through a combination of agreed upon measures in nuclear disarmament—first of all, in the elimination of nuclear tests and measures of control and confidence-building. In particular, Russia states that she sees in these measures the guarantee of successful conduct of a conference in 1995 at which will be decided the long-term fate of the NPT. At this conference, Russia intends to achieve an indefinite extension of the provisions of this Treaty. Russia values the role of the IAEA in enforcing observance of the NPT and supports the efforts taken by the Agency in perfecting the existing system of safeguards.

Russia shares the view of other nuclear weapon states that it is necessary to deprive weapons of mass destruction (WMD) of their "attractiveness." In the world of agreements on regional security, there exists a need for political conditions that lower tensions and allow countries, which still have not done this, to forswear the "nuclear option" and join the NPT. In this context, Russia intends, in particular, to continue taking an active part in efforts to regulate the situation in the Middle East and other "hot spots."

What is also very important from the point of view of international security is the clear-cut, position of Russia that from her territory there should emerge neither the threat of use of WMD nor the danger of their proliferation. That means, *inter alia*, that Russia fully intends to conduct a policy that meets international standards in the sphere of "dual-use" exports. In fact, she has recently taken "comprehensive safeguards" in this sphere and completed the adoption of domestic internal laws which strictly regulate exports from Russia of materials, equipment, technology and services, which could be used for creating WMD and "dual use" items. The creation of an effective system of state control of such exports has been completed.

The Russian leadership also pays particular attention to maintaining essential socio-economic and legal conditions, which in practice would counteract the flight of "sensitive" specialists abroad. In this context, it goes without saying, it would be of great importance if Russia, Germany, and other members of the EC, the U.S. and Japan continue to provide strong and effective support for the International Scientific Center in Moscow. An important direction in the joint projects undertaken by this Center should be the establishment of favorable conditions for the "conversion" of the work of scientists, for peaceful purposes—in particular, increasing the safe use of nuclear energy and clearing large-scale industrial regions in Russia of radioactive contamination.

However, despite some positive developments and encouraging statements by her policy-makers, Russia is still considered by many observers as a potential source of proliferation.

A National Export Control
System in Russia

The Russian export control system differs from that of the former Soviet Union. In the first place, the Russian export control system is being reoriented to cover primarily non-proliferation tasks. In the former Soviet Union, the system was used primarily as an instrument to prevent the sale of the most critical technologies and goods belonging to the national patrimony. In this sense, the Russian export control system is also a tool to protect national economic security interests, but, at the same time, it is much more political than economic in nature. That is why it is being formed from the very beginning as a comprehensive system to cover all of the non-proliferation regimes.

Secondly, the system in question is being adjusted to the market economy environment now forming in Russia. In the Soviet Union, it was a centralized, administrative, and rigid system based on state-owned defense industries. Perhaps, it is the most important problem faced by

Russia. Now she realizes the difficulty of finding an appropriate, delicate balance between the liberal principles of a free-market economy and effective regulation of export controls. Russia is really in need of Western technical assistance in this field.

Thirdly, the Russian export control system is still being developed, replicating the best features of Western systems. That is why now is the right time to hold bilateral and multilateral consultations, workshops and conferences with Russian participants on export control methods. It is now occurring.

The system is being developed together with the export control systems of the other countries of the Commonwealth of Independent States (CIS). Of course, the great advantage for Russia is that she has inherited all the bureaucracy of the former USSR including specialists in export controls—together with all associated buildings and agencies located in Moscow. This Russian advantage works to the detriment of the other CIS countries. But Russian authorities fully understand their responsibility to bring appropriate personnel and human expertise to the CIS countries with the assistance and political support from Western countries.

One should underline the importance of political support, particularly the effort made by a number of Western countries that brought a special team of export control specialists to Russia in May 1992 and other CIS countries with a mission to explain to appropriate authorities the importance of setting up effective export control systems. This extremely important and successful trip happened to be one of the major reasons for the constructive meeting of the CIS prime ministers in Minsk on June 26, 1992, and all subsequent meetings. As is known, a special agreement was signed in Minsk on CIS cooperation in the field of export controls, launching close cooperation between these countries. This interaction between experts was continued over the following years on many specific export control issues. The last event of its kind occurred September 1994.

In general, export control cooperation proves to be perhaps the least controversial and least politicized issue in Russia's relations with other CIS countries, as compared to other problems. A consensus was formed within the CIS that export control regulations should not be subject to political debate. This is a common achievement that Russia reached in collaboration with Western countries.

To meet COCOM requirements, Russia has introduced in its national practice and legislation a procedure of import certificate-delivery and on-site inspections at the request of the exporter. The required commitment letter was submitted last year to COCOM.

Furthermore, a unified customs space was introduced in the CIS and is now regulated by special agreement. The agreement has been effective despite the transparency of borders that exists in the CIS.

Thus, Russia is now establishing an effective export control system, one sufficient to remove the original concerns of Western countries, and one intended to eliminate completely trade restrictions.

Russia will put this system in place despite all attending difficulties and regardless of whether the assistance from the other countries will be forthcoming. However, it would be more rational to address and overcome this task through joint effort.

Shortcomings in the International Regimes

One of the most serious shortcomings in the current NPT regime is the absence in existing treaties of provisions ensuring the creation of an effective mechanism for verification of the development of prototypes of specific types of nuclear weapons and their components. Existing treaty provisions are limited to control over the use of nuclear materials and installations, and the official sale or transfer of related products and technologies to other countries.

For example, the system of IAEA safeguards, although it reinforces the regime of special inspections, is inadequate for the task of preventing attempts to produce nuclear weapons. Special inspections can be undertaken only, for example, after receipt of positive information of violations having occurred. This requirement makes such an IAEA inspection a rare occurrence and this creates a political "threshold of permission" for violators. Moreover, one can anticipate significant time delays between requests for a special inspection and the actual arrival of an IAEA inspection team in the target country.

In addition, the existing IAEA safeguards do not ensure timely warning regarding the use of plutonium and highly enriched uranium in civilian reactors for military purposes, which creates the potential for theft of nuclear raw materials.

The terms of the Universal Basel Convention for control over the transportation of dangerous waste are very weak. In this context, in particular, attention is drawn to the well-known Japanese "Plutonium Project," developed with the goal of accumulating in Japan colossal quantities of fissionable material.

The Convention on Prohibition of Biological Weapons does not provide for a control mechanism. On the positive side, the Convention on Chemical Weapons has greater potential.

Thus, existing international mechanisms and means are not sufficient for guaranteeing the implantation of effective non-proliferation regimes. There is an obvious need for such mechanisms and means.

Existing treaties, or those currently being negotiated, which limit the proliferation of WMD, do not contain synonymous provisions on what to do with already existing technologies for the development of nuclear, chemical or biological weapons amongst states that are signatory to the treaties. This places existing non-proliferation regimes in an ambiguous and uncertain situation with respect to the disposition of potential or existing weapons components.

Insufficiently effective are proposed sanctions against violators of the non-proliferation regimes. In effect, the main thrust of such sanctions are denial by international economic organizations of financial assistance to countries where there is proof or grave suspicions that they are manufacturing WMD. Among the most likely candidates as WMD violators in the Third World are those not experiencing shortages in liquid capital, are not in need of help from the IMF of IBRD and, finally, are not vulnerable to sanctions although they can, nevertheless, have a definite deterring affect.

However, it is impossible to close your eyes to the fact that the use of "comprehensive" sanctions, including economic blockade, impact adversely on the well-being of people—primarily simple people. As a rule, they will not place immediate, direct pressure on the leadership forcing it to abandon the production of WMD.

Finally, a serious shortcoming is the lack of access for all members of the international community to information about the real state of affairs in specific countries. Insufficient transparency precludes the possibility of making the non-proliferation regime comprehensive and adequate to meet the real threat.

The effectiveness of mechanisms for limiting the proliferation of WMD can be maintained only when they are based on a congruence of goals on the part of each state with the universal goals of the world community. Much in this area depends on how determined the major powers are to leave behind the hangups of the past, i.e. the division of "threshold" and "near threshold" states into "friendly" and "non friendly" with all the consequences of political double standards. Russia has started to depart from this path and expects the same of her partners.

"Passive" and "Active" Measures

Some people think that the situation in the sphere of non-proliferation has already reached a point beyond control. Of course, it is an overly pessimistic view, but such dangers have increased in recent years. Coordinated measures to combat proliferation of WMD and missile delivery means must be energetically pursued.

Recently it has become the convention to divide such measures into two basic categories "passive" (more close to non-proliferation) and "active" (more close to counter-proliferation).

The first category usually includes the following:

• Progressive strengthening of existing non-proliferation regimes, primarily the 1968 NPT;

• Further steps in the sphere of nuclear disarmament including, above all, a ban on nuclear weapons testing (agreements already reached in this context, including the START II Treaty, it should be recognized, are insufficient);

• Political measures to remove incentives to acquire nuclear weapons, including the lessening of tensions and settlement of conflict situations in various regions of the world;

• The development and strengthening of the system of IAEA safeguards;

• Strengthening and harmonizing national systems of export controls; and

• Measures to halt the dispensation of scientific expertise and knowledge in the sphere of WMD and their missile delivery systems through the creation of socio-economic and legal conditions which prevent the "export" of nuclear specialists to third countries.

Among recent initiatives on "passive" measures, one should mention UN-sponsored measures of "delimitization" of nuclear weapons, as well as China's proposal of a Conference of five nuclear power on non-first-use of nuclear weapons. Despite great political and emotional significance of such declarations one should not exaggerate their practical significance.

As far as the "delitimization" proposal is concerned, one should note that it is applied to international law, which has played a limited role in world politics as a rule. Non-first-use declarations, as practice has showed, were never treated as political or military obligations by the major nuclear powers. Non-first-use declarations were used by the powers, possessing conventional superiority, for political purposes. Of course, the implementation of China's proposal could be useful, but since the non-first-use obligation is not verifiable, such implementation is of little practical significance.

In the second category ("active measures"), which by the way are significantly less well formulated, one might include the following:

•   Increasing the effectiveness of control over proliferation, mutual exchange of data received through NTM, institutionalizing for the purposes of an international regime of "open skies," and of new technologies and systems of export control and non-proliferation, cooperation of the intelligence services of various countries;

•   Joint political counteraction by the nuclear powers of the nuclear ambitions of third countries;

•   Development of institutionalized economic and legal sanctions against violators of the non-proliferation regimes (Pakistan, Libya);

•   Threat of use of military (including nuclear) force against violators as a form of implementation of a new variant of the "deterrence" doctrine applied to non-proliferation (it is apparent that an international analysis of this issue should be conducted);

•   Formulating variants and scenarios for the conduct of nuclear powers in the event that deterrence fails, that is, variants of direct uses of military force (studies of this concept are also needed); and

•   Joint research in technology of remote disarmament (rendering harmless, or disabling) nuclear warheads, which may be in the hands of terrorists.

To this range of measures, the possibility of creation of BMD is also added.

It is obvious that all these measures can work only as an integrated complex. For example, a national system of export control, as experience shows, is not a panacea. As an end in itself, export controls cannot stop the proliferation of WMD. This is confirmed by the fact that Iran, Pakistan, North Korea and other acquirers of WMD have gotten around controls. Besides, strict export controls in many cases leads to the rapid creation of indigenous production or a search for alternative sources for acquiring needed materials.

The Case of Non-Russian
CIS Countries

Fears that the dispersal of nuclear weapons in several former Soviet republics would lead to the emergence of new nuclear weapon powers were bruited when, in January 1992, the Russian Federation formally declared that it was a "legal successor of the USSR from the stand-point of responsibility of the fulfillment of international obligations," covering obligations "under bilateral and multilateral agreements in the field of arms limitations and disarmament." These agreements include the NPT, under which Russia may not transfer control over nuclear weapons to any country "directly or indirectly."

The Russian declaration, of which the international community had taken note, was not challenged by the non-Russian republics at the time it was made. Subsequently, as is known under the Lisbon Protocol, Byelarus, Kazakhstan and Ukraine made a straightforward pledge to accede to the NPT as non-nuclear weapon states "in the shortest possible time."

However, as post-pledge developments showed, the question was not resolved at that time. Many economical, political and technical difficulties arose on the way to implementation. Among these, political difficulties dominated. In fact, despite the resemblance of common problems faced by all three ex-Soviet republics, each follows its own separate course: Ukraine—an offensive one; Kazakhstan—moderate; and Byelarus—clearly constructive.

It is obvious that failure by Byelarus, Kazakhstan or Ukraine to meet their denuclearization obligations could generate explosive antagonisms among the former Soviet republics and have disastrous effects for the NPT. The nuclear threshold counties would feel encouraged to cross the threshold and openly "go nuclear." The resulting arms race would reverse the present disarmament trend and carry new threats for international security.

However, such a development, while conceivable is not very likely for a number of technical, economical and political reasons. As far as tactical nuclear weapons are concerned, they were withdrawn from the territories of those countries in 1992. As for strategic nuclear weapons, they will be withdrawn from the territories of Ukraine, Kazakhstan and Byelarus by the end of implementation of the START I Treaty, that is to say by 1998. Right now these strategic nuclear missile forces are already being deactivated.

There should be no doubt that irrespective of domestic developments in the "geopolitical space," which used to be the Soviet Union, central control over strategic nuclear forces will be preserved. One hardly could imagine that Kazakhstan or Ukraine would be able to have their separate national strategic nuclear forces: in this case, they should build their separate national satellites, early-warning systems and many other things belonging to "military infrastructure" of offensive strategic forces. Although such a possibility could not be absolutely ruled out, there are doubts that such an option would be affordable for some of those sovereign states for financial reasons. One cannot ignore that those states will be heavily dependent in the years to come on Western countries, including the United States, which will apparently not be indifferent watching the emergence of new nuclear powers in Europe.

To put it another way, the three ex-Soviet republics can hardly afford to ignore overwhelming international opposition to a further spread of nuclear weapons. And, finally, there can be no doubt about the dubious character of claiming by those countries ownership of nuclear weapons and the materials within them from the legal point of view.

Although it is tempting for newly independent states to enter the international system and attempt to play the game of international politics by their own rules, experience suggests that in the long run they have to conform to the generally accepted norms of international law and relations. With respect to treaties already in existence, this means accepting their negotiating history as the basis for understanding their meaning.

The NPT was negotiated in the mid-1960s against a background of USSR concerns over discussions then taking place within NATO over sharing control over American nuclear weapons in Europe with its Western European allies, especially West Germany. In that context, the NPT was primarily intended to be a non-dissemination treaty. It outlawed any transfer of nuclear weapons between states, including nuclear weapon states—Article 1 being shaped around U.S. domestic legislation. At the same time, it permitted U.S. and Soviet nuclear devices to be deployed on the territory of allies, provided those nuclear weapon states retained physical custody and control over those devices. This required their own troops to guard nuclear storage facilities and the devices be designed so as to be incapable of operation without access to firing codes held by the custodial state.

The Treaty also specifically commits nuclear weapon states not to assist non-nuclear weapon states to acquire nuclear weapons. One implication of this is that the only type of monitoring of nuclear weapon dismantling that could be undertaken by a non-nuclear weapon state would involve a weapon "in-fissile material out process," since any more intrusive monitoring of dismantling might involve illegal dissemination of weapon design information.

The INF Treaty also has some bearing on these matters, as it involved the withdrawal and destruction of missiles owned by the U.S. and USSR stationed in other states, such as Germany, Italy and the United Kingdom. This was addressed by the Treaty between the U.S. and USSR, but with both nations negotiating subsidiary agreements with allies permitting each access to the territory of the other's allies for verification purposes.

Finally, it should be noted that at the end of January 1992, the UN Security Council produced an agreed statement specifying that nuclear proliferation was a threat to international peace and security under Article VII of the UN Charter. The implication of this is that any state or states involved in a process of proliferation or dissemination of nuclear weapons will confront extreme sanctions against them by the Security Council.

Objects and Subjects
of Nonproliferation

The end of the "Cold War" led to changes in the objects and subjects of non-proliferation policy. Now, the old division of states into East and West has been replaced by a more complex and more finely graded classification which includes:

1. The Coordinating States - these states (for example, the U.S. and Russia) are fully or partially members of all treaties on non-proliferation and export control (NPT, the Nuclear Suppliers Group, the Missile Technology Control Regime, the Australia Group and eventual post-COCOM mechanism).

2. The Cooperating States - these states (for example, China) participate in some, but not all, treaties on non-proliferation and export controls, and have announced their intention to join, in the future all four or cooperate with them.

3. The Sensitive States - some of these states (for example, India) have the legal and administrative basis for export control available but at this time see being drawn into the existing arrangements on export control as an infringement of their security and also of limited political and economic utility; these states however currently do not directly threaten the security of the Coordinating States.

4. The Threatening States - these states (for example, Iran and Iraq) are in need of sensitive technologies; they produce them and, in some cases, export them, ignoring the existing mechanisms of export control and conducting a security policy which threatens the interests of the Coordinating States.

The policy of the Coordinating States in the sphere of trade, technology transfer and export control in relation to different groups of states must be implemented differently. For example, the policy of the U.S. and Russia in relation to other Coordinating States should be carried out on a no restriction basis. As far as the Cooperating States are concerned, their policy should introduce some elements of control. As for the Sensitive States, the U.S. and Russia should introduce many elements of control and maintain many restrictive conditions. And, finally, the Threatening States must be the subject of maximum control including embargo.

Practical stimuli and comprehensive procedures should be used so that the Cooperative, Sensitive and Threatening States can shift to a more desirable position toward the Coordinating or other states. In the post-COCOM mechanism, the basic requirement should include:

1. A pledge to take corresponding measures of export strategy, including adoption of a system of import certification/control of delivery;

2. Guaranteeing that strategic goods and technologies imported from cooperating countries will be used exclusively to civilian purposes;

3. Assigning guarantees of final use, which would be supported by national governments and be confirmed by inquiries to the exporting country for information; and

4. Agreeing to on-site inspections upon request of the exporting country.

The creation of a comprehensive system of export control can lead to the dismantling of prohibitive lists.

The Nonproliferation Treaty: Prospects for 1995 Extension Conference

Speaking about the prospects for the 1995 NPT conference in general terms, one could predict that relaxation of international tensions, increasing stability and nuclear disarmament will lead to diminished general interest in nuclear weapons acquisition. However, for the universalization of non-proliferation and the unlimited extension of commitments, several things are needed. Requisite is global *detente*, but some regions remain exceedingly tense. Drastic nuclear disarmament has been agreed, but it is not yet accomplished. International verification is being strengthened to provide confidence that states might dare to live without, or with few, nuclear weapons—but the safeguards strengthening process is not complete. It is not naive to aim at the universalization of non-proliferation and at an unlimited extension of the NPT, but it is prudent to be aware of the considerable hurdles to be overcome.

To universalize reliable non-proliferation pledges *detente* will be needed in the Middle East, on the Indian subcontinent and on the Korean peninsula.

Accelerated nuclear disarmament measures by the nuclear-weapon states have great value *per se*, and will also do much to enhance the NPT Conference in 1995. However, the absence of CTB agreement could block its success. A cut-off in the production of direct-use nuclear material for weapons purposes would be a significant contribution to success of the conference.

It should be stressed that the major way to strengthen non-proliferation is to de-emphasize the role of nuclear weapons in defence postures and strategies of nuclear weapon countries. One should also prove that the Third World countries would not be serving their own interests by initiating the nuclear option taken by the nuclear-weapon states. Their own security could be impaired by triggering regional nuclear arms races and destabilizing the existing world order. Nuclear proliferation is likely to hurt the security interests of the Third World rather than punish the nuclear-weapon states for their failure to halt vertical proliferation.

It is necessary to do all that is required not only to extend the NPT but, later on, to jointly find a means to increase its effectiveness. In connection with this, it appears necessary to:

1. Fully clarify the question of the obligations in the Treaty to "not manufacture" nuclear weapons including a full ban on their manufacture, the pursuit of associated RDT&E, and the creation of warhead components. Such a prohibition would be aimed at all non-nuclear country members of the Treaty and states which have signed other agreements on non-proliferation.

Before joining the NPT, "unofficially" possessors of nuclear weapons, "threshold" and "near threshold" countries would have to make a special commitment to fully disclose past activities, directed towards the creation or possession of nuclear weapons. In addition, such states would have to show that they are no longer seeking to develop their own nuclear weapons, would have to reorganize and redirect efforts of associated scientific and technical groups, liquidate or render harmless installations where work was performed in creating nuclear weapons, also fully destroy all earlier manufactured (or inherited) components of warheads. This, naturally, also applies to those republics of the former USSR which still have not fulfilled the terms of the START I Treaty. For verification of stated declarations in international agreements, on its own initiative, the inspected country in a show of good will, would undergo a series of special inspections. Other countries, in the absence of information about work being conducted on nuclear weapons, would be considered observers of the regime.

Consolidating such an expanded interpretation of the NPT and other agreements should become one of the priority tasks of the IAEA. This approach might be placed before the Group of Nuclear Suppliers. It might be discussed at the UN Security Council as well.

2. Formulate and adopt an improved system of verification, to ensure observance of bans on development of nuclear weapons and to control basic forms of nuclear materials. The main instrument for maintaining such control should be the IAEA, whose functions in this case could be further elaborated and expanded.

The mechanism for NPT verification can be a strengthened inspection regime of nuclear installations "under suspicion." Such a regime can be made standard for all signatories of the NPT which had to have on their territory nuclear installations, not covered previously under IAEA safeguards, and also for countries suspected of clandestinely developing nuclear weapons. The creation of such a regime can be initiated by a corresponding resolution of the UN Security Council.

3. Expand the legal base for economic and political sanctions relative to states and private firms in violation of the non-proliferation regimes. This can acquire especial importance, for example, in connection with deviations—including collective or regional—from adherence to the convention on the destruction of chemical weapons which was concluded in January 1993. In addition, two things should be underscored: the introduction of sanctions should be implemented only by decision of the UN, and responsibility for breaches of the non-proliferation regimes should be borne not only by the buyer but also the seller. It may seem that the best way to bring all those changes about is to amend the NPT. Any amendment must be approved by a majority of the parties to the treaty, including the votes of all nuclear weapon parties and all other parties which, on the date the amendment is circulated, are members of the IAEA Board of Governors. These requirements would be very difficult to meet. It is especially unlikely that unanimity could be obtained on any significant amendment in such a large and hydrogenous group as the IAEA Board of Governors.

Therefore, it is safer for the integrity of the NPT, and certainly much simpler, to strengthen its provisions through common understandings, formal or informal, or supplementary agreements among the parties.

One of the issues related to non-proliferation, although of a more marginal character, is the concept of "negative" security assurances. Up to now such assurances have been given by the individual nuclear weapon states on different occasions, although China's assurances are generally viewed as unconditional.

However, the search for unconditional universal guarantees has proved fruitless to-date. Indeed, the latter would require fundamental changes in the postures and policies of the major powers. Some of these changes would be equivalent to a non-first-use obligation with regard to any state, not just to a state not possessing nuclear weapons. In the meantime, however, before the general non-first-use agreement is reached, the qualified "negative" security assurances already contracted could perhaps be incorporated into a formal international accord.

One should not, however, overestimate the significance of such measures. After all the assurances offered by nuclear weapons states to non-nuclear states under the terms of the NPT, these have not been sufficient incentives to those countries to abide by the NPT. At least, all "pre-nuclear" states like India, Pakistan and Israel haven't joined the NPT as non-nuclear states. One might conclude that they have decided that the political dividends they enjoy from their "pre-nuclear" status outweighs the anticipated risk of the potential use of nuclear weapons against them—especially in the post-Cold War environment.

Towards a New International Nonproliferation Mechanism

The field of non-proliferation is proving to be one of the most promising and important areas of cooperation between Russia and the Western countries. First of all, cooperation contributes heavily toward improvement of political relationships among these countries. This has been demonstrated on several occasions, even though we only began to discuss the most delicate and sensitive issues—the kind of interaction unimaginable in the recent past—just two years ago.

From a more general perspective, this cooperation reflects the major trends of global development. The fact of the matter is that Russia is not the only subject involved in great change. The changes in Russia represent only a part—however, not a marginal one—of overall global change. We are now entering an absolutely new world that is terra incognito to us. The problems of this strange new world should be tackled through a common effort. The revolution in Russia is obviously an accelerator or a catalyst for general change and development.

From this perspective, all instruments of the Cold War like COCOM should be transformed and adjusted. That is why Russia places such emphasis on a commitment by the U.S. and other ex-COCOM countries to reorient their approach to meet post-Cold War challenges and to establish a new multilateral body where Russia will no longer be viewed as a potential adversary but, rather, as a potential partner in combatting proliferation.

Russia took seriously the explanations of the COCOM countries put forward during the November 1992 cooperation forum meeting. There are no political reasons for the existence of trade restrictions, but there are still some concerns related to the effectiveness of the Russian export control system (so-called "technical reasons"). A great deal of work was carried out during the past two years to remove such concerns. One can see that an effective export control system has been put in place in

Russia, meeting all the requirements formulated by the ex-COCOM countries, in November 1992, as a condition for removal of all restrictions.

The new arrangement should not duplicate the work of other international regimes. It should complement existing control regimes for weapons of mass destruction and their delivery systems by focussing on the threats to international peace and security which may arise from transfers of armaments and sensitive dual-use goods and technologies where the risks are judged greatest. The new arrangement should not be directed against any state or group of states, and should not impede bona fide efforts to acquire legitimate means with which to defend themselves pursuant to Article 51 of the Charter of the United Nations.

The new arrangement should provide for an appropriate exchange—of information leading to discussions among all participating states on arms transfers, as well as on sensitive dual-use goods and technologies. To this end, parallel procedures should be developed, within the overall framework of the new arrangement, to deal with the differing requirements of trade in dual-use goods and technologies on the one hand and transfers of armaments on the other.

In respect of dual-use goods, the procedures should provide for a dialogue between Governments leading to an exchange of information to develop a common understanding of risks associated with transfers of such items, to assess the scope for coordinating national control policies to combat these risks and to ensure that trade in these items is carried out responsibly and in furtherance of international peace and security. In respect of arms transfers, procedures should also provide for appropriate information exchanges through normal diplomatic channels among a group of members which are the principal exporters of armaments belonging to the seven categories specified in the United Nations Register of Conventional Arms, appropriately defined.

What was also important was the decision taken to invite Russia to participate in the new arrangement from the beginning. It was also decided to encourage China's early participation as that of other potentially eligible states.

Russia considers all these developments to be of great importance since they implement the idea of the creation of an international organization which would include both states as well as those interested in obtaining access to high technologies. This would permit the modernization of the international non-proliferation regime in a manner consistent with significant weakening of suspicion that it is aimed at strengthening the monopoly of the "club" of industrially developed states.

Speaking in more general terms, an effective, practical tool for preventing the proliferation of WMD could be the creation and use of a global system of "early warning," resting on scientifically based criteria. Such a system would be organized to offer objective assessments of WMD threats and their missile delivery means by various countries. This global system of threat assessment could significantly strengthen and reduce the costs of such a multibillion dollar project as Global Protection System (GPS).

An international mechanism for control and surveillance should possess the ability to reach sound conclusions about the actions of states possessing WMD or developed technologies and production bases for their manufacture, and also about the plans of countries which may be interested in obtaining access to them. To an equal degree, this should apply to states that have an existing missile production capability or wish to possess missile technologies, including technologies for space research. In terms of creating such an international mechanism, several existing organizations—for example, the World Space Organization—can play a role. They are fully capable within their structures of carrying out verification in the sphere of preventing "switching" acquired missiles, their components and associated peaceful technologies for uses to purely military, or "dual use."

Here, a constructive role should be played by the UN. Under its auspices a, data bank could be established where information would be accumulated on WMD. A parallel bank could be filled with data from "contiguous" sectors focused on trade in conventional weapons and military technologies.

The possibility of creating an International Control Agency with the function of coordinating observance of agreements both of disarmament in general and non-proliferation, should not be ignored. Existing, probably as part of the Permanent UN Secretariat (or as an autonomous organizational unit), the International Control Agency based on special agreements, concluded with the UN, IAEA and other interested organizations could fulfill control functions.

The exposure of possible violators of agreed international regimes would be accompanied by possibly the suppression of further illegal activities, including recourse to economic sanctions or other forms of penalty enforcement.

Counteracting the Proliferation of WMD

Georgi E. Mamedov

Since the cold war and east-west confrontation came to an end, new threats to global stability have emerged. I have in mind the danger of proliferation of weapons of mass destruction at the time when major reductions in U.S. and Russian arsenals have just begun. Given the new challenges in the field of security which have emerged after the collapse of the totalitarian regimes in the Eurasian continent, and tensions and conflicts in various regions of the world, efforts to counteract the proliferation of WMD, primarily nuclear ones, are becoming increasingly urgent. It is important to ensure that the nuclear arms race, halted in one area, not be resumed in another one.

In their Joint Declaration of January 14, 1994, the Russian and U.S. Presidents expressed the commitment of the two countries to cooperate actively and closely with each other, as well as with the other states concerned, in order to prevent and reduce such a threat. In the Declaration, they also emphasized that proliferation of nuclear weapons posed a serious threat to the security of all states, and stated their intention to take rigorous measures aimed at preventing it.

In this connection, we believe that improving the situation both at the global and regional levels is the best way to prevent proliferation of weapons of mass destruction. Following this approach, President Yeltsin, in his address to the forty-ninth session of the UN General Assembly, set forth a program of action of the new Russia aimed at establishing a strong post-confrontation system of international security. This program

Dr. Georgi E. Mamedov is the Deputy Minister for Foreign Affairs of the Russian Federation. From 1981 to 1991, he was assigned to the USSR Ministry for Foreign Affairs, Department of the USA and Canada, and later became head of the Department. Dr. Mamedov earned his Ph.D. from the Moscow State Institute for International Relations of the USSR Foreign Ministry.

is to provide pre-conditions for progress in reducing the role of the nuclear factor in maintaining global and regional security and, finally, for full elimination of nuclear weapons all over the world as called for by UN decisions and stipulated in Russian military doctrine. It is important to create a global climate which prevents states from being tempted to acquire WMD, with a view to guaranteeing their own security and, which, on the other hand, encourages their voluntary and judicious rejection of the nuclear option.

The Search for Political Solutions

Russia believes that the search for political solutions to emerging problems, particularly by strengthening the already existing non-proliferation regimes, should be the main instrument of preventing the proliferation of weapons of mass destruction. However, under existing dynamically changing circumstances, we should be prepared that, at some stage, the international community will have to face a situation when "classic" non-proliferation will no longer be sufficient to ensure prevention of the spread of WMD and associated delivery systems.

Counterproliferation Concept

In this connection, it is expedient to pay attention to the so-called "counter proliferation concept"—i.e. the elaboration of a set of preventive and protective measures to avert WMD proliferation—which are to complement the "traditional" arsenal of non-proliferation efforts.

We believe that this idea, as a whole, is in line with our understanding of counterproliferation of WMD and their delivery systems and could, in principle, open new opportunities in the field of control. Specifically, such aspects as timely identification of potential violators of the non-proliferation regime and improvement of our respective defense potentials are of utmost military and strategic urgency for Russia, given its geopolitical situation. And, here, we are interested in developing international cooperation, *inter alia*, within NATO, which would help us to elaborate common approaches to this problem.

ABM Regional Systems. This involves, first of all, the interaction in the establishment and deployment of "non-strategic" ABM regional systems. We are prepared to discuss joint efforts in this field with the

U.S. and other states. Consultations could, *inter alia*, include examination of "non-strategic" ABM regional systems concepts, identification of opportunities for joint research, and ongoing experiments in this field.

Here, we proceed from the principle of unchangeability of the ABM Treaty of 1972 and the absolute need of Russian participation in efforts aimed at creating "non-strategic" ABM regional systems. Without Russia's participation, such systems, whether deployed in the European region or in the North Pacific, could hardly play, in these regions, the stabilizing role which they are intended to play.

Joint research and experimentation could provide impetus for further cooperation which has already begun in the field of "non-strategic" ABM systems, and which now manifests itself in preparations for a joint Russian-American exercise using such systems.

UN Security Council. At the same time, other elements of the "counterproliferation" concept give rise to a number of questions. It is obvious that aspirations for unilateral use of armed forces without a UN Security Council decision, and only on the basis of intelligence data concerning the appearance of WMD or their delivery systems in a certain region of the world, does not fit in with existing norms of the international law. Besides, implementation of concrete measures to elaborate new high-precision systems of weapons designed to provide for the implementation of the "counterproliferation" idea will inevitably result in a new spiral in the world arms race and adversely affect present strategic stability.

Such an approach to the problems of counteracting proliferation could provoke a negative response on the part of a number of regional states whose cooperation is necessary for the implementation of a multilateral strategy in the field of non-proliferation; such negative response can jeopardize the success of the 1995 Conference on Review and Prolongation of the NPT.

Conclusions. Thus, we believe that there are a number of very serious issues requiring more thorough discussion and coordination. Our fundamental position on this question is that priority in the struggle against proliferation of WMD and their delivery systems should address political methods, while at the same time we do not exclude a combination of political and diplomatic approaches with coercion measures (economic in character) and other restrictive strategies. As to the use of military force, we believe that resorting to this measure may be considered only in exceptional circumstances, and only when sanctioned by the UN Security Council.

Enhancement of the Regime Based on the Treaty on the Nonproliferation of Nuclear Weapons (NPT)

In this respect, we highly appreciate the Joint Declaration made by the Presidents of Russia and the U.S. on September 28, 1994, on the twin issues of strategic stability and nuclear security, wherein they stressed the special responsibility of nuclear powers in this field. This document underlines that both countries, in cooperation with other permanent members of the UN Security Council, as well as other countries, will initiate efforts to ensure the success of the 1995 Conference of the NPT Participating States and the adoption of the decision concerning the indefinite and unconditional prolongation of this Treaty. Such a decision would add to the efficiency of the NPT and its universal nature; it also would accelerate the process of reducing and eliminating nuclear arsenals and strengthen international stability. Russia regards the adoption of this decision as a high responsibility of states, and we are ready to continue active cooperation in this field with all the countries sharing this approach.

Comprehensive Nuclear Test Ban Treaty

Striving to promote the creation of favorable international conditions for the prolongation of NPT, Russia advocates the speeding up of multilateral negotiations aimed at *concluding the comprehensive nuclear test ban treaty* (CTB) so that it could be signed in 1995, thereby marking the 50th anniversary of the UN—thereby abandoning efforts at qualitative improvement of nuclear weapons. We believe that this task in no way makes the prolongation of the NPT the hostage of concluding the CTB Treaty. On the contrary, such a position testifies to seriousness of intentions to achieve a nuclear test ban at the earliest possible time. It is apparent that, to achieve such a result, serious discussion is required, first of all with China and France, who have not yet taken a political decision on this question.

Strengthening of the Nonproliferation Regime

At the same time, we presume that, to dissipate the concerns of a number of non-nuclear states that criticize the efforts of nuclear powers in the field of nuclear disarmament and the pace at which far-reaching measures should be taken in this direction, the nuclear "five" could initiate additional steps during the period preceding the 1995 Conference. This does not mean that we are ready to question the importance of what has already been achieved by Russia and the USA in the implementation of their obligations under Article VI of the NPT and, naturally, it would be a mistake on the part of non-nuclear states to try to use our proposals for presenting new claims to the nuclear powers. We proceed from the fact that strengthening of the non-proliferation regime is not less but, rather, even more important for the security interests of non-nuclear states.

Increased and Intensified Dialogue

Russia and the U.S.A., as was agreed in the course of the meeting of the Presidents of these two countries held in Washington on September 27-28, 1994, will intensify their dialogue in the field of nuclear disarmament in order to compare conceptual approaches and to elaborate specific steps to adapt the nuclear forces and practices of the two sides to a new situation in the field of international security and to the present spirit of Russian-American partnership, including the possibility of further reductions and limitations respecting the remaining nuclear forces after the ratification of the START-II Treaty.

Participation of all Nuclear States

At the same time, our opinion is that the new international realities require participation of all nuclear states in the process of reductions and limitations of nuclear weapons. The experience gained, indicates that there are limits inherent in the method of solving the nuclear weapons problems through separate, although extremely important, agreements. The interrelationship of nuclear problems calls for a complex approach in seeking their solution.

It is exactly these considerations that underlie the proposal of the President of Russia concerning the elaboration by the five nuclear weapons states of a treaty on nuclear security and strategic stability. The advantage of such a treaty would be that its subject could constitute the most important link of the nuclear chain, i.e., the material and technical basis of nuclear weapons. This treaty would solve, in whole, the following problems: termination of production of fissile materials for weapons purposes; ban on repeated use of fissile materials released as a result of disarmament for weapons production; further elimination of nuclear munitions; and reduction of nuclear weapons delivery systems.

These measures could be implemented on a step-by-step basis taking into account the specific characteristics of the nuclear potential of each country. In order to take into consideration the positions of other nuclear countries, an asymmetry in commitments would be tolerated.

The proposed "Five" treaty, together with a comprehensive ban on nuclear tests, while not serving as a substitute for existing efforts underway at the Geneva Conference on Disarmament, would facilitate practical decisions in this sphere on the part of all nuclear countries and would make a significant contribution to the strengthening of the non-proliferation regime.

Extended Security Committments to Nonnuclear States Through the NPT

Russia also stands for granting to the NPT non-nuclear participating states which have voluntarily rejected the nuclear option and duly respect their commitments under the Treaty, more precise security assurances on the part of the UNSC in case of nuclear threat or blackmail. This underlies the proposal made by the President of Russia to convene in the nearest future a special meeting of the UNSC at the level of foreign ministers to come to an agreement on a new resolution by that body, further elaborating the provisions of the well-known UNSC resolution 255 of 1968.

Russia is prepared to work actively on the issue of strengthening security assurances for non-nuclear states from the use or threat of use of nuclear weapons against them, i.e. the so-called "negative" assurances. These concerns, in particular, both necessitate elaboration of an international convention and agreement on an assurances formula covering all nuclear states, which might be reflected in an appropriate UNSC resolution.

More Active Role for IAEA

Moreover, a positive role could also be played by joint and parallel efforts of the interested parties in the following directions. *Active interaction with the IAEA*, taking into account the role, played by the Agency in providing for successful operation of a control mechanism, mainly in the context of the verification of the treaty's observance. Improvement of the international regime of control over export of nuclear material assuming that all countries able to export nuclear technology, materials and equipment agree to be guided by the principle of full scope IAEA safeguards. Development of international cooperation in order to oppose smuggling and illegal traffic of nuclear materials is also essential.

Narrowing Sphere of
WMD Proliferation in FSU

Efforts aimed at the geographical narrowing of the sphere of the WMD proliferation are also an essential component of Russian politics.

The break-up of the Soviet Union in December 1991, and the formation in its place of more than a dozen independent states and formation of the CIS, resulted in a number of complicated problems associated with non-proliferation of nuclear weapons, which needed immediate resolution. The Soviet strategic and tactical nuclear arsenals turned out to be deployed on the territory of all the new states. Many were involved in different aspects of the nuclear cycle. Unstable conflict situations in some of the former territory of the Soviet Union posed a real threat to the physical security of nuclear weapons, as well as posing the risk of uncontrolled export of raw nuclear materials, equipment and technologies. Moreover, the end of the USSR as a subject of international law gave rise to problems of succession to international obligations, as regards nuclear weapons, including questions relating to the NPT regime.

It was clear—and Russia proceeded from this understanding—that it was inadmissible to allow several new nuclear weapon states to appear in place of one former Soviet Union and, thus, to undermine the international regime of non-proliferation of nuclear weapons, which is of vital importance for peace and security.

The Russian leadership was well aware of how serious the emerging problems and potential dangers were, and, from the very first days of its independence, Russia vigorously sought to seek their urgent settlement. With the support of the world community, including that of the states formed out of the territory of the USSR, Russia, as a successor-state of the Soviet Union, assumed the responsibility for the Soviet nuclear arsenal and for the implementation of corresponding international obligations of the USSR

For these reasons, Russia withdrew all its tactical nuclear forces from Eastern Europe and "post-Soviet" space, and now is systematically withdrawing to Russia strategic nuclear weapons from the three CIS countries where these weapons are still deployed.

Important in this respect was the signing, on May 23, 1992, between Russia, the U.S., Byelorussia, Kazakhstan and Ukraine, of the Lisbon Agreements including the Protocol to the U.S.-Soviet Treaty on the Strategic Arms Reduction (START I) of July 31, 1991.

According to the Lisbon Agreements, Byelorussia, Kazakhstan and Ukraine, together with Russia and the U.S., became Parties to the START I Treaty. These three states have undertaken to free their territories, within the seven-year period provided for in the START-1 Treaty, from all strategic nuclear warheads and to join, as soon as possible, the Non-Proliferation Treaty as non-nuclear states.

Lisbon Agreements and Declaration of Heads of CIS States

On July 6, 1992, the heads of the CIS states, including Ukraine, Byelorussia and Kazakhstan, signed a declaration in which only the Russian Federation, from the successor-states of the Soviet Union, was formally recognized as a nuclear state, while the other CIS states proclaimed their decision to join the Non-Proliferation Treaty as non-nuclear states.

The Lisbon Agreements and the Declaration of the Heads of the CIS states of July 6, 1992, have created a political and international legal framework according one state—i.e. the Russian Federation—the function of control over nuclear weapons, thus ensuring their non-proliferation in the territory of the former Soviet Union. In pursuance of the Lisbon Protocol, Russia, together with Byelorussia, Kazakhstan and Ukraine, have worked out a number of agreements and accords aimed at the implementation of the START I Treaty and the non-nuclear status of these states. Schedules for removal of nuclear weapons from these countries to Russia for their destruction and disposal have been agreed upon.

Denuclearization of Ukraine

The most difficult problems have arisen in connection with the denuclearization of Ukraine as a result of positions taken by the former leaders of this country on nuclear issues. However, at the meeting of the Presidents of Russia, Ukraine and the U.S., which took place in Moscow in January, 1994, a major break-through was achieved. In the tripartite declaration signed at the conclusion of this summit on 14 January, 1994, President Kravchuk confirmed his previous assurance that Ukraine would join the Treaty on the Non-Proliferation of Nuclear Weapons as a non-nuclear state and that all nuclear weapons would be removed to Russia in accordance with agreed time schedules. The three Presidents recognized that it was important that Ukraine receive compensation for the value of the enriched uranium used in the nuclear devices located in its territory. It is envisaged that, in return for the removal of nuclear arms, Russia will provide to Ukraine compensation in the form of supplies of fuel to meet the requirements of the Ukrainian nuclear power sector during a fixed period of time.

Tripartite Declaration

As a follow-up to the tripartite declaration of January 14, 1994, agreements have been concluded with Ukraine which make it possible to proceed with deactivation of strategic offensive weapons on its territory, as well as the removal of nuclear warheads to Russia for their subsequent dismantlement and disposal. At this time, Russia has received 360 nuclear warheads. In turn, Russia has supplied three lots of fuel assemblies for Ukrainian plants as compensation for the dismantled nuclear warheads.

Discussions with Byelorussia and Kazakhstan are underway concerning issues relating to appropriate compensation for the removed nuclear weapons on their territory.

Taking into account the wishes expressed by Byelorussia, Kazakhstan and Ukraine concerning provision of security assurances to these states in connection with their non-nuclear status, the Depositories of the Treaty on the Non-Proliferation of Nuclear Weapons have agreed to provide such assurances and have agreed upon the text thereof, the essentials of which are reflected in the aforementioned declaration of the three Presidents.

Notwithstanding all the progress which has been achieved, the START I Treaty, cannot enter into effect without Ukraine's joining the NPT as a non-nuclear state (Byelorussia and Kazakhstan joined the Treaty under such status in February 1993 and in February 1994 respectively) which, in turn, blocks the START II from implementation.

Regional Aspect of Nonproliferation

Along with recent encouraging developments, there are some serious problems in this domain. Favorable trends are emerging in Africa. The Republic of South Africa's adherence to the NPT has played a key role in this context. It represented the beginning of a new era on the continent—that of freedom from nuclear threat. It is important that South Africa not only joined the Treaty, but, also, made a positive decision regarding the transparency of its former nuclear arms development program. We welcome the Republic's readiness for cooperation with the IAEA. We hope that South Africa's new policy will bring the whole of Africa into a nuclear-free zone.

Nuclear Free Zone

"Nuclear-free" standards are gaining acceptance in Latin America. Growing cooperation between Argentina and Brazil, and their common achievement of mutual transparency and confidence-building measures, remove the nuclear arms race threat between them and are good examples of their political wisdom in embracing responsible conduct. We hope that these processes will result in the earliest implementation of the provisions of the Treaty for the Prohibition of Nuclear Weapons in Latin America (Tlatelolco Treaty) by all the states in the region. We welcome Cuba, which has declared its decision to join the Treaty.

The process of political settlement has begun in the Middle East as well, which actually makes it possible to take a new look at ways and means of settling non-proliferation issues. The idea of creation of a nuclear-free-zone in the region may gain a second breath. We support efforts, including those which are being undertaken under the auspices of the IAEA, aimed at practical implementation of this idea. However, the problem of Israel's joining the Treaty on the Non-Proliferation of Nuclear Weapons remains to be solved, and, no doubt, the settlement of this issue requires ours the joint efforts.

The situation in South Asia remains alarming. The two largest states, India and Pakistan, are not Parties to the NPT and do not implement the principles of IAEA full scope safeguards as regards their nuclear activity. To solve the problems accumulated here, an overall settlement of the situation is necessary. Real chances for settlement could be enhanced by an international meeting, with the participation of Russia, the U.S., China, India, Pakistan, and other interested parties.

Speaking about Asia, we cannot avoid mentioning the nuclear problem of the Democratic People's Republic of Korea. On the whole, we are positive with respect to the recently concluded agreement between the U.S. and North Korea. It is a document which may benefit the normalization of the situation on the entire Korean peninsula. We share the conclusions and assessments regarding this agreement provided by Mr. H. Blix, Director General of the IAEA, at the recent session of the UN Security Council. But, nevertheless, we also have certain apprehensions as to the consequences of this document for the regime of nuclear weapons non-proliferation.

Control Over Proliferation of Missiles and Missile Technologies

We consider control over proliferation of missiles and missile technologies as an important factor for consolidating the regime of non-proliferation of WMD and their delivery systems. For Russia, as well as for a number of other countries, the problem of non-proliferation of missile delivery systems of WMD is of special importance. Failure to solve this problem might objectively endanger Russia's security interests to a greater extent than those of many other countries on other continents. In some regions, situated in immediate proximity to Russia's frontiers seized by increased tension, we are witnessing noticeable manifestations of a desire to have in their arsenals combat missiles and a potential for their domestic production. The problem is aggravated by the fact that it is precisely in such regions that the danger of WMD spread has not been removed.

Modern world realities determine our interest in blocking missile weapons proliferation through coordination of national export policy through rules worked out within the Missile Technology Control Regime (MTCR). That is why Russia decided to accede to this regime.

Chemical and Biological Weapons

We assume that the best guarantee against proliferation of these types of WMD would be prompt entry into force of the Convention on the Prohibition of Chemical Weapons, the participation in it of all states, as well as strengthening of the 1972 Biological Weapons Convention by establishing a corresponding mechanism of efficient international verification. Russia is making active efforts in all these fields.

SECTION III

Preventive Approaches

Preventive Approaches: Expectations and Limitations for Inspections

David A. Kay

Historical Precedent

THE IMPORTANCE ASSIGNED TO ON-SITE INSPECTIONS IN ARMS control efforts has waxed and waned over the years. Although it is now generally ignored in discussions of inspections, the Versailles Peace Treaty enshrined a tough, coercive regime based on intrusive on-site inspections to ensure effective German disarmament and marked a high point in expectations for on-site inspection. The Inter-Allied Commissions of Control established under the Treaty were given sweeping rights of access, "anytime, anywhere, with anything," and carried out inspections designed to: collect information on the location and amounts of treaty restricted items; compile baseline information to verify information provided by Germany; take possession of surplus or prohibited items; supervise the destruction of these items; identify military factories that will be permitted to continue production; supervise the destruction or conversion of all other military production facilities; and provide for the long-term monitoring of Germany's military activities.[1] Between 1919 and 1927 almost 34,000 on-site inspections were carried out by 400 Allied officers and 1000 additional support

Dr. David A. Kay is Assistant Vice President of Science Applications International Corporation in the Negotiations and Planning Division. Prior to his present position, from 1992 to 1993 he was Secretary General at the Uranium Institute, London, UK. Dr. Kay earned a Bachelors degree from the University of Texas, Austin, and a Masters and Ph.D. from Columbia University.

personnel. To anyone familiar with the course of inspections in post-Gulf War Iraq, there is a striking similarity with many aspects of the Versailles regime:

- For a variety of reasons associated with the delayed entry into force of the Versailles Treaty and German reluctance to cooperate. As with Iraq, the crucial first phase of baseline data collection was delayed until after the Germans had demobilized and disposed of a number of weapons without any Allied inspectors being present.

- A continuing source of friction was and is whether dual purpose equipment and arms were included in treaty limited items.

- Both Germans and Iraqis is resisted the Allied interpretation that long-term monitoring should be understood to permit the stationing of permanent monitors in key facilities.

- The on-site inspection mechanism was and is seen as a continuing and very visible reminder of their defeat. The closure and destruction of military factories was claimed to be a cause of major unemployment and general economic difficulties. Cooperation was limited and substantial arms caches were hidden.

- A divisive issue for the Allies was and is how German and Iraqi non-compliance should be met. In the former case of Germany, the French argued that noncompliance should be met by military occupation of territory, while the British argued in favor of a more diplomatic approach and direct negotiations. Further, when Franco-Belgium occupation of the Ruhr occurred, on-site inspection effectively ceased for a period of two-years in the face of massive passive resistance.

This dredging up of what must seem to many today as the ancient history of the Versailles period is intended to remind us that the specific verification environment—that is, the political context within which inspections take place—has varied over time and between arms control agreements and influences significantly the way in which inspections operate in a verification system.[2]

The Verification Environment and Its Impact on Inspections

A useful way to slice the arms control verification environments, and what can be expected of on-site inspection, is by the extent to which cooperative, adversarial and coercive elements dominate.

Cooperative, Adversarial, and Coercive Verification

Most recently two wars, the Cold War and the Gulf War, have had dramatic impacts on the process of verification including the role on-site inspections play in arms controls agreements. Arms control treaties such as INF, START, CFE, and CWC, negotiated in the last years of the Cold War when the parties still had reasons to be suspicious of each other's intentions, were accompanied by calls for stringent, intrusive, complex verification. The oft-repeated motto, "Trust, but Verify," or its Soviet version, "Verify, then Agree," underlined an insistence on proof of compliance.

Within a short period, however, implementation of the INF and CFE Treaties demonstrated a high level of compliance on the part of the FSU and the former Warsaw Pact countries. Treaty-related activities, in particular on-site inspections, were characterized by good cooperation, verification proceeded in a satisfactory manner, and the atmosphere was one of transparency and confidence. This type of verification environment became characterized as generally "cooperative" and the importance attached to ensuring compliance through on-site inspection declined.

Cooperative Inspection. The IAEA/NPT safeguards system, as it existed before the Gulf War, can be considered the model of cooperative inspection, because safeguards were primarily intended to provide assurance to neighbors of a country's peaceful intentions not to seek out violations. Those countries that were not prepared to give such assurances, or that simply wanted to maintain their options and some degree of ambiguity about their nuclear intentions, stayed outside of the NPT safeguards system.[3] This system is "cooperative," in that Member States have agreed to submit to inspections of their declared nuclear facilities that are designed to confirm their safeguards undertakings. The dominant expectation before the Gulf War was that any state that wanted to seek nuclear weapons would not join the NPT, or if it had joined the NPT, would either withdraw or pursue its weapons efforts through a clandestine program that would not be detected through inspections of declared facilities. As a result of this dominant belief as to the purpose of nuclear safeguards, they came to be viewed before the Gulf War largely as confidence-building measures carried out in a cooperative verification environment. IAEA/NPT inspections were to serve the purpose of confirmation of self-proclaimed good behavior, and not of a search for evidence of treaty violations. Anomalies when they occurred were viewed, more often than not, first as errors of methodology or omission, not of deliberate evasion. Inspections, in a cooperative verification environment, are not discoverers of fact, but confirmers of evidence presented by those subject to inspection.

Adversarial Inspection Environment.   A second type of inspection environment can be termed adversarial. In an adversarial inspection environment, the arms limitations or nonproliferation commitments are entered into freely, but the level of suspicion between the parties is sufficiently great that the parties view non-compliance as a realistic possibility and seek verification measures that will detect such noncompliance.[4] If no violations are found over a long period or if basic political relations change in major ways—as they did with the end of the Cold War—then the adversarial verification environment may move toward the cooperative end of the spectrum.

Before the end of the Cold War, relations between the United States and the FSU could be generally characterized as adversarial, and arms control measures of that period reflected this fact. Many of the global and regional arms control agreements now being sought (e.g., a nuclear weapons free Middle East or fissile material cut-off) will, if successfully concluded, be signed by parties that share considerable suspicions of the intentions of other parties to conduct non-compliant activities.   Any inspections carried out to verify these agreements, at least until the underlying political dynamic between such countries changes, will be conducted in an adversarial environment.

Under such conditions, the adversarial inspection environment will have three primary characteristics: verification methods, including inspections, will be extensive and intrusive because some parties may not comply with the agreement; there will be anomalous events and ambiguous activities requiring investigation; and since there can be no absolute guarantee to prevent, or even detect all non-compliance, the level of intrusive verification agreed to should, at the very least, raise the political and economic costs of large-scale, clandestine non-compliance by making it probable that major violations will be detected. On-site inspection, operating in conjunction with national technical means, will be a necessary instrument of ensuring the parties that their interests are not being adversely effected by the cheating of the other party.

On the other hand, the fact that each side is presumed to have an equal initial interest in seeing the arms control arrangement work, and each is open to reciprocal demands for inspection, will tend to put some limits on the intrusiveness and aggressiveness of the inspection process. The process is adversarial, but each side is presumed to want the regime to continue and realizes that all demands for access, inspection rights and information will apply equally to itself as well as other parties to the treaty.

Coercive Inspection Environment. The end of the Gulf War has signalled an entirely different context—and as already noted, one that resembles the Versailles regime—in which inspection activities can take place. The verification environment in which the Iraqi inspections have taken place can be termed a coercive inspection environment.

A coercive verification environment is dominated by two factors. First, the arms limitation itself is imposed and is not a voluntary undertaking. Secondly, the working assumption is that non-compliance and active deception measures to avoid detection will be so intrusive that extensive verification methods must be employed. While the exact context in which the Iraqi inspections have taken place is unique, many of the verification lessons may have application to other agreements where the basic agreement is established through coercion or imposition (e.g. by victorious states or the UN Security Council) where there is strong reason to suspect non-compliance.

Conclusions

While arms control agreements reflect the verification environment at the time they were concluded, this environment may change with considerable impact upon the inspections that operate under a given agreement. The clearest example of such change is the pre-versus-post Gulf War IAEA/NPT safeguards. In the pre-Gulf War, the dominant verification environment was cooperative. After the discoveries of the extent of Iraq's clandestine nuclear program emerged from the aftermath of the War and the possibility of non-compliant behavior became recognized as a realistic possibility, numerous changes in the IAEA/NPT safeguards regime were instituted and the environment became more generally adversarial. The bulk of the U.S.-Soviet agreements that were signed in the Cold War era provide additional examples of changes in the verification environment that are moving in a more hopeful direction from adversarial to cooperative.[5]

The Impact of Environmental
Expectations Upon Inspectors

Inspectors operating in cooperative, adversarial, and coercive verification environments will have widely different expectations and experiences, which can have both positive and negative effects on the way they carry out their work. With an increasing emphasis on confidence-building and transparency in East-West arms control agreements, U.S. inspectors may begin to operate under the assumption that compliance will be the norm and that anomalies are simply "mistakes," or the result of the disorganization that generally characterizes the FSU, and not the result of deliberate decisions to act contrary to a treaty obligation. This assumption could well lead to less vigorous efforts to find evidence of non-compliant activities or to recognize such evidence as non-compliant behavior.

Political Environment

In a cooperative verification environment, inspectors may let down their defenses and be more susceptible to deception measures. The inspector also faces the temptation of being "charmed" by the hospitality of an inspected country to the point where his or her alertness to anomalous activities or events may be dulled. The political pressures to maintain an atmosphere of cooperation for larger political purposes may well influence the thoroughness of the on-site inspection process and the seriousness with which indications of non-compliance are treated. How suspicious or defensive should an inspector be? While the desirable attitude may be one of inquisitiveness, respectful questioning, and skepticism, the expectation of cooperation and the policymakers' lack of enthusiasm for creating new problems can, over time, shift such inspections toward pro forma reassurance.

IAEA Approach

An inspector's reaction to anomalies and possible violations of agreements will depend greatly upon the dominant verification environment within which he or she operates. In the IAEA inspectorate, the traditional approach to resolving anomalies has been incremental: the procedure starts within the organization, moving through prescribed review channels, and, if necessary, then follows a prescribed path in relations between the Agency and the state involved. Efforts to resolve or clarify anomalies are done quietly and within house—not with public display in the political limelight—and with a fundamental assumption that such anomalies arise from factors other than intentional violation of nonproliferation obligations. The effort is to seek the cooperation of the state involved in clarifying discrepancies and uncertainties, because a primary purpose of IAEA safeguards is to facilitate demonstration by a state of its compliance with its international undertakings.

Cooperative Environments. In cooperative environments, if the detection of anomalies is followed with public accusations of deliberate violations, the result is likely to be a hostile reaction which discourages increased transparency and access. In a cooperative verification environment, inspectors are more likely, if faced with anomalies, to seek better clarification of treaty obligations, than to pursue confrontational approaches.

CFE Treaty inspection experiences have argued for more detailed definitions of treaty-limited equipment, allowing for a clearer distinction between limited and permitted "look alike" weapons to avoid such interpretational differences. Inspectors noted that they would have benefitted by having detailed photographic catalogues of the weapons in both categories.

Adversarial Environment. In contrast, in the adversarial environment which marked the beginning of the INF inspections, American inspectors operated in a system in which evidence of non-compliance, however militarily-insignificant, was made public by reports to Congress and given media attention. Similarly, IAEA discoveries of discrepancies during *ad hoc* inspections in North Korea were well-publicized. The adversarial environment became clear as North Korea denied IAEA requests to conduct special inspections to clear up this matter, even though Pyongyang is obligated under its agreement with the Agency to accept such inspections.

Anomalies found by UNSCOM and IAEA inspectors in Iraq, caused by the limited, incomplete, or deliberately inaccurate Iraqi declarations, created a situation in which the relationship between the inspectors and Iraqi officials was filled with friction and distrust. In this coercive verification environment, recourse to a unified UN Security Council which could enact further sanctions and threaten military actions was crucial to the successful completion of the inspections.

Changes in the Verification Environment. The Iraqi and DPRK experiences have underlined for the IAEA a new international environment where looking for undeclared nuclear activities and early warning indicators of nuclear programs will be more important, and where the degree of confidence in detecting diversions will not be as high as that associated with traditional safeguards.   In other words, the verification environment is changing from cooperative toward adversarial and the demands on inspectors will be different. To the extent that the old cooperative environment continues to exist for some states side-by-side with more adversarial inspections, one can expect additional tensions and stress on safeguard inspectors and the IAEA as a whole.

Little analytical attention has been paid over the years to the process of on-site inspections in highly adversarial conditions. One area that needs to be assessed, for example, is the impact on the inspection process that the repeated cycles of confrontation with Iraq over the rights of inspectors has had. These cycles have involved Iraq blocking inspectors for the full exercise of their rights, the Security Council and member states threatening, and occasionally taking, military action to punish the most serious violations. Iraq has been forced to back down repeatedly on major violations, but has gained time in each case to delay or even prevent the inspection of sites and materials of interest to UNSCOM. In addition, Iraq has persisted in a pattern of more minor violations, getting away with a wide variety of interfering and delaying tactics which are not individually serious enough to provoke a military response. The net effect has been to slow down the inspection process and, in some cases, to allow Iraq enough warning time to destroy or remove important evidence of its prohibited activities. Even more serious, but much harder to document, is the impact that Iraq's tactics may have had on the conduct and course of the inspection activities. Faced with constant harassment and a tenuous underlying political consensus in the security Council supporting the inspection and long-term monitoring of Iraq's weapon's capability, UNSCOM and IAEA inspection missions have tended at times to become as interested in seeking to avoid confrontations with Iraq as in discovering any remaining hidden arms.

Lessons of Intentional Interference. The UNSCOM/IAEA inspections provide a number of useful lessons on the impact of intentional interference with inspections. Broadly these lessons fall into three categories: First, obstruction works. Iraqi harassment and interference have seriously impaired inspections efforts, reducing their efficiency and, delayed and almost certainly, prevented the discovery of important information about Iraq's weapons of mass destruction. Second, in addition to a general level of interference, Iraq has been able to interfere selectively with inspections of important sites and programs. The overall lack of inspection results in uncovering the Iraqi biological weapons program has, to a large extent, resulted from such selective interference. Third, the international community has not been able to develop an effective response to much of the low-level physical harassment, obstruction, and intimidation. Many of the low-level harassment techniques lend themselves to denial of government responsibility and to cheat-and-retreat strategies, and in isolation may seem so trivial that it is difficult to make a political case for enforcement action based on their persistence. Nonetheless, even low-level harassment has helped to erode inspection effectiveness.

Inspections and the Future

There are two conflicting lessons from on-site inspection over the last decade that deserve attention. The first is that on-site inspection can fail to detect even massive violations of an arms control agreement—this is the case of NPT inspection in pre-Gulf War Iraq. While the reasons for this failure will continue to be argued for years—and some will even argue that it was not a failure, as these inspections were not designed to uncover the particular approach to cheating that the Iraq's employed—it should give all of us pause as we seek security through arms control arrangements. On-site inspection by itself does not necessarily ensure compliance or early detection of an agreement.

The second and contrasting lesson—and one that holds far more hope—is that on-site inspection can, under certain circumstances, uncover even well hidden arms programs and carry out a more thorough disarming of an aggressor government than even military action. This is the hopeful lesson of the Iraq experience. The verification environment was clear, the inspection mechanism focused on a single purpose.[6] The inspection process had a direct and very supportive link with the Security Council, and national intelligence information was made available to directly support inspection in the field. In retrospect, the decision to place the inspections in Iraq in the hands of a body, UNSCOM, created for just that purpose appears to have made the decisive difference. UNSCOM, as a subsidiary organ of the Security Council, was able to break or simply ignore the ossified procedures of the UN Secretariat and get on with its task of dismantling Iraq's WMD program. Its status as an organ of the Security Council means that the inspection process would remain before the Security Council and any Iraqi act of defiance would be seen as direct challenges to the members of the Security Council. When Iraq tried on several occasions to bring the inspections to a halt, the Council demonstrated its willingness to use military action to ensure that the inspections would continue.

Most importantly, UNSCOM became the vehicle through which national governments could pass intelligence information to the international inspection effort. While Iraq has no doubt come to view the Special Commission as just an agent of the coalition powers, and particularly the United States, from the inside its role has been much more complex. First of all, UNSCOM, and this really means its Chairman, Rolf Ekeus, has had the necessary but unenviable task of vetting and maintaining a sense of proportion in the face of intelligence reports that often overstate what is known as opposed to what is simply suspected, or judged possible. In the face of the highly efficient Iraqi deception activities, the inspections could not have gone forward without accurate intelligence. On the other hand, if every intelligence lead had been chased down by an inspection team, the operation would have ground to a halt in its first few months. National governments have developed various means for coping with the propensity of their intelligence services to overstate the capabilities of opponents, but UNSCOM was the first international arms control arrangement to have to come to terms with the problem of vetting intelligence estimates. UNSCOM also played a vital role in legitimizing the passage of national intelligence information to inspectors in the field. In the early days of the Iraqi inspections in 1991, I often wondered which would force us to grind to a halt first: the fear of national intelligence services that sources and methods would be irreversibly compromised if valuable intelligence passed into the hands of a group of international inspectors or the fear of colleagues at the IAEA and the UN that their moral purity would be forever ruined if they allowed those of us engaged in the inspection effort to have access to national intelligence data. That these mutual barriers have largely now been overcome is due principally to the tact and intelligence of Rolf Ekeus and his colleagues on the Special Commission.

If the optimistic note that comes from post-Gulf War Iraq is to dominate the more pessimistic caution of pre-war Iraq, then attention must focus on the following key elements that relate to inspections:

• Ensure that the inspection mechanism matches the task and the environment that actually prevails. Do not expect that an inspection mechanism designed for a cooperative environment will be adequate for an adversarial situation—particularly if it must play by the rules and management constraints of a cooperative system.

• Recognize the impact that can be had by coupling national intelligence information to an international inspectorate equipped by doctrine and training to use such information. The cautionary corollary is not to expect that intelligence information turned over to an inspectorate not trained in how to use such information will result in anything more than grief and mutual recrimination.

• Inspection regimes must better understand that knowledgeable and determined deception can often defeat both on-site inspections and national technical means. Inspections in an adversarial or coercive environment must be sensitive to the many opportunities that a skillful proliferator has for engaging in deception activities and, above all, avoid drawing sweeping conclusions of innocence from quick visits and partial information.

• Much more work needs to be done to understand how best to support on-site inspections that ensure a maximum contribution to effective arms control. Little is known, for example, about the human factors that affect inspector performance and relatively little has been done to develop technologies that can support on-site inspections.

Notes

1. For a short introduction of the Allied activities after World War I see Fred Tanner (ed.), *From Versailles to Baghdad: Post-War Armament Control of Defeated States*, United Nations Institute for Disarmament Research, Geneva, 1992.

2. I would like to thank a colleague, Patricia McFate of SAIC, for emphasizing the importance of this distinction.

3. See, Allan McKnight, *Atomic Safeguards: A Study in International Verification*, New York: United Nations Institute for Training and Research, 1971 and Lawrence Scheinman, *The International Atomic Energy Agency and World Nuclear Order*, Washington, D.C.: Resources for the Future, 1987.

4. In the case of the *Convention on the Prohibition of the Development, Production and Stockpiling of Bacteriological (Biological) and Toxin Weapons and on Their Destruction* [more widely know as the Biological Weapons

Convention], the combined impact of the technical difficulties of obtaining verification and the certainty that one party intended to continue violating the Treaty's provisions resulted in the adoption of an arrangement without any verification provisions.

5. While it is at least theoretically possible that one agreement can embody more than one verification environment, the experience of the IAEA/NPT safeguards would argue that this is very difficult. Various proposals have been made over the years for differing levels of rigor in the safeguards applied to a State according to the likelihood that it might violate the NPT, but they have all floundered on the shoals of demands for equality of treatment among States. Also much of the tension between the IAEA and the UN Special Commission for Iraq (UNSCOM) over the inspection process being imposed in Iraq grew out of the extent to which these procedures fundamentally conflicted with the operating premises and modalities of IAEA/NPT safeguards.

6. Much of the tension that has tended to crop up between the IAEA and UNSCOM are rooted in the multiple missions of the IAEA—both promoter of nuclear energy and enforcer of safety and safeguard norms—and the fact that the IAEA could not be exclusively focused on Iraq. The IAEA had to worry as to whether inspection techniques pioneered in Iraq would be seen as appropriate for other countries and how those countries might react to such a prospect.

Preventive Approaches:
The MTRC Regime

Janne E. Nolan

Efforts to control the proliferation of proscribed military technology have traditionally centered on protectionist instruments imposed by advanced nations on smaller states.[1] The Missile Technology Control Regime, for example, an industrial country supplier cartel to restrict missile technology exports to the Third World, is the centerpiece of the current efforts to stop the spread of ballistic and cruise missiles.[2] The main premise underlying this approach is that industrial nations can still exert decisive influence over developing countries' military programs by imposing controls on the international flow of technology.

Such efforts have been increasingly criticized by some Third World nations as discriminatory, based on the perception that such regimes leave developing countries vulnerable to economic and political manipulation with no demonstrable pay-off. The idea that industrial countries can still exert meaningful control over developing countries' technology acquisitions, moreover, also is being tested by the increased sophistication of Third World defense industrial bases, the growing availability of dual-use technologies globally, and the demise of institutionalized export control arrangements such as the Coordinating Committee for Multilateral Export Controls (COCOM).

Dr. Janne E. Nolan is a Senior Fellow at the Brookings Institution and an Adjunct Professor at Georgetown University. She served in the Executive Branch during the Carter Administration in the U.S. Arms Control and Disarmament Agency and was a delegate to the U.S.-Soviet negotiations on arms transfers limitations. Dr. Nolan holds Ph.D. and Masters degrees from the Fletcher School of Law and Diplomacy at Tufts University and a B.A. from Antioch College.

The following analyzes how the MTCR currently operates to stem the flow of missile-related technologies, the implications of the regime's strengths and weaknesses for overall counterproliferation policy, and alternative ways in which this regime might be improved.[3]

The Control of Missiles

Ballistic missiles traditionally have been singled out in the United States for more stringent export control than is applied to other technologies, including high performance aircraft and naval platforms, in part because of the linkage between nuclear proliferation and advanced missile delivery capabilities.   Surface-to-surface missiles were discussed as possible candidate systems for bilateral export restraint in the U.S.-Soviet Conventional Arms Transfer negotiations during the Carter Administration, for example, and both the United States and the Soviet Union observed tacit restraint in transferring long-range missiles to allies in Korea and the Middle East throughout the 1960s and 1970s.

U.S. policy has been particularly stringent with regard to sales of potentially nuclear capable surface-to-surface missiles or related technology to any countries outside of NATO and Japan. Although Israel received the Lance missile, for instance, its request to purchase the Pershing Ia intermediate-range missile in the early 1970s was denied. The U.S. also discouraged Indian efforts to acquire the U.S. Scout space launch vehicle for its civilian space program in 1965, recognizing that it could have military applications. The U.S. did permit the sale of the Nike-Hercules surface-to-air missile to Taiwan and South Korea, which led to South Korea's successful conversion of this system to a surface-to-surface configuration despite strict end-use assurances from the Korean government.

The Soviet Union, for its part, transferred hundreds of SCUD-B ballistic missiles to its clients in the Third World beginning in the 1970s, and provided Syria with the more advanced SS-21 ballistic missile. European suppliers also have proven quite permissive about missile-related exports, including missile systems, space launch vehicles (SLV), and associated manufacturing technologies. French assistance helped Israel to build the Jericho I in the 1960s, and there have been numerous European programs to assist states with the development and production of SLVs, such as the provision of the French Mammoth propulsion system for production by Pakistan and India. European commercial ventures have been vital to missile programs in India, Brazil, Israel, Argentina, Iraq, and even Libya. In furtherance of traditional U.S. policy, President Ronald Reagan signed National Security Decision Directive (NSDD)-70 in November 1982, calling for the investigation of ways to control missile proliferation. This led to agreement among seven industrial countries to establish consensual restraint guidelines for missile-related exports, formalized as the Missile Technology Control Regime in April 1987. Over time and particularly after Operation Desert Storm, the restraint of missiles has become a far more central element of the international diplomatic agenda, on a par with the international nuclear non-proliferation regime, efforts to control chemical weapons, and discussions with key states about ways to contain regional military tensions. The regime now has a total of twenty-five members.

Prior to the initiation of the MTCR in 1987, there was no formal international apparatus to guide transfers of conventional technologies to developing countries. Given the history of failed efforts to craft even modest agreements to control conventional arms sales, the MTCR is a significant achievement. Judging from the experience of developing "trigger lists" for restricted equipment in nuclear non-proliferation efforts, which has always proven highly contentious domestically and internationally, the MTCR also should be seen as a triumph of unusual technical consensus. Those who crafted the regime have gone a long way in identifying the inputs which can contribute to missile development, and in securing agreement from twenty-five countries about guidelines to control their dissemination. The MTCR also has helped to pinpoint the most difficult aspects of missile design and target these for special scrutiny. Guidance technology is generally agreed to be the most important "enabling" technology for countries aspiring to develop missiles.

The MTCR led to the development of a new bureaucratic infrastructure for monitoring one aspect of North-South missile technology flows, and to try to understand the synergism among particular dual-use technologies which, added together, could augment missile production capabilities.[4] The MTCR already has had some success in impeding missile programs. It is credited with helping to stop the Argentinean-Egyptian-Iraqi CONDOR II program, delaying although not prohibiting Chinese sales of the M-series of missiles, encouraging the cancellation of two Brazilian missile systems, and forcing the German government to crack down on private firms engaged in missile development efforts in Libya and Iraq.

Developing a missile technology export dialogue with the former Soviet Union has been particularly important now that industrial production in the former Soviet bloc is no longer dominated by centralized, state-run enterprises. Governments are facing the difficult task of developing domestic guidelines and enforcement mechanisms to monitor their newly commercial activities. Liberalized trade between East and West could have serious implications for developing countries' access to technology. Given the high level of export dependency among most industrial countries, the easing of trade barriers among developed nations could significantly raise the level and volume of missile technology available for purchase globally if not monitored cooperatively.

Constraints on the Effectiveness of the MTCR

Unlike agreements in the nuclear area, such as the London Suppliers' Group, the MTCR has no international agency to monitor compliance, no enforcement mechanisms, and no institutionalized arrangements for regular meetings among participants. Despite its modest scope, the MTCR has nevertheless been mired in some serious disputes over its implementation virtually since its inception.[5]

There are four major elements of the MTCR which have given rise to controversies since 1987. First is the question of civilian space cooperation and what is and is not considered permissible under MTCR guidelines. Although the text of the MTCR states specifically that it is not designed to interfere with "legitimate" space programs, the agreement also states that such efforts cannot be associated with the development of weapon delivery capabilities. Since many of the technologies for space launch vehicles and ballistic missiles are virtually indistinguishable, determining what is precluded for export is inherently difficult and contentious.

Given the political sensitivity of a supplier cartel among developing countries, some ambiguity may be a virtue. No supplying government wants to state outright that Third World space ventures are wholly illegitimate, and some flexibility in the application of guidelines is needed to accommodate differences among sovereign countries.[6]

Still, the ambiguity about controlled technologies raises the related question of national obligations imposed as a result of signing the MTCR. From its inception, the regime was designed to be consensual, with participating governments interpreting and adapting guidelines as part of national export codes. The MTCR was not intended to override national policy but rather to leave it to individual states to provide assurances about the destination and intended uses of technology exports. France's proposed sale to Brazil of liquid-fuel motor technology which could be useful for ballistic missile production in the late 1980s, however, provoked intense U.S. opposition. The contract was suspended only after two years of dispute. Similarly, a Russian space enterprise proceeded with a sale of cryogenic and rocket technologies to an Indian company in 1992, prompting the U.S. to invoke mandatory trade sanctions against both entities.[7]

The issue of MTCR enforcement is highly controversial. On the one hand, obvious violations of the MTCR, like China's sale of M-11 series missiles to Pakistan and other publicized disputes over apparent violations of the letter or spirit of the MTCR, damage the credibility of the regime. The lack of binding enforcement authority prompted several pieces of legislation in the U.S. Congress over the last few years imposing punitive measures on countries and companies engaged in MTCR-restricted trade. Although different in the scope and nature of sanctions that could be invoked, these initiatives shared the common view that penalties on MTCR violators must be stiffened, in some cases whether or not the exports in question originate in a country which had signed the agreement. Supporters of sanctions argue that trade restrictions are meaningless if they can be readily circumvented by renegade companies or countries, and that the large powers have the leverage to enforce compliance by threatening penalties which exceed the perceived benefits of violations.[8]

Despite fairly broad bipartisan support in the U.S., some of these provisions have prompted criticism from foreign governments. Imposing trade sanctions on foreign nationals, for example, including denying access to U.S. government contracts and licenses to violators, commits the U.S. to rely on coercive means to persuade states to comply with the MTCR, and thus, it is argued, hinders the regime's ability to elicit the support of additional countries. Japan has tried to avoid the use of sanctions, for example, emphasizing a non-coercive approach to the

MTCR and promoting transparency in international technology trade on behalf of non-proliferation norms.

A third area of discussion is the relative priority governments will give to national and international regulatory mechanisms for stemming missile proliferation as compared to countermilitary responses, such as promoting anti-tactical ballistic missile programs for key allies or even deploying strategic defenses nationally. Although these instruments are not mutually exclusive, they represent different approaches to the problem which may not necessarily be politically or bureaucratically compatible in the long-term.[9] Decisions to transfer ATBM technology, for example, will have to take into account the potential for diversion of ATBM technology to offensive missile programs in certain countries, as well as the possibility that deployments of defensive systems could exacerbate regional military rivalries.

Finally, a fundamental weakness of the MTCR is the relatively small number of adherents. Eliciting enduring support for the MTCR is hindered by the absence of a common perception of the risks posed by missile proliferation or the benefits to be derived from membership in the cartel. Leaving aside opposition from states which perceive it as discriminatory, the MTCR still lacks a publicly compelling rationale. As Joseph Nye has argued, the regime has inherently limited legitimacy because ballistic missiles, unlike nuclear or chemical weapons, are not widely perceived to carry "a moral stigma."[10]

Improving the Regime

The states which retain a margin of control over sensitive technologies can influence demand by raising the financial and political costs of their acquisition, and thus dissuading states from proceeding with problematic military programs. There is little question that technology eventually will proliferate to countries which are determined to achieve certain military capabilities. But the capability to produce and launch advanced missiles is still centered in a handful of nations, even if additional states, including rogue countries such as North Korea, are beginning to produce such goods and may in time be able to undercut the current market hierarchy.

Trade restrictions can only delay this process and buy time to devise ways for better managing the potential risks posed by the diffusion of advanced weapon technologies. There are a number of ways the MTCR might be strengthened. Three priorities include expanding membership by enhancing the incentives to join, shifting the emphasis of the regime from supply side controls to more liberalized trade based on safeguards, and defining control guidelines more clearly.

One avenue for enhancing incentives to adhere to the MTCR is to grant states wider access to technology in return for agreements to submit to inspections aimed at preventing diversion of technologies to proscribed ends. This would require established verification procedures and a system safeguards to monitor the disposition of technology, including on-site inspections. There are already some modest precedents for this under the MTCR. In the case of Argentina, for example, the U.S. inspected missile production facilities to verify that Argentina had in fact lived up to its pledge to terminate its missile development program.[11] In another instance, the Indians and Russians jointly agreed to allow on-site inspections of the cryogenic rocket engine technology slated for sale to India to demonstrate that it was intended strictly for a peaceful space launch program, although the U.S. did not respond favorably to the offer.[12]

The latter case demonstrates the need for better instruments to monitor MTCR compliance. Had the MTCR contained established procedures for inspections, the dispute over the Indian-Russian contract could have been resolved with far less tension and controversy. Whatever the merits of the intended sale, the way in which it was actually managed instead reinforced a perception among Russians and Indians that the United States' objections were economically motivated and wholly self-serving. Rightly or wrongly, the legitimacy of the regime was put into question.

In the current international political environment, an effort to broaden the MTCR into an international treaty seems for now quixotic. It would founder on objections by developing countries about its discriminatory nature, and from the difficulties of making the case that ballistic missiles are worthy of universal controls even though other delivery vehicles, such as advanced aircraft, are not. To the degree that the MTCR has been successful, in fact, its success has derived from the regime's modest and consensual nature, and from the fact that it was negotiated out of the glare of the international spotlight.

But there are important similarities between a space cooperation treaty aimed at stemming missile diffusion and other non-proliferation regimes, such as the chemical weapons convention, making the possibility of such an agreement, however remote, worthy of further examination. In all areas of non-proliferation policy, there is general consensus that militarily-related technologies should be controlled but that peaceful uses should be encouraged. In the case of chemical or biological technologies, the key challenge is to identify relevant inputs and materials and target these for scrutiny without harming free commerce in legitimate items. If countries could be persuaded that involvement in an international space regime, as such, brought with it guarantees of needed technology and the potential for greater security, it might be possible to persuade some states to join in.[13]

The difficulties of distinguishing between military and non- military space technologies may seem overwhelming, but similar challenges have plagued the CWC for years. Most chemical products and production processes have both civilian and military applications. It has been agreed among the parties to the treaty, however, that it will be possible to institutionalize safeguards against targeted technologies, and to protect against diversion from civilian to military purposes through monitoring and on-site inspection. The experience in the nuclear area suggests that safeguards have never been completely successful, but major reforms and advancement in inspection techniques suggest they may become more effective in the coming years.

It is not inconceivable that a system of international safeguards could be developed as part of a space cooperation regime, with states permitting on-site inspections of space facilities in return for satellite data, launch services and other forms of technology access. An agency comprised of multinational inspectors, like the IAEA used for nuclear proliferation, could serve as the umbrella organization to conduct international inspections and verify compliance with the agreement.

There would be several, potentially intractable problems. The degree to which countries would be willing to forgo efforts to acquire independent space launch capabilities would depend in part on the degree of concessionary assistance given to them by advanced countries. Given the problems faced by space industries in the developed nations, such subsidies are difficult to envision. More importantly, every developing country which currently has a space program also has a missile program, and these states may not want to abandon their ambitions to be freed of great power control. An agreement on space activities, moreover, would not address other, equally vital channels of missile-related technology diffusion.

Still, consideration should be given to elevating a missile and other proscribed military trade regime to the status of an international agency, even if membership remains strictly consensual. Such an apparatus could serve as the source of expertise to anticipate the kinds of futuristic technology transfers which could have adverse consequences for global stability, such as precision-strike systems, biotechnologies, or anti-satellite systems, and to try to manage their dissemination in a more structured way.

In addition, members could make a concerted effort to share technical expertise on devising national export laws and other regulation and enforcement mechanisms with other states. The MTCR is already a potential mechanism useful for conducting stricter oversight of the end-use and end-user of dual-use exports. The U.S. has long been actively engaged in exchanging information with other MTCR members about monitoring exports, including trying to elicit support from China, North Korea, Argentina, Brazil and the republics of the former Soviet Union—albeit with mixed success. In principle, the lists of controlled items compiled for the MTCR could in time also be the basis for a more comprehensive approach to North-South technology diffusion, were there political support for such an objective. The demise of COCOM, with no successor institution yet in place, suggests no immediate prospects for such a development. Still, there is sufficient flexibility in the existing MTCR guidelines to include new kinds of high risk technologies which may become more widely available in coming years in a safeguards regime, including equipment pertinent to warhead design, improvements in missile accuracy and range, targeting capabilities, and anti-satellite operations.[14]

With the exception of a relatively few categories of items which could be restricted *a priori*, such as advanced guidance technologies, decisions about what constitutes sensitive technologies will increasingly have to be more sensitive to the specific conditions in recipient states, including relative industrial capabilities, local or regional enmities, other military forces, and overall foreign policy objectives.

The sheer complexity of the international technology market, with its vast networks of legal and illegal suppliers, already are overwhelming the modest resources available in government to track technological developments and to develop effective policy instruments. With the growing international commercialization of inputs needed for modern weapon production, far greater cooperation between industry and government may be necessary simply to identify technologies deemed vital to security. As the European countries move to rationalize their high technology industries by melding commercial and defense activities, for instance, industry will have to play a larger role to ensure the security of defense-related innovations.

This kind of cooperation may be especially important in cases involving information technology, an area which has become a central factor in a wide range of advanced military missions, including command and control, intelligence, targeting, and guidance. Absent joint industry and government support, any technology regime could be readily subverted by commercial exploitation of market opportunities if undertaken without adequate consideration of the collective security interests of other industrialized states. The U.S. has already undertaken sweeping export control liberalization for many sensitive technologies, largely without formal advance consideration of safeguards.[15] Future policies will need to take the proliferation implications of trade liberalization far more into account.

As the industrial countries move to greater integration of their defense industrial sectors, they will have to forge common agreements about the disposition and security of their shared technologies. Defense companies will have a direct interest in these agreements. Industry participation and support for such arrangements may be necessary both to help compile information about sources of technology and to help design and implement workable security safeguards which do not interfere unduly with desirable private enterprise.

A practical model for government-industry cooperation might be found in the area of chemical weapons. The Chemical Manufacturers Association, whose member account for almost ninety percent of all chemical production in the U.S., has been an active participant in devising the terms and mechanisms of a treaty to ban chemical weapons. Without the assistance of industry, it is safe to say that there would not have been the requisite resources and expertise to identify the thousands of items relevant to chemical weapons production and where they are produced, nor to evaluate the risks and benefits of alternative approaches to treaty limitations and their verification.

The chemical producers model may be particularly apt for the space industry. Commercial interests involved in promoting peaceful space cooperation have the most to lose from international opprobrium about the diversion of space technology for ballistic missiles or other offensive military uses. It may be in the immediate self-interest of such companies to assist governments to restrain missile programs in problematic states, by helping to identify relevant technological inputs needed for missile development and in devising safeguards which can discourage the adaptation of civilian equipment for military programs. Although some might see this as undue encroachment on sovereignty, this is one area in which a few suppliers still do have the leverage to influence the pace and content of space-related production programs.

Enforcing the MTCR may also require greater intelligence resources than are currently dedicated to this objective. Improved intelligence capabilities could help enforcement by shifting the emphasis of restraint policies towards prevention of proliferation, rather than the more demanding process of inflicting punishment after the fact. This is an important issue which should be raised with allies, in order to establish procedures for pooling intelligence assets. The economic and defense integration of Europe, along with the declining demands of East-West defense, may make this kind of collaboration easier in the future.

Whether the industrial countries are prepared to offer client states incentives for their forbearance in missile acquisition, and, if so, what kind, is another unresolved question. Agencies with responsibilities for international debt management and other concessionary transactions need to be brought into the policy process to see if there may be ways to link financial incentives to desirable military restraints. At a minimum, the policies of the international lending agencies, such as the World Bank and the International Development Agency, should be reviewed to ensure that their assessments of countries' eligibility for credits and loans take into account the influence of the military sector, including the nature and relative burden of weapon development and production programs.

Conclusion

As important a challenge as controlling missiles is finding the means to anticipate future technological change which could have even more pronounced effects on international security, including the diffusion of new generations of weapons such as precision strike systems. A more focussed strategy for managing the missile trade could help begin to address several such security challenges, identifying futuristic technologies whose significance to national security warrant efforts to protect them from market forces and encouraging accommodations among adversarial states to contain the demand for advanced weapons.[16]

The MTCR has been plagued by its image as an idealistic arms control initiative designed to save the Third World from itself, rather than a prudent gesture to stem the deterioration of military environments. Although it should be obvious, it perhaps needs to be reiterated that countries have abided by export restraints in the past because of an interest in containing military developments in areas in which their own interests might be placed at risk. This may not be an argument which wins supporters in developing countries, but it does have the virtue of reflecting the pragmatic self-interests embodied in the MTCR for industrial states.

In the future, alternative policy options to address the problems posed by missile proliferation will have to recognize the extent to which missile proliferation is already deeply rooted in international politics, and, as such, may not be seriously attenuated by selective supplier controls. The very limited number of examples of conscious military restraint among developing countries, including regional agreements such as the Treaty for the Prohibition of Nuclear Weapons in Latin America, does not inspire great optimism for restraint regimes which elicit the support of recipients. But no such system of international controls has ever been fully articulated, or been deemed a sufficient international priority to warrant concerted negotiations among governments.

In the immediate future, the MTCR could be strengthened by seeking agreement for more formal guidelines, along the lines of the London Suppliers' Group controlling nuclear exports, establishing routine procedures for consultation among participants, sharing intelligence, and developing durable international norms for broader areas of technology diffusion. To be credible, such a regime must be adhered to by a larger group of nations, and need to elicit the support of developing, as well as developed states. The majority of existing proposals for international agreements to control weapon technologies tend to reflect a great power bias, often with little sensitivity for the ambitions of developing states to become more equal partners in the international system. Although the larger powers still have some capacity for exerting some leverage over smaller states, the perception of discrimination may become the greatest impediment to achieving more far-reaching cooperative efforts in the coming years.   Building common norms which can elicit genuine international support will require taking the objectives of developing countries seriously, and recognizing that those interests are as enduring as they are diverse.

Notes

1. This paper is adapted from an essay prepared for the U.S.-Japanese Study Group on Arms Control and Non-Proliferation After the Cold War, sponsored by the Carnegie Endowment for International Peace and the International House of Japan.

2. Signed in 1987, the MTCR had seven original members, including the United States, Japan, Canada, France, Germany, Italy and the United Kingdom. By consent, the states agree to abide by prohibitions on the sale of ballistic and cruise missile systems capable of carrying 500 kilograms of payload to a range of 300 kilometers or more. Eleven additional countries, including Austria, Australia, Belgium, Denmark, Finland, Luxembourg, the Netherlands, New Zealand, Norway, Spain and Sweden have joined as formal adherents since 1987. The Soviet Union, Israel and China are not members but have agreed to comply with MTCR strictures. With the breakup of the Soviet Union in late 1991, international efforts were underway to try to induce newly independent republics such as Ukraine and Kazakhstan also to acceded to these norms.

3. The following is adapted from the author's study *Trappings of Power: Ballistic Missiles in the Third World* (Washington, D.C.: Brookings Institution, 1991).

4. The list of restricted technologies was modestly updated and revised in November 1991. See "Missile Technology Control Regime (MTCR) Equipment and Technology Annex," November 4, 1991.

5. For information on specific disputes such as French plans to sell Brazil critical technology that were subsequently thwarted by the threat of U.S. penalties, see Ian Anthony, "Missile Technology Control Regime," in *Arms Export Regulations*, (Oxford: Oxford University Press, 1991), p. 226.

6. The issues of equity and non-discrimination are particularly pronounced in the former Soviet bloc. Ukrainian officials, for example, have explicitly stated that they will reject the missile regime if they are not treated as an equal partner by existing members. Ukraine has expressed concerns about what it perceives to be the propensity of nations to use the MTCR as a protectionist instrument to promote narrow economic interests. See Ozga, *A Chronology*, p. 87.

7. See, for instance, Ian Anthony, "Missile Technology Control Regime," in *Arms Export Regulations*, (Oxford: Oxford University Press, 1991), p. 226.

8. Senator Jeff Bingaman (D-N.M), the principal sponsor of a bill in 1989 to impose sanctions of violators of the MTCR argued that legislation to stem missile proliferation is no different than legislation on behalf of nuclear nonproliferation, including the 1978 Nuclear Non-Proliferation Act. See

Statement of Senator Jeff Bingaman, *National Security Implications of Missile Proliferation*, Hearings before the Senate Committee on Foreign Relations, 101 Congress, 1 sess, (Washington, D.C.: U.S. Government Printing Office, 1989, pp. 34-35.

9. The United States recently proposed two options for Japanese missile defense, primarily as a countermeasure to North Korea's missile capabilities and nuclear program. The U.S. has offered to sell a complete Theater Missile Defense (TMD) system to Japan, but would rather enter into a codevelopment program in which the U.S. would contribute military technologies in exchange for Japanese dual-use technologies that the U.S. could in turn market.

10. Joseph S. Nye, Jr., "Arms Control After the Cold War," *Foreign Affairs*, vol. 68 (Winter 1989-90), p. 60.

11. Ozga, *A Chronology*, p. 86.

12. For more information on the Indian-Russian cryogenic rocket engine deal, see Sanjoy Hazarika, "Moscow Affirms Sale of Technology to India," *New York Times*, May 7, 1992, p. A7.

13. This has led some to advocate the establishment of an international space organization to provides launcher services to countries which do not have their own space programs, or to those willing to abjure diversion of their space investment to military uses.

14. The acquisition of even rudimentary anti-satellite capabilities among a wider number of countries could certainly complicate, if not vitiate, any international agreement to develop a space operations regime or to limit space weapons. Even if the possibility of offensive space activities is still remote, the possession of such systems in additional countries may impose new complications in trying to develop international norms for the management of military space operations. Given its disproportionate reliance on space-based assets for a variety of security objectives, the U.S. has every reason to pay close attention to the global diffusion of space technology.

15. See, for instance, Andy Pasztor and John J. Fialka, "Economy: Export Controls On Computers to be Relaxed," *Wall Street Journal*, September 20, 1993, p. A2.

16. The implications of non-nuclear counterforce capability accorded by precision-guided specialized warheads has been a subject of discussion in U.S. strategy for several years. Unencumbered by the taboos associated with nuclear or chemical weapons, the   proliferation of such systems may be difficult to prevent. The acquisition of such systems could be destabilizing in regional contexts if they accord states with the ability to launch preemptive strikes and encourage aggressive military operations which would otherwise be seen as too risky with nuclear or chemical warheads.

Rethinking U.S. Proliferation Policy for the Future

William C. Martel
William T. Pendley

A Note on Proliferation Choices

ONE OF THE TENETS OF INTERNATIONAL RELATIONS IS THAT states act in accordance with their perception of their interests and power. A state's actions and policies clearly reflect its interpretation of the dangers inherent in the international system and the responses that are necessary to protect the state. A discussion of political choices provides a framework for understanding the forces that motivate states to possess nuclear weapons in the context of global nuclear proliferation.

First, states make the decision to possess nuclear weapons because they are convinced that these weapons will improve their overall security. The history of the Cold War demonstrates that the possession of nuclear weapons directly enhanced the security of the United States, Soviet Union, China, and western European states, principally because the

William C. Martel is Associate Professor of International Relations and Russian Studies in the Department of Regional and Warfare Studies at the Air War College. He received his doctorate from the University of Massachusetts (Amherst) and was a Post-Doctoral Research Fellow and MacArthur Scholar at Harvard University's Center for Science and International Affairs in the Kennedy School of Government and at the Center for International Affairs.

William T. Pendley is Associate Professor of International Relations and Asian Studies in the Department of Regional and Warfare Studies at the Air War College. Prior, he was Deputy Assistant Secretary of Defense for East Asian and Pacific Affairs and served as Acting Assistant Secretary of Defense for International Security Affairs for the Clinton Administration during the transition. He was an officer in the United States Navy for 32 years, retiring as a Rear Admiral.

costs of war were disproportionately higher than the gains. States also understand that nuclear weapons impose fearfully high costs on potential aggressors and equally increase their freedom of maneuver against non-nuclear states.

The implicit theme in U.S. policy has been that most states simply do not have legitimate reasons for possessing nuclear weapons, or at least their reasons are not as legitimate as those that motivated the United States to develop nuclear weapons. While this is not the same as arguing that states have frivolous reasons for nuclear proliferation, this reasoning effectively rejects all incentives for nuclear ownership as contrary to the interests of the states themselves and to the conditions necessary for international security. This political calculation becomes problematic, and undermines the logic behind nonproliferation efforts, once states posit that there are compelling reasons for states to own nuclear arsenals.

Second, the decision to possess nuclear weapons will be taken only after a state's leadership has engaged in a careful and prudent consideration of relevant political, military, and economic factors. States clearly understand that, just as nuclear weapons can reduce reliance on other states and can enhance their security, they also can heighten tensions in a region and increase the chance of war. This is particularly true during the developmental stage of a nuclear weapons program when nuclear weapons have security tradeoffs, including the risk of preemptive attacks, regional hostility, and war. But states that make the decision to possess nuclear weapons do not operate in a strategic on politico-institutional vacuum. They are acutely aware that the presence of nuclear weapons will elicit reactions from regional and global powers.

Third, each state is the best judge of its security interests and the power necessary to protect those interests. The presumption is that states are uniquely qualified to judge their interests, the potential of other states to interfere with those interests, and the ability to defend their interests. The corollary is that foreigners are not capable of judging a state's interests, and thus are not in a position to declare when states should or should not possess nuclear weapons. Because states carefully weigh their power in comparison with that of other states, they are attuned to imbalances that weaken their ability to serve those interests. Nuclear ownership, therefore, constitutes a prudent exercise in balancing their strategic interests with the power they marshal to defend those material interests.

Fourth, the proliferation of nuclear weapons reflects a consensus among the "proliferators" that international security is enhanced by the existence ofthese weapons. States define security on an individual basis, which suggests that the global proliferation of nuclear weapons reflects agreement among many states that nuclear weapons contribute not just to national but international security in a non-bipolar world.

Political Realities and Nuclear Imperatives

There are three changes in international politics that mandate a fundamental change in U.S. policy. First, the number of nuclear weapons states is on the rise.[1] In the last several years, Pakistan, India, and Israel joined the nuclear club not to mention the active efforts of North Korea. Each developed nuclear weapons indigenously or with the direct or indirect support of at least one of the major nuclear powers, and often at costs in the realm of $10-20 billion.

Second, there are instances in which it is difficult for the United States to prevent further cases of nuclear proliferation unless military intervention is envisioned. While the cornerstone of U.S. nonproliferation policy during the last several decades was to prevent the spread of nuclear weapons, this policy is fundamentally at odds with the established reality that states increasingly have the wherewithal to develop nuclear weapons on their own. Iran, Iraq, North Korea, Pakistan, India, Israel, South Africa, and others demonstrated that middle-range powers can develop nuclear weapons if they exercise the determination to do so.

Third, the international mechanisms for controlling nuclear weapons technologies, principally export controls and nuclear regulatory regimes such as the NPT[2] and IAEA[3], no longer are sufficient to prevent all nuclear proliferation. Iraq was developing nuclear weapons while it was under inspection by the IAEA as a signatory to the NPT. North Korea also pursued its weapons development program as a signatory to the NPT. Only recently the IAEA dismissed reports about a secret Iranian nuclear program after it conducted inspections of selected nuclear facilities in Iran.[4]

The evidence is that the normal instruments for controlling access to nuclear technologies and materials are grossly inadequate for preventing states from developing nuclear weapons.

Rethinking U.S. Policy

The fundamental problem with U.S. proliferation policy, however, is that it is at odds with these principles of state behavior. To be frank, neither the United States nor any other state is in a position to condemn another state's decision to possess nuclear weapons. Yet, U.S. policy has precisely this effect when it declares that non-nuclear states are not entitled to possess nuclear weapons. The philosophical foundation of U.S. policy operates on the assumption that the United States is best suited to judge the merits of a state's decision to "go nuclear." But this study argues that the United States faces the challenge of mutual security in an era in which nuclear-armed states must coexist with one another without the umbrella of Cold War institutions and policies. If U.S. policy creates a situation where stability is preserved among all nuclear powers, then such a world corresponds with its long-term interest in security. The crux of the problem is for the United States to learn to deal with the new nuclear states as the path to building a stable political order.

In the face of evidence that ten to twenty states believe that the possession of nuclear weapons offers greater security than conventional forces alone, the policy of the United States needs to be aligned more precisely with the broad security interests of these states. While U.S. efforts during the Cold War to control proliferation were largely successful, U.S. policy is bound to fail because it runs directly counter to the growing consensus among states which believe, rightly or wrongly, that nuclear weapons enhance their security. North Korea's behavior provides vivid evidence of a stunning reproach of the United States for the continuing failures in its proliferation policy.

There is a tendency for states to follow policies that were established in earlier times for reasons that include the overwhelming weight of bureacratic inertia and political convenience.

While there are occasions that justify adherence to traditional policies, there are other times when the past is not a sufficient guide to action in the future. It is time to re-examine the core beliefs that define the role of nuclear weapons in international security. This study argues that U.S. proliferation policy is a clear candidate for reexamination.

The Clinton Administration defines preventing proliferation as one of six priorities for American foreign policy, and argues that the United States has an obligation to resist proliferation, as the daily struggles since 1991 with Ukraine and North Korea demonstrate. The problem is that

U.S. proliferation policy is still committed to essentially the same principles that governed U.S. actions for decades, despite their growing irrelevance in the 1990s. U.S. policy must be tailored to fit the new strategic reality of the late twentieth century, as underscored by the inability of the United States to prevent proliferation short of extraordinary measures, including intervention.

The aim of this study is to articulate a new framework for the United States as it reshapes nuclear proliferation policy in the closing years of the twentieth century. The United States must strike a balance between the aspirations of states that deem the possession of nuclear weapons to be in their national interests, and the U.S. interest in shaping an international order that is consistent with its interest in the preservation of political, economic, and military security.

Toward New Thinking on Nuclear Proliferation

Rethinking U.S. Interests and Policy

Several decades of policymakers defined and conducted policy on the basis of the proposition that any proliferation of nuclear weapons was inimical to U.S. interests. The argument was that additional nuclear powers meant a concomitant increase in the probability of nuclear war. Thus, it followed that restraining the number of nuclear powers would decrease the danger of nuclear war.

The United States invested considerable resources in attempts to limit the number of states as nuclear signatories of the Nuclear Nonproliferation Treaty, which included the United States, Soviet Union, France, Britain, and later, China.[5] The United States also availed itself of various international regimes to enforce the ban on the spread of nuclear technologies and materials and the means to deliver such weapons.

This policy was sensible and effective for three reasons. The first was the reasonable expectation that the process of nuclear proliferation could be contained, largely because of the great economic and technological cost associated with the early development of nuclear weapons. Very few states, the proliferation community reasoned, could marshall the resources necessary to build nuclear weapons. The second reason was that the

United States and the Soviet Union provided tight security guarantees for many states.   Any transgressor against states was unlikely given the superpowers' tightly circumscribed areas of interest. States reasoned that an attack against them would bring the wrath of the superpowers upon the transgressor. The third was the escalatory danger posed by nuclear weapons in a tight bipolar world, in particular the fear that nuclear weapons in the hands of regional powers could provoke a "catalytic" nuclear war between the superpowers.[6] Indeed, these escalatory dangers still exist between regional nuclear powers.

In effect, U.S. proliferation policy was sound because it flowed from two sensible propositions about its ability to contain nuclear technologies. U.S. policy, therefore, was consistent with the ability of the United States to prevent the spread of nuclear weapons.   It was also a policy that fundamentally supported international stability during the Cold War that existed for nearly fifty years. But this reality no longer exists.

U.S. Power to Control Proliferation is Limited

The ability to control nuclear proliferation is limited, as states amass the scientific, technological, and economic wherewithal to develop nuclear weapons in direct opposition to the best efforts of the international community to prevent it.[7] The experience of Iraq, until the 1991 Persian Gulf War and subsequent United Nations special inspections, demonstrates that a determined and rich state can assemble the technological complex needed to develop nuclear weapons.

Neither the United States nor the international community has the ability to prevent these efforts if a state decides that the possession of nuclear weapons serves its national interests.   The examples of Israel,India, and Pakistan exemplify the condition in which the rhetoric of nonproliferation policy is not consonant with the existence of indigenous nuclear programs. This is true for three reasons.

First, nuclear weapons technologies have existed for nearly fifty years, which means that the requisite scientific talent can be assembled by states that possess sufficient resources. There are more than enough physicists and engineers who understand nuclear physics to assemble nuclear weapons. Second, states determined to develop nuclear weapons can circumvent IAEA controls established by the Nonproliferation Treaty to control the fissile materials produced by civilian nuclear facilities. In the case of Iraq, it produced fissile material in calcutrons, while South

Africa produced fissile materials in civilian research reactors which they had not declared to the IAEA. Both cases of nuclear development occurred under the eyes of IAEA inspectors. Third, the collapse of the former Soviet Union raises the inevitable prospect of a flood of fissile materials, scientists, and possibly nuclear weapons to states desirous of possessing nuclear weapons.

The emerging reality is that the United States simply cannot prevent all cases of nuclear proliferation, but this raises the question of why the United States continues to declare that nuclear nonproliferation is a vital national interest when the ability to stop the spread of nuclear weapons is limited. More worrisome still is the prevalence of old thinking about nuclear proliferation in the United States, as exemplified by discussions about nonproliferation.

States See Value in Nuclear Weapons

The behavior of states in recent years suggests that many believe that nuclear weapons have immense security value. The rush by North Korea and Iran to possess nuclear weapons underlines the point that nuclear weapons have value for these states. The immense cost and risk associated with nuclear proliferation is more than most states would accept, unless those states believed that nuclear weapons would make a significant contribution to their security.

The decision to possess nuclear weapons, once shorn of theoretical arguments, is largely driven by the belief that nuclear weapons offer security. The ability to threaten devastating retaliation unmatched by conventional forces and alliances offers an unparalleled measure of security. This is precisely the experience of the United States, Soviet Union, China, and their respective allies, when states believed that nuclear weapons enhanced security because they increased the costs of war. The United States found security in nuclear weapons, and so too do others. Of course, the United States found insecurity when certain states acquired nuclear weapons, and so it attempted with considerable success to curb the spread of nuclear weapons.

What remains perplexing is the dogma surrounding nuclear weapons. An axiom of U.S. proliferation policy is that nuclear weapons are unacceptable for states which do not currently possess them or, more accurately, for states that are not closely allied with the United States. While ultimately accepting nuclear ownership for the permanent members of the United Nations Security Council, the U.S. has really only been comfortable with proliferation in states with whom we have a special relationship such as Britain at the end of World War II and Israel in the 1970s.

The developed states appear to believe that only certain states can be trusted with nuclear weapons, and that all the rest are suspect in this regard. Yet states continue to behave in ways that contradict this belief, particularly when they look the other way in certain cases of proliferation. As long as U.S. thinking reflects the view that nuclear weapons should be possessed only by the states that already possess them, it severely weakens U.S. leverage in the politics of nuclear proliferation. A discriminatory policy that accepts the "Haves" but rejects all "Have-Nots" will not be effective, supportable, or credible in the evolving international security environment. The ideal solution was to favor the spread of nuclear weapons to U.S. friends and allies only, but this solution is no longer relevant in a world in which the United States cannot control the process of nuclear proliferation.

The United States has an extremely limited ability to influence the interests of states that are contemplating the development of nuclear weapons. For now, the message is a discriminatory one that specifies who may, and may not, possess nuclear weapons. Worse, the United States has the tendency to elevate the importance of nuclear weapons in its diplomatic strategy by the constant fixation on nonproliferation. The central emphasis in U.S.-North Korean relations in 1994 on whether North Korea should possess nuclear weapons elevates the value of nuclear weapons. When the United States issues condemnations against North Korea, it focuses attention on the importance of nuclear weapons. This has the effect of reinforcing the role of nuclear weapons, when a policy of denuclearization should strive to minimize their role by demonstrating that nuclear weapons are not the essential measure of power.

The proper theme in U.S. policy should be nuclear weapons have obvious security value for states. Because the objective is to de-emphasize the importance of nuclear weapons, U.S. policy ought to curtail severely the rhetoric about nuclear proliferation. If the United States and other states believe nuclear weapons have security value, then other states will follow suit. If the hope is to reduce the role of nuclear weapons, then the United States must shape a policy that lessens the importance attached to nuclear weapons. For now, U.S. rhetoric has little impact on the process by which states judge whether the value and cost of nuclear weapons is consistent with their interests.

A circumspect policy regarding the possession of nuclear weapons will be more credible to states that attach security to the possession of nuclear weapons. For now, the fixation in U.S. proliferation policy on prevention strengthens the case of the proponents of the argument that nuclear weapons are needed to counteract the power of the United States. As the Indian Army Chief of Staff General K. Sundarji observed, "The lesson of Desert Storm is don't mess with the United States without nuclear weapons." Indeed, the current emphasis in U.S. policy on nonproliferation elevates the role of nuclear weapons at a time when the United States hopes to achieve precisely the opposite effect.

Rethinking Security in a Proliferated World

The present formulation of U.S. policy is that the process of nuclear proliferation jeopardizes international security. The corollary is that there must be widespread efforts to avert further proliferation, as indicated by Secretary of State Warren Christopher's statement that nuclear proliferation is one of the six priorities of American foreign policy.There are several factors that strengthen the alternative concept that some cases of nuclear proliferation reinforce international security.

First, the process of nuclear proliferation over the last two decades, as Israel, India, Pakistan, and South Africa (albeit temporarily) joined the nuclear club, did not demonstrably diminish international security. Fortunately, there have not been any nuclear wars among these states. In the case of the sub-continent, there is no empirical evidence that nuclear proliferation destabilized the situation. On the contrary, the de-escalation of the crisis in the spring of 1990 between India and Pakistan probably was the result of mutual fears of nuclear war. The concomitant increase in the risks of confrontation for these states corresponds with the onset of simple nuclear deterrence. Just as the United States and Soviet Union experienced inhibitions on their actions because of the existence of nuclear weapons, the same probably is true for these states. The inhibitions imposed on states by nuclear weapons are not demonstrably different from the pressures that increased the stability of regional politics in the aftermath of World War II.

Second, the prohibitions on nuclear proliferation are a shibboleth of the past. During the Cold War, the addition of nuclear powers complicated the alliances of the superpowers because the escalation of regional conflicts threatened to engulf the world in a nuclear conflagration. But with the relaxation of the superpowers no-longer overlapping spheres of interest, nuclear proliferation can offer the benefits of greater security.

The time is right to re-examine the proposition that every case of nuclear proliferation leads to instability and is inimical to U.S. interests. At its core, this principle reflects the belief that only current nuclear weapons states and, more narrowly, the victorious states of World War II, as permanent members of the UN Security Council, are entitled to possess nuclear weapons. The reality is that the first generation of nuclear powers was not willing to renounce the possession of atomic arms. Therefore, the powerful states attempted to keep a monopoly on nuclear weapons and reduce threats to themselves and, perhaps, certain regions. There is nothing wrong with major powers seeking to protect their own interests.

While neither historical evidence nor detailed analysis is cited to support the assertion that more nuclear weapons states are destabilizing, this assumption is deeply ingrained in the underlying philosophy of proliferation. The United States has a unique historical opportunity to consider how to enhance stability among states that possess nuclear weapons. The moment is right to rethink U.S. policy, largely because this new policy would match the realities of nuclear proliferation in the 1990s with the evolving international security environment. This is the proper time to rethink the notion of stability in a multi-nuclear world.

Reorienting the basic philosophy behind U.S. proliferation policy poses significant intellectual and emotional challenges. Those who have devoted time and energy to preventing proliferation will find the notion that nuclear proliferation is largely beyond control a counter-intuitive exercise in heresy. A new policy for proliferation will involve radical changes in the beliefs that govern nuclear proliferation, and alter the fundamental conduct of the proliferation "business."

Reshaping Perceptions About Proliferation

There are three separate steps that the United States should take to redefine the old thinking about the nature of stability in a multi-nuclear world.

The first involves the thinking of the governmental, academic, and research communities. Nuclear proliferation specialists need to broaden their thinking about the terms of stability in a world in which ten or twenty nuclear powers, rather than the eight or so that exist in the mid 1990s, is the norm. The terms of reference in proliferation have been the use of all available peaceful mechanisms to avert the spread of nuclear weapons, despite growing skepticism about the ability to achieve this objective. This belief has a pernicious effect on the basic design and function of the governments and international regimes that seek to restrain the spread of nuclear weapons. By contrast, there is a need to concentrate on the nature of coexistence in a stable global security system consisting of 10 or even 20 nuclear weapons states. The United States has learned to coexist with the current members of the nuclear club, but has not learned to institutionalize policies for encouraging nuclear-armed states to abort their behavior in ways that reinforce regional or global stability.

Second, the structure and function of various international regimes responsible for controlling proliferation are necessarily obsolete.[8] Before there is an effort to reorganize these institutions, such as the IAEA, there has to be a consensus on the fundamental objective of nuclear proliferation policy and the support these institutions can provide to that policy. The roles of non-proliferation institutions must be consistent with their capabilities and objectives if their credibility is to be preserved. The United States is uniquely positioned to begin a debate that leads to a reorganization of the institutions whose purpose is to create stability where none may exist. The LAEA has this role, but remains a vestige of the near-absolute restrictions on nuclear ownership that emerged from the Cold War.

Third, the United States cannot accomplish this fundamental change in beliefs about proliferation without a vigorous and sustained public discussion on the matter. There must be deeper public support before a new policy can be put in place. For nearly half a century, the public debate in the United States and among the developed states reflected a reflexive fixation on the destabilizing effects of proliferation.   The developed states must craft a policy that balances the contemporary reality of proliferation, which is that not all states which possess nuclear weapons necessarily will be a force for instability, while taking the necessary steps to build coexistence in a safer and more stable world of multiple nuclear states.

The thrust of U.S. policy must be to build a consensus smong the constituents on the desirability and practicality of new approaches to nuclear proliferation.   When proliferation occurs despite policies of blanket opposition by major states and international institutions, it undermines the credibility of all efforts and policies to shape a stable world of coexistence among nuclear powers.

Nuclear-Free States can be Major Powers

There are several impediments to changing perceptions about the purpose behind proliferation policy.   In addition to political and bureaucratic obstacles within governments and societies, a significant impediment involves the perception that major-power status is defined by the possession of nuclear weapons.

To deny that nuclear weapons strengthen the security, power, and status of states raises the question whether nuclear-free states can be major powers in the current international system.   It is possible for non-nuclear states to be major powers, even though the current emphasis of nuclear proliferation policy creates the opposite impression.   Germany and Japan exemplify the cases of major powers that do not possess nuclear weapons.

The emphasis on preventing nuclear proliferation has the unintended consequence of enhancing the value of nuclear weapons.   To engage in protracted policy debates about preventing North Korea from possessing nuclear weapons reinforces the message that nuclear weapons are an important determinant of national power and prestige. If nuclear weapons were not significant, then by definition the United States and others would not expend so much political capital on nuclear proliferation. The tone of international rhetoric about proliferation leads states to infer that the United States believes nuclear weapons are significant.

This argues that the United States should aspire to create the opposite impression, that one's status as a major power is derived from nuclear ownership.   Germany and Japan illustrate the case of states that have

enormously powerful economies and exercise considerable influence in
Europe and Asia, respectively. Each state clearly possesses the ability to
produce nuclear weapons, and yet each chose to forego nuclear weapons
for its own reasons.[9] Because neither state is a global military power,
and each relies on the U.S. security guarantee and nuclear umbrella, each
state can afford to be militarily weak and non-nuclear. Under these
terms, their actions implicitly support the view that their status as major
powers is secure by their non-nuclear status. While both states are
members of the Group of Seven industrial nations (G-7), their status as
major powers is diminished somewhat by the absence from the permanent
membership of the UN Security Council.The presence of nuclear weapons
states on the permanent membership of the Security Council symbolizes
the role of nuclear weapons in defining major power status in security
matters since 1945.

U.S. policy further undercuts the arguments of states, like Germany
and Japan, that major powers do not necessarily need to possess nuclear
weapons. One way to strengthen this view is to eliminate the passionate
talk of averting proliferation from policy, while enhancing the role of
non-nuclear major powers such as Germany and Japan. If one lesson of
the experiences of Germany and Japan is that neither states possesses
nuclear weapons in large measure because the United States extended a
security guarantee to them, then the United States might consider security
guarantees for other states. Only then will it be true that one's status as
a major power is influenced only peripherally by nuclear ownership.

The United States needs to take the lead in advancing the view that
nuclear proliferation poses both risks and benefits. While the risks can be
greater than the benefits in some instances, such as the spread of nuclear
weapons to rogue states, in other cases, nuclear weapons are a force for
stability, as demonstrated in the case of Pakistan and India. A new U.S.
policy must rest on the realization that nuclear proliferation is proceeding
despite the active resistance of the international community. In an ideal
world, some might prefer to see the abolition of nuclear weapons, while
others might prefer to see them concentrated in the hands of a few states.
Neither condition is ever likely to exist again.

The policy of the United States must rest on the philosophical view
that this state has an interest in shaping a stable and peaceful world. We
have the singular obligation to manage the inevitable process of
proliferation toward the creation of stability. To accomplish this objective,
the United States must promulgate new concepts for guiding proliferation

policy. The next section outlines several conceptual steps for coping with all nuclear states.

Four Principles of U.S. Proliferation Policy

The challenge for the United States is to define a new policy that governs nuclear proliferation, while recognizing that its ability to dissuade states from developing nuclear weapons is limited. This new policy must focus on shaping stable nuclear arsenals and political institutions in the societies that possess these weapons. The conceptual foundation for this new U.S. nuclear proliferation policy rests on four principles.

Nuclear ownership by any state is an open issue, contingent upon behavior that conforms to international standards.

During the Cold War, the United States reflexively categorized virtually all instances of nuclear proliferation as inherently destabilizing, and used its resources to avert proliferation. This new policy contrasts with the existing policy on several levels.

First, the United States will view efforts at nuclear ownership with an open mind, judging the merits of each case. This policy rests on the judgment that the United States is not inherently opposed to nuclear proliferation on the part of any state. This new U.S. policy will reflect judgments about the stabilizing or destabilizing consequences of nuclear ownership for the present and the foreseeable future. It is important to note that this policy rejects the view, enshrined in earlier policy, that all cases of nuclear proliferation are inherently destabilizing and contrary to U.S. interests.

Further, this new policy bases U.S. judgments about the effect of nuclear ownership on a state's actions, past and present, and judgments about the likelihood that it will conform to accepted standards of international behavior. This policy is open with respect to the willingness of the United States to support nuclear ownership by states that demonstrate a willingness to abide by the norms of stabilizing behavior. In contrast with the past, the United States does not define all proliferation as inimical to its interests, but will focus only on those instances which pose a "clear and present danger" to the interests of the United States.

The new policy is not meant as a mask for the unstated preference for a non-nuclear world, or a world in which only a few states possess nuclear weapons. Such a reality is no longer attainable. This policy accepts the view that it is reasonable to believe nuclear weapons are an enduring aspect of international politics, and that the challenge of policy is to make the reality of nuclear ownership consistent with peace and security for all states. It also focuses on maintaining international stability, which is not synonymous with a foreign policy that attempts to indefinitely preserve the *status quo*.

The United States seeks to reduce the incentives that drive states toward nuclear ownership.

Nuclear ownership does not occur in a political or strategic vacuum, but reflects the judgment that nuclear weapons enhance a state's security. The challenge for the United States is to reduce the incentives that drive states toward nuclear ownership.

The problem with the current U.S. approach is that policy has focused primarily on negative disincentives. While the United States has offered security guarantees to North Korea in exchange for terminating its nuclear weapons program, the implicit element in U.S. policy is the threat of sanctions and intervention. The United States cannot depend exclusively on the old policy that sought to make the cost of nuclear ownership so burdensome that states would refrain from the possession of nuclear weapons. The new policy, by contrast, envisions a range of incentives that diminish the importance of nuclear ownership as a fundamental determinant of great power status. While this change represents a major hurdle, the objective is to diminish the belief that cannot be a great power unless it possesses nuclear weapons because nuclear weapons are seen as the measure of power. The elevation of states, such as Germany and Japan, to the ranks of permanent members of the United Nations Security Council would go a long way to demonstrate that nuclear ownership is not a prerequisite of membership. Their prominence as economic powers strengthens the argument that nuclear ownership is not the *sine qua non* of recognition as great states.

An element of this approach is to reduce the incentives for nuclear ownership through security concerns. Because states see nuclear weapons as the ultimate security guarantee, the United States needs to strengthen the role of unilateral and multilateral security guarantees to lessen the incentive of nuclear ownership. During the Cold War the United States extended security guarantees to a panoply of states as a way to diminish their need for nuclear weapons. Germany and Japan remain non-nuclear states to this day precisely because they derived security from their alliances with the United States. An effective policy of extending security guarantees is one part of a broader foreign policy architecture for involvement by the United States in a range of regional issues. In this sense, U.S. proliferation policy must be more comprehensive than issuing denunciations against states that are moving toward nuclear ownership. It is imperative for the United States to redress the worries of states that see nuclear ownership as the solution to vexing security concerns.

The United States will employ measures to avert nuclear ownership by states that manifest destabilizing behavior.

In the past, the United States focused indiscriminately on slowing or preventing most, if not all, cases of nuclear proliferation. In the future, an essential theme of U.S. proliferation policy must be to concentrate on averting nuclear ownership in cases that have the potential to exhibit destabilizing behavior. The principle for U.S. policy is to avert ownership on the basis of a state's behavior, rather than resisting nuclear ownership on the basis of universal opposition to all proliferation. This means that in the cases of nuclear ownership which enhance regional peace and security, the developed states must nurture those cases. This policy recognizes, however, that the United States reserves the right to judge whether nuclear ownership by any state is potentially destabilizing, and to respond with the appropriate steps. The United States will need to resist some nuclear proliferation efforts if it is to affirm the principle that there are destabilizing cases of nuclear proliferation.

The implementation of this new principle of U.S. proliferation policy encompasses the entire range of traditional nonproliferation policies that were in force during the Cold War. The instruments for averting ownership are national and international regimes for controlling nuclear materials, including export control mechanisms and punitive political, economic, and military sanctions. Many of the existing governmental mechanisms are entirely appropriate for this purpose.

This new principle seeks to be less discriminatory as it selectively weighs the risks of nuclear ownership, in contrast with the *carte blanche* opposition to nuclear ownership that characterized the earlier policy. States are perfectly free to possess nuclear weapons, and are not discouraged from doing so as long as their behavior comports with accepted standards. At the same time, however, it would be the height of folly for the United States or other states to support the possession of nuclear weapons by states which support international terrorism or whose national policy is animated by the desire to foment international instability. In cases where a state's behavior raises such concerns, the United States either on a unilateral or multilateral basis, reserves the right to respond for the purpose of averting nuclear ownership.

This argument does not presume that the "rogue" states will accept this formulation, cease their nuclear programs, or stop accusing the developed states of discrimination. The aspiration, however, is to narrow the gap between the rhetoric and practice of U.S. proliferation policy, and thus to imbue U.S. policies with greater coherence and credibility.

A more equitable policy on nuclear ownership places the emphasis on security and safety.

The burden on states that decide to possess nuclear weapons is to develop the policies and practices that lead to the safe and secure custody of nuclear forces. With the expertise gained over nearly fifty years, the United States has the ability to assist the new nuclear states develop the appropriate mechanisms and institutions that are prerequisites of nuclear stability. Unless states have secure command and control, established lines of authority between political and military echelons, a tradition of military subordination to political authorities, there are no guarantees that they will have the ability to establish safe and secure nuclear forces.

The United States can provide technical support in an number of areas to help these states ensure that their nuclear forces are under proper command and control. The existence of safe and secure nuclear forces rests on more than technical knowledge or engineering, but on a broad array of approaches to managing nuclear forces. It is virtually certain that most nascent nuclear states will not have the specialized knowledge or skills that are necessary to ensure that nuclear forces are under tight political control.

U.S. policy cannot be paralyzed by the fear that nuclear forces will fall into the hands of destabilizing leaderships. The hope is that safe and secure forces (SSF) will coincide with the emergence of stable leaderships in the states that possess nuclear weapons. Yet, the fact that there will be cases in which nuclear forces are controlled by destabilizing leaderships reinforces the logic of supporting measures that lead to safe and secure forces. Such forces in the hands of destabilizing leaderships still create a more stable situation than forces that do not meet this criterion. Safe and secure forces are always better than the alternative.

Reshaping Proliferation Policy for the 21st Century

There is some merit to the criticism that the United States opposes nuclear proliferation with the usual array of rhetoric and sanctions, but does not appear to have the political will to use force. It is imperative that the United States establish a new policy before the uncontrolled process of nuclear proliferation leads to a complete erosion of American credibility. To realign the rhetoric and substance of proliferation policy, there are several conceptual steps that the United States needs to make to shape a fundamental shift in the political and intellectual climate. More specific recommendations are presented in Part V.

Reject Dual Standards of Nuclear Ownership

The intellectual foundation for nonproliferation policy during the Cold War legitimized the division of the world into nuclear "Haves" and "Have-nots," and enshrined this distinction in the Nuclear Nonproliferation Treaty. This dual standard of nuclear ownership was recognized by many states as inherently discriminatory, and contributed to the impression that U.S. nonproliferation policies were unjust.

The proposition that only some states ought to possess nuclear weapons is no longer intellectually sound[10], as the cases of Israel North Korea, and Pakistan so vividly demonstrate. The belief that all forms of proliferation are destabilizing is an artifact of a time when nuclear weapons were an historical and operational oddity. The proliferation of nuclear weapons states attests to the growing normality of nuclear weapons, and to the futility of policies that hope to halt all proliferation.

Strengthen Stabilizing Cases

There is a need to broaden international thinking to build on the success of stabilizing instances of nuclear proliferation. We offer a contemporary example that should redefine how states think about the effect of nuclear proliferation.

Pakistan's putative nuclear arsenal directly and absolutely deters Indian aggression, and the same logic applies to the deterrent effect of India's nuclear arsenal on Pakistan. These states are now locked in a permanent "nuclear embrace." Neither state can risk nuclear armageddon, and hence must live with constraints on their behavior similar to those on the United States and the Soviet Union during the Cold War.

Once the United States admits the possibility of stabilizing cases of nuclear proliferation, and that the logic of nuclear ownership is equal for all states, many of the self-inflicted encumbrances on U.S. policy will disappear. Just as the United States argued that the development of nuclear weapons in the 1940s had a stabilizing effect on international politics, the question is how different will the possession of nuclear weapons be for subsequent generations of nuclear powers. The next logical step is to define the essential conditions for nuclear stability, and the path that states must follow to create stability. This realization will stimulate a long-overdue revolution in the way the government and society in the United States think about nuclear proliferation.

There is an urgent need for the United States to confront the dangers posed by existing nuclear forces which are not controlled or maintained under the same types of safeguards that kept U.S. forces secure for decades. Nuclear ownership demands that states establish mechanisms and procedures for ensuring that tight control is exercised over nuclear forces. Safe and secure nuclear forces are essential elements of global stability in a multi-nuclear world, and vastly more needs to be done in this regard.

Focus on Destabilizing Proliferation

It is evident that nuclear proliferation can have profoundly destabilizing consequences. The possession of nuclear weapons by some states will threaten U.S. interests and allies, and thus demand policy responses by the United States. We offer three contemporary examples of destabilizing proliferation.

First, Iran's apparent decision to become a nuclear-weapons power has profound consequences for regional stability in the Middle East. The prospect of a nuclear-armed Iran is a cause for great concern, and will generate reactions from Israel, Iraq, and other states which believe that Iran will use nuclear weapons to intimidate its enemies. These concerns could escalate into preemptive attacks against Iran in a period of greater tensions.

Second, North Korea's nuclear program is seen as a destabilizing development in the region. The destabilizing element of North Korean nuclear ownership is the risk of war that engulfs the region and demands U.S. intervention. A nuclear-armed North Korea also could elicit nuclear responses by South Korea and possibly Japan, thus locking North Korea into a deterrent relationship with regional powers as well as the United States. What is a destabilizing development on the Korean Peninsula in 1994 could evolve into the destabilization of Northeast Asia if a nuclear-armed reunified Korea were to emerge in the future.

Third, there is the possible danger of terrorist organizations that are armed with nuclear weapons. One of the major destabilizing aspects of the development of nuclear weapons by both Iran and North Korea is their long history of terrorism and their support of terrorist organizations. It is unlikely that nuclear weapons will be made available to terrorist organizations in the immediate future. This development would cross a new and fundamentally destabilizing threshold in proliferation. The greater risk may be actions by the security services of these states, rather than transfers of nuclear weapons to sub-state groups. This condition would elevate concerns about the dangers of Iran's and North Korea's nuclear programs from a regional to a global problem.

North Korea is especially dangerous since its economic situation increases the pressure to provide weapons or technology to other terrorist states or organizations in return for hard currency or energy resources. While it is highly unlikely that nuclear weapons will be developed in the workshop of some terrorist, and even more unlikely that terrorist organizations can develop the "suitcase bomb" so often written about, policymakers cannot dis-miss the dangers of states that are less inhibited providing weapons and technology to such terrorist organizations.

The challenge for the United States is to focus its efforts on the destabilizing cases. Some cases will raise the specter of military intervention, others may result in the risk of war or unilateral military action, and still others will be resolved through the quiet, yet aggressive, channels of diplomacy. We should remind ourselves that it took a war to halt the development of Iraq's extremely destabilizing nuclear weapons program. In an historical context, the partial destruction of Iraq's nuclear program was more significant than the expulsion of Iraqi forces from Kuwait. It is essential that the United States have the political will to act early in the development of nuclear weapons so that it does not put itself in the position of the recent situation with North Korea. The most dangerous situation is that which exists when U.S. rhetoric exceeds its will to act.

Diminish Value of Nuclear Weapons

The United States needs to establish the principle that all states have the inherent right to possess nuclear power and technology. Furthermore, it needs to state clearly that other states should not interfere with decisions to possess nuclear weapons by states that contribute to stability. This new policy will have two beneficial consequences.

The first is to diminish the incentive to possess nuclear weapons. When states realize that nuclear ownership is not a central feature of international politics, and thereby does not automatically generate opportunities for extracting gains from the international community, an advantage of nuclear ownership will fade. Second, if the United States and the international community downplay the role of nuclear weapons, it will lessen their political utility as an instrument for diplomatic leverage.

The problem is that current proliferation policy enshrines nuclear weapons as a critical determinant of diplomatic relations. North Korea, Pakistan, Iran, and Iraq are daily reminders of the failure of policies to avert nuclear proliferation. It takes no great strategic insight on the part of these states to realize that nuclear weapons assure a prominent place on the U.S. agenda.

There are several steps that the United States can take to diminish the value of nuclear weapons. An important element is to link political and economic support with decisions to remain non-nuclear. This policy was employed in the case of Ukraine when the United States linked economic assistance with pressure on Ukraine to relinquish its nuclear weapons. While this particular case raises a number of serious concerns, it exemplifies a general approach to reducing the incentives to possess nuclear weapons. A corollary of this policy is to use security assurances, whether on a bilateral or multilateral basis, to establish a foundation for security for states that look to nuclear weapons as a protector of their interests.

A further step that the United States must contemplate is the development of defensive systems to protect the United States, its allies, and U.S. forces in overseas operations against limited nuclear attacks. These systems are critical if the United States is to preserve its ability to protect its interests abroad and those of its allies in a multi-nuclear world. Such defensive systems are clearly feasible and will play an essential role if the United States is to reduce the military effectiveness of nuclear weapons. Effective defensive systems can be a major disincentive to nuclear proliferation. Nuclear weapons have little value if they are vulnerable to preemptive attack by smart conventional munitions or nuclear weapons and, in turn, cannot be effectively delivered on target. A combination of effective defensive systems and an enhanced intelligence capability to defeat other more surreptitious forms of nuclear weapons delivery are essential elements of a comprehensive policy on nuclear proliferation.

Summary

The benefit from drawing a distinction between stabilizing and destabilizing cases of nuclear proliferation is to establish a basis for coexistence among nuclear-armed states. The strategy of nuclear coexistence avoids the expenditure of precious political credibility on proliferation cases that do not harm vital U.S. interests. This strategy also helps the United States focus its diplomatic efforts on the cases that deserve the most attention. The United States cannot afford to waste political credibility and governmental effort on proliferation activities that do not affect vital U.S. interests. Throughout the 1990s and beyond, the United States needs to focus nuclear proliferation efforts on the states that represent a threat to coexistence among nuclear-armed states. The discourse on nuclear coexistence must be a careful blend of positive and negative sanctions to alternatively reward and punish states that threaten to disrupt the nuclear peace. A state of nuclear coexistence can endure only when the policy of resisting proliferation with maximum rhetoric is coupled with the political will to act politically, economically, and militarily to prevent the proliferation of nuclear weapons to states that nolate standards of acceptable international behavior.

Notes

1. See Graham, "Winning the Nonproliferation Battle."

2. The argument that the NPT is broken is, itself, contentious. For the views that it is broken, see "It's Broke, So Fix It: The Nuclear Nonproliferation Treaty is in Urgent Need of Repair," *The Economist,* July 27, 1991, p. 13; Ashok Kapur, "Dump the Treaty," *Bulletin of the Atomic Scientists,* July-August 1990, pp. 21-23. For the contrary view, see Lewis A. Dunn, "It Ain't Broke Don't Fix It," *Bulletin of the Atomic Scientists,* July-August 1990, pp. 19-21.

3. See Ann Marie Cunningham, "Wanted: An Astute Nuclear Detective," *Technology Review,* October 1993, p.13, for criticisms about the LAEA's performance. The alternative view is that the flaws in the IAEA safeguards system have been repaired, and that the United States should increase its support for the IAEA. See Robert L. Gallucci, "Nuclear Situation in Iraq," U.S. *Department of State Dispatch,* July 5, 1993, p. 483.

4. See "UN Reports on A-Arms Threat," *Facts on File,* March 5, 1992, p. 157.

5. China, which is not an original signatory to the NPT, only agreed to adhere to the Nuclear Nonproliferation Treaty in 1992.

6. See Henry A. Kissinger, *Nuclear Weapons and Foreign Policy* (New York: Harper & Row, 1957).

7. While we disagree, for a careful account of the argument that the essential logic of nonproliferation remains unchanged, see Thomas W. Graham, "Winning the Nonproliferation Battle."

8. Ibid.

9. The consensus is that Germany and Japan did not produce nuclear weapons as a result of U.S. pressure. See Graham, "Winning the Nonproliferation Battle," p. 12.

10. Some observers argue that no states are sufficiently mature to possess nuclear weapons, and therefore that the existence of any nuclear-armed states weakens international security. This view, however, does not address the reality that whether one considers states mature or not, they will possess these weapons. Moreover, such arguments, while supporting discriminatory norms, are largely irrelevant and gratuitous.

Appendix

FIGURE: *Where are the Soviet nuclear weapons? (December 1993)*

WHERE ARE THE SOVIET NUCLEAR WEAPONS?

STRATEGIC: Eighty percent of all Soviet strategic nuclear weapons are located in the Russian republic, with the remaining 20% stationed in Ukraine, Byelorussia and Kazakhstan.

TACTICAL: About 10,000 Soviet tactical nuclear weapons are based in the Russian republic. The remaing 5,000 are in other republics.

0   500
MILES

IN THE RUSSIAN REPUBLIC:
■ 12 of 16 fields for silo-based ICBMS
■ 10 of 12 mobile ICBM bases
■ All six ports for nuclear armed submarines
■ 11 of 26 medium and heavy bomber bases
■ The only anti-ballistic missile site
■ The majority of nuclear weapons storage sites

IN BYELORUSSIA:
■ 2 fields of mobile SS-25 ICBMs
■ 5 bomber fields

IN KAZAKHSTAN:
■ 2 of the 6 SS-18 ICBM field maintained by the USSR
■ 50 SS-18s based at Imeni Gastello and 50 SS-18s at Zhangiz Toba
■ 1 heavy bomber base

IN UKRAINE:
■ Entire Soviet stock of SS-24 silo-based ICBMs, 56 located in Pervomaysk
■ 60 SS-19 ICBMs deployed in Derazhnya
■ 8 nuclear bomber bases
■ In its declaration of independence Aug. 24, 1991, Ukraine claimed control of all military installations on its soil, but the Ukraine has requested removal of all Soviet nuclear weapons from its territory.

SOURCE: Center for Defense Information

THE WASHINGTON POST

233

TABLE 1. *Ballistic missiles by countries (August 1994)*

	Alternative Name	Range (km) Maximum	Payload (kg)	Status
AFGHANISTAN				
SS-1 SCUD B	T7-B300	300	985	**In Service**
ALGERIA				
SS-1SCUD B	T7-B300	300	985	**In Service**
ARGENTINA				
CONDOR 2		900	500	*Terminated*
AZERBAIJAN				
SS-1SCUD B	T7-B	300	985	**In Service**
BELARUS				
SS-21 SCARAB	TOCHKA	120	480	**In Service**
SS-1SCUD B	T7-B	300	985	**In Service**
SICKLERS-12M	SS-25	10,500	1,200[T/W][1]	**In Service**
BRAZIL				
MB/EE-150		150	500	*Terminated*
SS-300		300	450	*Terminated*
SS-600		600	500	*Terminated*
SS-1 000		1,200	n/k	*Terminated*
VLS / SLV	[SLV1]	5,000	500	Development
BULGARIA				
SS-1SCUD B	T7-B	300	985	**In Service**
CHINA				
CSS-2	DF-3/3A	2,800	2,150	**In Service**
CSS-3	DF-4	4,750	2,200	**In Service**
CSS-4	DF-5/5A	13,000	3,200 [T/W]	**In Service**
CSS-6	DF-21/A	1,800	600	**In Service**
CSS-N-3	JL-1 [SLBM]	1,700	600 [T/W]	**In Service**
DF-11	M-11	290	800	**In Service**
DF-15/M-9	SST-600	600	950	**In Servlce**
DF-31		8,000	700 [T/W]	Development
DF-41		12,000	800	Development
JL-2	[SLBM]?	8,000	700 [T/W]	Development

	Alternative Name	Range (km) Maximum	Payload (kg)	Status
EGYPT				
SS-1 SCUD B	T7-B	300	985	**In Service**
VECTOR		900	500	*Terminated*
CZECH REP				
SS-21 SCARAB	TOCHKA	120	480	**In Service**
SS-1 SCUD B	T7-B	300	985	**In Service**
FRANCE				
HADES		480	400	In Storage
SSBS S-3D		3,500	1,800	**In Service**
MSBS M-4A/B	[SLBM]	5,000	1,200 [T/W]	**In Service**
MSBS M-5	[SLBM]	6-11,000	n/k	Development
GEORGIA				
SS-1 SCUD B	T7B	300	985	**In Service**
HUNGARY				
SS-21 SCARAB	TOCHKA	120	480	**In Service**
SS-1 SCUD B	T7-B	300	985	**In Service**
INDIA				
PRITHVI 1	SS-150	150	1,000	**In Service**
PRITHVI 2	SS-250	250	500	**In Service**
PRITHVI 3	SS-350	350	500	Development
AGNI [2]		2,500	1,000	**Prototype**
ASLV	[SLV]	4,000	500	**In Service**
PSLV	[SLV]	8,000	n/k	Development
GSLV	[SLV]	14,000	n/k	Development
IRAN [3]				
8610		130	500	**In Service**
MUSHAK 120		120	190	**In Service**
MUSHAK 160		160	190	**In Service**
MUSHAK 200		200	500	Development
M-11	DF-11	290	800	**In Service**
SS-1 SCUD B	T7-B	300	985	**In Service**
SCUD C		550	500	**In Service**
TONDAR 68	M-18	1,000	400	Development

	Alternative Name	Range (km) Maximum	Payload (kg)	Status
IRAQ [4]				
SS-1 SCUD B	T7-B	300	985	**Prohibited**
AL HUSSEIN		650	500	**Prohibited**
AL ABBAS		900	350	*Terminated*
BADR 2000		900	500	*Terminated*
TAMMUZ 1		2,000	750	*Terminated*
ISRAEL				
LANCE	MGM 52	130	450	**In Service**
JERICHO 1	YA-1	500	500	**In Service**
JERICHO 2	YA-2	1,500+	1,000	**In Service**
SHAVIT	[SLV]	4,500	1,100	**In Service**
JAPAN [5]				
M-3	[SLV]	4,000	500 [T/W]	**Capability**
H-1	[SLV]	12,000	n/k	**Capability**
H-2	[SLV]	15,000	4,000 [T/W]	Development
KAZAKHSTAN				
SS-21 SCARAB	TOCHKA	120	480	**In Service**
SS-1 SCUD B	T7-B	300	985	**In Service**
SATAN RS-20	SS-18	11,000	7,600 [T/W]	**In Service**
NORTH KOREA				
SS-1 SCUD	T7-B	300	985	**In Service**
SCUD C		550	500	**In Service**
NODONG 1 [6]		1,000	1,000	Development[7]
NODONG 2		1,500	1,000	Development[8]
TAEPO DONG 1 [9]		2,000	1,000	Development[10]
TAEPO DONG 2 [11]		3,500	1,000	Development
SOUTH KOREA				
HYON MU	NHK1	250	300	**In Service**
LIBYA [12]				
SS-21 SCARAB	TOCHKA	120	480	**In Service**
SS-1 SCUD B	T7-B	300	985	**In Service**
SCUD C		550	500	**In Service**
AL FATAH	ITTISALT	950	500	Development
PAKISTAN [13]				
HATF 1		100	500	**In Service**
HATF 2		300	500	**In Service**
HATF 3		600	500	Development
M-11 [14]	**DF-11**	**290**	**800**	**In Service**

	Alternative Name	Range (km) Maximum	Payload (kg)	Status
POLAND				
SS-21 SCARAB	TOCHKA	120	480	**In Service**
SS-1 SCUD B	T7-B	300	985	**In Service**
ROMANIA				
SS-21 SCUD B	T7-B	300	985	**In Service**
RUSSIA				
SS-1 SCUD B	T7-B	300	985	**In Service**
SS-11 SEGO	RS-10	13,000	1,000 [T/W]	**In Service**
SS-13 SAVAGE	RS-12	9,400	500 [T/W]	Retired
SS-17 SPANKER	RS-16	10,000	2,400 [T/W]	Retired
SS-18 SATAN	RS-20	11,000	7,600 [T/W]	**In Service**
SS-19 STILETTO	RS-18	10,000	3,600 [T/W]	**In Service**
SS-21 SCARAB	TOCHKA	120	480	**In Service**
SS-24 SCALPEL	RS-22	10,000	3,200 [T/W]	**In Service**
SS-25 SICKLE	RS-12M	10,500	1,200 [T/W]	**In Service**
SS-N-6 SERB		3,000	650	**In Service**
SS-N-8 SAWFLY		9,100	1,100 [T/W]	**In Service**
SS-N-18 STINGRAY	RSM-50	8,000	1,600 [T/W]	**In Service**
SS-N-20 STURGEON	RSM-52	8,300	2,500 [T/W]	**In Service**
SS-N-23 SKIFF[a]		8,300	2,800 [T/W]	**In Service**
SAUDI ARABIA				
CSS-2	DF-3/3A	2,800	2,150	**In Service**
SLOVAKIA				
SS-21 SCARAB	TOCHKA	120	480	**In Service**
SS-1 SCUD B	T7-B	300	985	**In Service**
SOUTH AFRICA				
ARNISTON [15]		1,500	1,000	Development
SPAIN				
CAPRICORNIO	[SLV]	1,300	500	Development
SYRIA				
SS-21 SCARAB	TOCHKA	120	480	**In Service**
SS-1 SCUD B	T7-B	300	985	**In Service**
SCUD C		550	500	**In Service**
M-11	DF-11	290	800	**In Service**
M-9	DF-15	600	950	**On Order**

	Alternative Name	Range (km) Maximum	Payload (kg)	Status
TAIWAN				
GREEN BEE	CHINGFENG	130	400	**In Service**
SKY HORSE	TIEN MA	950	500	Development
UKRAINE				
SS-21 SCARAB	TOCHKA	120	480	**In Service**
SS-1 SCUD B	T7-B	300	985	**In Service**
SCALPEL	SS-24	10,000	3,200 [T/W]	**In Service**
STILETTO	22-19	10,000	3,600 [T/W]	**In Service**
UNITED ARAB EMIRATES				
SS-1 SCUD B	T7-B	300	985	**In Service**
UNITED KINGDOM				
POLARIS A-3 TK	[SLBM]	4,700	c. 500 [T/W]	**Retiring**
TRIDENT C5	[SLBM]	12,500	2,800 [T/W]	**Entering Service**
UNITED STATES				
ATACMS	MGM 140	135	450	**In Service**
MINUTEMAN 2	LGM 30F	11,300	737	**Retiring**
MINUTEMAN 3	LGM 30G	14,800	1,088 [T/W]	**In Service**
PEACEKEEPER	LGM 118	11,000	3,175 [T/W]	**In Service**
TRIDENT C4	UBM 93A	7,400	1,5OO [T/W]	**In Service**
TRIDENT C5	UBM 133A	12,500	2,800 [T/W]	**In Service**
VIETNAM				
SS-1 SCUD B	T7-B	300	985	**In Service**
YEMEN [16]				
SS-21 SCARAB	TOCHKA	120	480	**In Service**
SS-1 SCUD B	SS-1	300	985	**In Service**

1.   [TW] Indicates that the figure quoted is for throw-weight

2.   Agni is described as a "technical demonstrator," produced with Russian assistance [ibid].

3. Approximately 100 Scud Bs were delivered by North Korea to Iran in July 1987 and were launched at Iraq in 1988 ("The War of the Cities"). North Korea also assisted in establishing a Scud B production assembly facility in Iran, and subsequently a similar facility for Scud Cs. Iran is also reported to be co-operating with Pakistan on missile development.

4. UN Resolution 687 prohibits Iraq from using, developing or otherwise acquiring

ballistic missiles (or related items) with ranges greater than 150 km, although it may have retained a number of missiles in violation of these terms.

5. All Japan's rockets are designed as Space Launch Vehicles [SLVs], but could be adapted to carry military payloads.

6. The Nodong (ND is also known as Rodong.

7. Believed to be single stage, Scud based. Launched from a mobile launcher.

8. It is possible that the Nodong 2 programme includes work on a two-stage missile.

9. Sometimes known as Nodong 3.

10. The TD 1 is believed to be based on a ND 1 first (launch) stage and a modified Scud warhead and second stage.

11. Sometimes know as Nodong 4.

12. Libya is reported to be co-funding the N. Korean Nodong programme and North Korea to be building a production facility for the Nodong 1 in Libya.

13. Pakistani officials visited N. Korea in 1992 to discuss the Nodong project and view a test-launch.

14. RUSI (May 1994) reports that China is supplying M-11s to Pakistan.

15. Arniston status see: "Missile and Space Launch Capabilities of Selected Countries," *The Nonproliferation Review*, Vol 1, No 3, 1994, p.86

16. All Yemini figures quoted are pre-civil war.

NOTE: This table was compiled by Dr. Robin Ranger and David Bosdet from categories and arrangements by Humphry Crum Ewing. Our thanks to the National Institute for Public Policy, Fairfax, VA for their assistance and suggestions.

TABLE 2. *Major multilateral arms control treaties and agreements*

Date	Agreement	No. Signatories, 1994	Principal Objectives
1959	Antarctic Treaty	40	Prevents the military use of the Antarctic, including the testing of nuclear weapons
1967	Outer Space Treaty	93	Outlaws the use of outer space for testing or stationing any weapons, as well as for military maneuvers
1967	Treaty of Tlatelolco	24	Creates the Latin America Nuclear Free Zone by prohibiting the testing and possession of nuclear facilities for military purposes
1968	Limited Test Ban Treaty	120	Prohibits nuclear weapons in the atmosphere, outer space, and underwater
1968	Nuclear Nonproliferation	163	Prevents the transfer of nuclear weapons and nuclear weapons production technologies to non-nuclear weapon states
1971	Seabed Treaty	88	Prohibits the deployment of weapons of mass destruction and nuclear weapons on the seabed beyond a 12-mile coastal limited
972	Biological Weapons Convention	126	Prohibits the production and storage of biological toxins; calls for the destruction of biological weapons stocks
1977	Environmental Modifications Convention	57	Bans the use of technologies that could alter the earth's weather patterns, ocean currents, ozone layer, or ecology
1981	Inhumane Weapons Convention	35	Prohibits the use of such weapons as fragmentation bombs, incendiary weapons, booby traps, and mines to which civilians could be exposed
1985	South Pacific Nuclear Free Zone (Roratonga) Treaty	11	Prohibits the testing, acquisition, or deployment of nuclear weapons in the South Pacific
1986	Confidence-Building and Security-Building Measures and Disarmament in Europe (CDE) Agreement (Stockholm Accord)	29	Requires prior notification and mandatory on-site inspection conventional military exercises in Europe
1987	Missile Technology Control Regime (MTCR)	25	Restricts export of ballistic missiles and production facilities
1990-92	Conventional Armed Forces	30	Places limits on five categories in Europe (CFE) of weapons in Europe and lowers balance of forces
1990	Confidence- and Security-Building Measures (CSBM) Agreement	53	Improves measures for exchanging detailed information on weapons, forces, and military

241

			exercises
1991	UN Register of Conventional Arms Transfers	173	Calls on states to voluntarily establish universal and non- discriminatory register that introduces greater openness about arms transfers and facilitates monitoring excessive arms build-up in any one country
1992	Open Skies Treaty	25	Permits flights by unarmed surveillance aircraft over the territory of the signatory states
1993	Chemical Weapons Convention (CWC)	147	Requires all stockpiles of chemical weapons to be destroyed within ten years
1993	UN Register of Conventional Arms	80	Requires states to submit information on seven categories of major weapons exported or imported during previous year

TABLE 3. *Major bilateral arms control agreements between the United States and the Soviet Union/Russia*

Date	Agreement	Principal Objectives
1963	Hot Line Agreement	Establishes a direct radio and telegraph communication between the governments to be used in times of crisis
1971	Hot Line Modernization Agreement	Puts a hot line satellite communication system into operation
1971	Nuclear Accidents Agreement	Creates a process for notification of accidental or unauthorized detonation of a nuclear weapon; creates safeguards to prevent accidents
1972	Anti-ballistic Missile (ABM) Treaty (SALT I)	Restricts the deployment antiballistic missile defense systems to one area and prohibits the develops the development of a space-based ABM system
1972	SALT I Interim Agreement Offensive Strategic Arms	Freezes the superpowers' total number of ballistic missiles launches for a 5-year period
1972	Protocol to the Interim Agreement	Clarifies and strengthens prior limits on strategic arms
1973	Agreement on the Prevention of Nuclear War	Requires superpowers to consult if a threat of nuclear war emerges
1974	Threshold Test Ban Treaty with Protocol	Restricts the underground testing of nuclear weapons above a yield of 150 kilotons
1974	Protocol to the ABM Treaty	Reduces permitted ABMs to one site
1976	Treaty on the Limitation of Underground Explosions for Peaceful Purposes	Broadens the ban on underground nuclear testing stipulated in the 1974 Threshold Test Ban Treaty; requires on-site observers of tests with yields exceeding 150 kilotons
1977	Convention on the Prohibition of Military or Any Other Hostile use of Environmental Modification Techniques	Bans weapons that threaten to modify the planetary ecology
1979	SALT II Treaty (never ratified)	Places ceilings on the number of strategic delivery vehicles, MIRVed missiles, long- range bombers, cruise missiles, ICBMs, and other weapons; restrains testing

Date	Agreement	Principal Objectives
1987	Nuclear Risk Reduction Centers Agreement	Creates facilities in each national capital to manage a nuclear crisis
1987	Intermediate-range Nuclear Force (INF) Treaty	Eliminates U.S. and USSR ground-level intermediate- and shorter-range nuclear weapons in Europe and permits on-site inspection to verify compliance
1990	Chemical Weapons Destruction Agreement	Ends production of chemical weapons; commits cutting inventories of chemical weapons in half by the end of 1999 and to 5,000 metric tons by the end of 2002
1990	Nuclear Testing Talks	New protocol improves verification procedures of prior treaties
1991	START (Strategic Arms Reduction Treaty)	Reduces arsenals of strategic nuclear weapons by about 30 percent
1992	START I Protocol	Holds Russia, Belarus, Ukraine, and Kazakhstan to strategic weapons reductions agreed to in START by the former USSR
1993	START II	Cuts the deployed U.S. and Russian strategic nuclear warheads on each side to between 3,000 and 3,500 by the year 2003; bans multiple-warhead land-based missiles

GLOSSARY

ABM	Anti-Ballistic Missile system; 1972 U.S.-Soviet Treaty
AACNM	Agency for Accounting and Control of Nuclear Materials
ALCMs	Air-Launched Cruise Missiles
AEA	Atomic Energy Act (1946 and 1954)
BMD	Ballistic Missile Defense
BMDO	Ballistic Missile Defense Organization
CBO	Congressional Budget Office
CSBMs	Confidence and Security Building Measures
CTB(T)	Comprehensive Test Ban (T) Treaty
ENDS	Enhanced Nuclear Detonation Safety System
GPALS	System for Global Protection Against Limited Strikes
GPS	Global Positioning System
IAEA	International Atomic Energy Agency
ICBMs	Intercontinental Ballistic Missiles
LTB(T)	Limited Test Ban (T) Treaty
LNSG	London Nuclear Supplies Group
MTCR	Missile Technology Control Regime
NEST	Nuclear Emergency Search Team
NPT	Non-proliferation Treaty
NSG	Nuclear Supplies Group
NWFZ	Nuclear Weapons Free Zone
NWS	Nuclear Weapons States
PAL	Permissive Action Link
SALT(A)	Strategic Arms Limitation Treaty (A) Agreements
SDI	Strategic Defense Initiative
SDIO	Strategic Defense International Organization
SLBMs	Sea-Launched Ballistic Missiles
START	Strategic Arms Reduction Treaty
THAAD	Theater High Altitude Area Defense system
TMD	Theater Missile Defense
WMD	Weapons of mass destruction

ABOUT THE EDITORS

Dr. Stuart E. Johnson is currently the Director of Research of the Institute for National Strategic Studies at National Defense University. He joined the staff at the NDU in 1985, when he directed the Command and Control Research Program. Dr. Johnson also has a part-time faculty appointment at the School of International and Public Affairs at Columbia University and at the George Washington University School of International Affairs in Washington, DC.

Dr. Johnson graduated from Amherst College in 1966, where he was selected for Phi Beta Kappa. He received his Ph.D. from Massachusetts Institute of Technology in 1971 after which he spent a year as a NATO Fellow at the University of Leiden in the Netherlands.

Dr. William H. Lewis is a Senior Fellow of the Institute for National Strategic Studies at the National Defense University. He recently retired from the George Washington University where he was appointed Professor of International Relations in 1981 and subsequently organized and served as Director of the Security Policy Studies Program. He has held a number of senior level appointments in the U.S. Government. Dr. Lewis has published widely in national security affairs journals and has edited and co-authored eight books in this field, the most recent being "Riding the Tiger: The Middle East Challenge After the Gulf War" (*Westview*, 1993).

*U.S. G.P.O.:1995-387-330:20004